Dark Places

Politics, Literature, & Film

Series Editor: Lee Trepanier, Samford University

The Politics, Literature, & Film series is an interdisciplinary examination of the intersection of politics with literature and/or film. The series is receptive to works that use a variety of methodological approaches, focus on any period from antiquity to the present, and situate their analysis in national, comparative, or global contexts. Politics, Literature, & Film seeks to be truly interdisciplinary by including authors from all the social sciences and humanities, such as political science, sociology, psychology, literature, philosophy, history, religious studies, and law. The series is open to both American and non-American literature and film. By putting forth bold and innovative ideas that appeal to a broad range of interests, the series aims to enrich our conversations about literature, film, and their relationship to politics.

Recent Titles

Dark Places: Crime and Politics in the Personal Noir of James Ellroy edited by Darrell A. Hamlin and Joseph Romance

The Architecture of Survival: Setting and Politics in Apocalypse Films by Erik Trump and Jake Parcell

Come With Me If You Want to Live: The Future as Foretold in Classic Sci-Fi Films by Michael Harris

The Dissident Politics in Václav Havel's Vanek Plays: Who Is Ferdinand Vanek Anyway? by Carol Strong

Irony, Liberalism, and Fantasy in the Films of Christopher by Jesse Russell

Magic in Early Modern England: Literature, Politics, and Supernatural Power by Andrew Moore

Philosophical Perspective on Film by Pedro Blas Gonzalez

Dark Places

Crime and Politics in the Personal Noir of James Ellroy

Edited by
Darrell A. Hamlin and Joseph Romance

LEXINGTON BOOKS
Lanham • Boulder • New York • London

Published by Lexington Books
An imprint of The Rowman & Littlefield Publishing Group, Inc.
4501 Forbes Boulevard, Suite 200, Lanham, Maryland 20706
www.rowman.com

86-90 Paul Street, London EC2A 4NE

British Library Cataloguing in Publication Information Available

Library of Congress Cataloging-in-Publication Data Available

ISBN: 978-1-66692-600-2 (cloth)
ISBN: 978-1-66692-601-9 (electronic)

Contents

Introduction

Darrell A. Hamlin and Joseph Romance

James Ellroy has envisioned the darkest corners of the American experience, public and private, to paint a landscape of corrupt hearts, minds, and institutions. Ellroy is particularly notable for exploring the connection between the murder of his own mother, when he was ten years old, and his career as a sexual deviant and petty thief in his early adulthood. "Dead people belong to the live people who claim them most obsessively," he wrote in the memoir *My Dark Places*.[1] Ellroy's obsession with the murder of his mother led to one of his most famous novels, *The Black Dahlia*, a fictionalized representation of the brutal and infamous unsolved murder of Elizabeth Short in 1947.[2] In his "USA Underworld Trilogy," Ellroy again provides a fictional solution to an even more famous unresolved crime, the assassination of President John F. Kennedy in 1963.[3] In these stories and others, Ellroy invents characters to interact with historic figures, repurposing facts and conjecture into fictional narrative to reclaim histories that he believes were never properly documented or expressed. This volume will explore connections between crime, politics, history, and memory in what we call Ellroy's *personal noir*.

A reader seeking exhaustive biographical treatment of James Ellroy can hardly do better than Steven Powell's recent book, *Love Me Fierce in Danger: The Life of James Ellroy*.[4] Our treatment of the author's life, as it relates to the themes and arguments of this volume of essays, is a more hard-boiled narrative.

On March 4, 1948, Lee Earle Ellroy was born in Los Angeles. He later chose the pen name James Ellroy. His parents divorced during his childhood. Post-divorce, he lived mostly with his mother, a nurse Ellroy later came to realize was amply focused on his well-being and growth into decent, socialized adulthood. Also according to Ellroy, Jean Hilleker Ellroy liked to dance and date and have a few drinks on the weekends when Ellroy was with his father.[5] It is impossible to encounter the work of James Ellroy without absorbing, on some level, that he has fashioned his art from an excavation of this tragic, complex, and lifelong evolving relationship. A dark destiny bound them.

When he was ten, the cataclysmic event of Ellroy's life occurred: his mother was murdered, and her body was dumped not far from where they lived.[6] Jean Ellroy's murder was somehow related to a sexual encounter on a date, and it remains unsolved to this day. Ellroy went to live full-time with his father, an accountant who sometimes worked as a business manager for Hollywood industry types, among them Rita Hayworth. By this time, Armand Ellroy's career was not a happy success story; he was unreliably employed, prone to grandiosity, providing marginal living arrangements for James as a child and adolescent. No sane person would nominate him as 1959's Father of the Year. That was the year James Ellroy turned eleven and was gifted Jack Webb's *The Badge* from his father, a book that included the story of Elizabeth Short.[7] More widely known, then and now, by the tabloid moniker of *The Black Dahlia*, Elizabeth Short was tortured and her grotesquely mutilated remains were found dumped in a field near a suburban housing development. This is one of the most renowned unsolved murders in U.S. history, probably the most notorious in the city of Los Angeles, and it was featured in a book given to Ellroy by his father when the boy's own transition to manhood was beginning. The force it commanded in a boy's mental and sexual development took a horribly unsurprising course. In adolescence, Ellroy obsessed over the sadistic murder of Elizabeth Short, conflating it in his mind with the murder of his mother, about whom he nurtured an ungenerous view throughout his childhood and teen years.

Fast forward to the late 1960s, Ellroy's father is dead, and Ellroy is fully committed to only one thing: prowling the homes of young women, breaking in to steal booze, prescription drugs, and underwear. He continues this career trajectory until his late twenties, when his physical and mental health reaches a breaking point and he somehow emerges from a tormented journey to sobriety. His obsession with the city and with its sustaining balance of violent crime and violent law enforcement, and the history and lore surrounding each, leads him to what is ultimately an extremely successful life as a crime writer. These crime stories are presented most famously in what is known as the LA Quartet of novels: *The Black Dahlia, The Big Nowhere, L.A. Confidential,* and *White Jazz.*[8] The *Black Dahlia*, of course, is a fictionalized attempt by Ellroy to look at the available perspectives on Elizabeth Short's murder, filtered through a tabloid and noir lens, to fashion a narrative that "solves" the crime with a bestselling story that somehow makes sense of it as both history and fiction.

This description of Ellroy's life and commercially successful artistic career may seem like ham-handed psychoanalysis. Yet we have paraphrased from

Ellroy himself, who turned his attention in the 1990s to memoir. The most famous of which is *My Dark Places*, the story of his work with a retired LA County detective, churning cold leads and archived evidence to try to solve the murder of his mother. While he was unable to solve the crime, he made sense of the event and its dominating effect on his own life. In a moving way, Ellroy recounts an achievement of respect and a complex love for his mother. But there is also the obvious: this memoir, and its meaning, is constructed for the audience by an admitted house-creeper and celebrated fiction writer whose memory recounts a period of life that was drug-addled, alcohol-fueled, and powered by an all-consuming masturbatory fantasy life that seems the only constant for Ellroy up until his late twenties. If that early narrative seems unreliable to us as an accurate account, it is the story he chooses to tell, and that project of personal history is a huge part of why we find it valuable to explore our own reading of Ellroy's work. He has deliberately entangled narrative with major reference points from his own life. Thus, that is the site of excavation for the scholars digging here in this book.

In the 1990s, Ellroy turned his attention to fashioning an epic, secret history of America, in a series of novels known as the USA Underworld Trilogy. These books—*American Tabloid, The Cold Six Thousand,* and *Bloods a Rover*—span from 1958 to 1973 to excavate connections between organized crime, institutional corruption, and covert government and military operations. It is a challenging, provocative story of America. In this sense, Ellroy's fiction and nonfiction are forensic in nature, his work a kind of autopsy on the self and society. As a nexus between crime and politics, Ellroy's work represents an American *noir* that is both public and private.

Recognizing explicit and implicit connections to the *noir* genre in both literature and film, the essays in this volume present the vision of scholars from political science, criminal justice, philosophy, literature, and history. The common thread running through the scholarship relates to a conceptual perspective on Ellroy we are calling *personal noir*, understood broadly, through a layered and overlapping expression.

- *Noir* as Personal Memory and History
- *Noir* as Political Memory and History
- *Noir* as a Clarifying Narrative Force

On the personal side, Ellroy has referred to his inner world as two things that jump out: "My Weird Shit"[9] and "My Dark Places." He has described the "weird shit" and the "dark places" as a lifelong obsession fusing his inner world with a professional passion for the criminal underworlds of individuals, institutions, and society. This volume seeks to make sense of Ellroy's *personal noir* as a kind of fast-burning jet fuel of obsession at the center of his life, and the work that has emerged from that life. Because Ellroy's fiction is drawn around real people and places, it is more than memory. It is a kind of history. Ellroy himself has defined his inner world as organized by weird, dark obsessions. This collection of essays will analyze a personal basis for the worldview of an artist, digging as much as identifiably possible in the areas of his life and work where Ellroy has aimed his readers through memoir.

This volume is also about the blurred lines of memory and history in his argument that America is a crime story. We want to emphasize and identify this on Ellroy's own terms, in his epitaph from *American Tabloid*, the first book in the Underworld Trilogy.

> *America was never innocent. We popped our cherry on the boat over and looked back with no regrets. You can't ascribe our fall from grace to any single event or set of circumstances. You can't lose what you lacked at conception.*
>
> *Mass-market nostalgia gets you hopped up for a past that never existed. Hagiography sanctifies shuck-and-jive politicians and reinvents their expedient gestures as moments of great moral weight. Our continuing narrative line is blurred past truth and hindsight. Only a reckless verisimilitude can set that line straight.*
>
> *The real Trinity of Camelot was Look Good, Kick Ass, Get Laid. Jack Kennedy was a mythological front man for a particularly juicy slice of our history. He talked a slick line and wore a world-class haircut. He was Bill Clinton minus pervasive media scrutiny and a few rolls of flab.*
>
> *Jack got whacked at the optimum moment to assure his sainthood. Lies continue to swirl around his eternal flame. It's time to dislodge his urn and cast light on a few men who attended his ascent and facilitated his fall.*
>
> *They were rogue cops and shakedown artists. They were wiretapper and soldiers of fortune and faggot lounge entertainers. Had one second of their lives deviated off course, American History would not exist as we know it.*
>
> *It's time to demythologize an era and build a new myth from the gutter to the stars. It's time to embrace bad men and the price they paid to secretly define their time.*
>
> *Here's to them.*[10]

Ellroy's is a deliberate project. Provocative. Stylistic. Offensive. Ellroy is clearly generating a Great Man theory of history, and the Great Men of American history, for Ellroy, are often most effectively the Bad Men.

It is also clear, from Ellroy's project, that he harbors complex admiration for these Bad Men, sees them as somehow great, for two reasons. First, because there is a kind of integrity to their raw purposes that is more honest than what we ever absorbed from our institutions and from our professed values. Second, these Bad Men were great because they bent history to their purposes. They have owned and steered America from the inside out all along.

Like his LA *noir* fiction, where people who lived interact with fictional characters for the purpose of solving an infamous, real crime, Ellroy has real historic figures doing the same thing to "solve" or "explain" the most infamous unsolved political crime of our history—the assassination of President John F. Kennedy. For Ellroy, this is not about gunshots on Dealey Plaza. It is a criminal cosmos, where the event of Dealey Plaza is but a necessary, inevitable feature of business, the business of owning America.

This weird, dark place—Ellroy's *personal noir*—is a form of energy that has fueled his inner world and his professional performance in the world we share with him.

This is the world where he really did lose his mother to an unsolved, sexually drenched murder.

The world where he carries an arrest record.

The world where words may never be adequate to tell the story of Elizabeth Short's life, dismembered in private and reassembled in tabloid publicity, where no one has yet been held responsible for her final torments.

The world where President John F. Kennedy was assassinated in a political crime for which only a minority believe that all the guilty have been definitively identified, and where it remains a fact that no one has ever been convicted as public justice for what the Warren Commission's first paragraph calls that "cruel and shocking act."[11]

In Ellroy's journey—which has also been a dark, mesmerizing journey for his reader—the history of that world, like the history of his inner world, has been energized, cauterized, and driven forward by a *personal noir* that has been a clarifying narrative force. A reason to keep living, to keep writing, provoking, offending, entertaining himself and his audience.

While each essay here contributes a unique understanding of Ellroy's writings and their importance, we believe that they can be grouped into three broad tiers of analysis.

The first four essays provide an overview of Ellroy and his fixations. In this sense, the essays map a terrain of Ellroy's disturbing world. The landscape drawn is geographical, biographical, psychological, and artistic. Real places, inside-out. The features of this topography are distinct, but at times overlapping, areas that are fraught for Ellroy's characters, fraught for his readers. We believe these first essays provide a foundation of background and insight for our own readers.

We start with Susan McWilliams, who argues that it all starts with California. Ellroy is the product of the state as an idea and a reality. Thus, an initial grasp of Ellroy is the grasp of California upon him; how he views California and his place within it is essential. As McWilliams observes, "California is central to the psychology of his work." California attracts migrants and its allure is, in part, based on the common human desire to start over again. Many who seek to begin anew have something they hate about themselves. However, while California offers this chance, it is unlikely that a healthy remaking will occur. Augmented by the opportunities and disappointments of the entertainment industry, such people are prone to criminality and violence. "California breeds the habits, and hunger for, crime," McWilliams writes. For many writers, crime is a theme, a subject, a genre of inspiration. Through a careful analysis of novels and autobiographical works, McWilliams demonstrates that Ellroy's focus on crime is a unique Californian product.

For Deirdre Condit, to make sense of Ellroy, readers must confront the gendered nature of his views. Wounded deeply, disturbingly influenced by the horrific murder of his mother, the tragedy led to a lifelong struggle with understanding what is most essential about being a woman or a man. Just as this singular crime visited on a woman and her son is a foundational source of the man's art, Condit argues that a primary source of distress for readers is a prevailing Ellroy view of what it means to be a man—a protector or predator of women. Resolving that requires Ellroy to hold women accountable for the violence done to them by men. This view of women subordinates them in either case, generating unstable and often violent force on women and their stories. Reinforcing McWilliams' essay, Condit reminds us that California is a promise to remake oneself into someone new. Damaged in childhood yet remaking himself as a successful writer, Ellroy's art expresses a warped masculinity that accounts for women as elements of a man's life he must shape, dominate, and control if he hopes to protect them.

As with most crime writers, death figures large in Ellroy's work. Unlike most crime writers, death is more than a plot device in the stories that emerge as a world from within his world. Erik Anderson explores the importance of death for understanding Ellroy's storytelling. For Anderson, murders are particularly expressive in Ellroy's world, and the murderous deeds in his art should be regarded in aesthetic terms apart from traditional literary approaches. Most prominently, Ellroy's framing of the murders—the bodies themselves—force us to consider the relationship between aesthetic crimes and moral issues raised by Ellroy's portrayal of death in *The Black Dahlia*. Anderson's essay is a meditation on the relationship between aesthetic and morality. Anderson takes us through that complicated relationship to conclude that "the immoralist account of the relationship between aesthetic and moral values help us to understand how some aesthetic crimes might nevertheless result in aesthetic triumphs."

The grounding tier of the book concludes with Lexey Bartlett's chapter and the role of the reader. As is well-known, and shown in all these essays, Ellroy paints a very dark version of humanity. It is a world of brutality, without conventionally drawn heroes or moral guidelines, with only rare hints of redemption. Indeed, the blood and body parts pile up like surgical aftermath in a civil war field hospital. Following Anderson's essay on the treatment of Elizabeth Short's humanity, Bartlett asks a pivotal question: *What does such literal and inexplicable violence do to the reader?* There is a relationship between the author and his audience. Given the darkness that Ellroy draws over us, Bartlett argues, "that the reader must reread against this text's assumptions, must resist or even refuse this text to avoid being erased." Bartlett offers a close reading of several texts, most centrally *The Black Dahlia*, to reflect on what it means to be a reader, particularly in the context of reading the violent world that Ellroy creates. In this sense, a reader must maintain personal and ethical boundaries to even encounter the symphonic violence Ellroy composes.

A second level of this book deals with the forces of law and order operating in Ellroy's work. These essays address what many expect when they read Ellroy—law, police, criminals. Ellroy gives us men with badges, yes, but even the best of them performs with confused, if not contemptible, motives. Darkness pervades every corner of his systems of justice. And yet, cheapened, malignant institutions of justice are still important institutions in human affairs. Several essays shed light on the individual and systemic corruptions a reader should expect from Ellroy's art.

Caitlin B. Coulter's chapter on the representations of Los Angeles detectives demonstrates how Ellroy subverts the traditional notions of crime-solving in a setting famous for detectives. Coulter traces the rich heritage of LA detective literature with analysis grounded in the articulated mastery of crime writer Raymond Chandler. The chapter argues that while Ellroy inherits the treasury of the detective genre, he also creates an "existential nightmare" of that career. As tough as Chandler's world is, the kind of loyalty and honor at the heart of his novels is extinct among Ellroy's LA detectives. In her analysis of *L.A. Confidential,* Coulter argues there is no honor for Ed Exley, Bud White, or Jack Vincennes as they use any means necessary to pull themselves out of the violence they have created and perpetuated. Not just searching for means of survival, these men of authority consciously utilize systems of harm to move up, lash out, and get off. Chandler's urban *noir* grows darker through Ellroy's dismal lens of hypocrisy and corruption. That some of the corruptions are tragic intersections of character and circumstance only strengthens the undertow of inevitability. When Ellroy regenerates the eternally recurring moral conundrums of hard-boiled protagonists, the stakes are higher than previously imagined. Yet without a foundation of integrity, or motivation outside their own passions, the three detectives regress to the choice of victim or victimizer. The violence inherent in a rewarded detective career, however, reduces the application of justice to a system of inescapable harm.

In his chapter, Jeffrey Becker burrows into the world of the police and, typically for Ellroy, there are no unsullied good guys. At a time when the state-sanctioned use of force by police and intelligence agencies has come under heightened scrutiny, this essay uses the *LA Quartet* novels by James Ellroy to examine the lines between enforcing the law, and the way the use of force (and torture) corrupts the ideals that law is meant to serve. For Becker, Ellroy's novels show how a political community defines crime, yet also makes exceptions to violations of the law to maintain a degree of peace within the emerging multicultural city of Los Angeles. The essay develops a broader argument about the relationship between violence, vice, race relations, social mores, and criminality in contemporary American democratic politics. Becker shows us that policing in America reflects contradictory impulses of American politics: the containment of vice and violence to maintain "law and order," but also the deployment of vice and violence to maintain political norms that shift and change depending on who is policed.

Several of Ellroy's books have been adapted into films, *L.A. Confidential* being the most famous and successful of the movie versions. Paul Babbitt explains how *L.A. Confidential* as a film differs in important ways from the novel, also bringing important context from the time of production and release. Themes of corruption and violence remain from the book, but as Babbitt observes, a film version is a unique framing of events and themes, essentially telling a different story. Babbitt reminds us that while the movie portrays Ellroy's novel, it is also a work of art that must be understood on its own terms.

In what we see as a third tier of essays in this book, political history in Ellroy's world is the central focus. At this level of analysis, American politics and history are stripped to a fully naked view of criminal complicity under the dressing of myth. For Ellroy, the story of America we advance and protect is an agreement of lies. He berates the sentimental version of textbooks and hero worship to make way for the dark truths of American ascendance.

W. John Green's chapter demonstrates that Ellroy's Underworld USA Trilogy includes the political violence of John Kennedy's assassination but is more insightfully read as the merging of criminality across borders. The story of transformation Green tells is entrepreneurial, epic, and subterranean. "In his Underworld USA Trilogy," Green writes in the language of political violence, "Ellroy exposes the fully integrated and interconnected world of wetwork throughout the Americas." As a historian, Green demonstrates how Ellroy's fictional world tracks with documented knowledge of that period, including the disturbing relationship of the US government to Latin American political violence. The purposeful violence underlying much of US covert policy from the 1950s and 1960s has come home in explicit ways today. Ellroy excavates this active trendline throughout his Underworld USA Trilogy. In Ellroy's revealed underworld, "the CIA, the FBI, the Mob, criminals of various stripes, intelligence operatives, the military, law enforcement, Latin American *pistoleros*, right-wingers, thugs, paramilitaries, *narcos*, wise-guys, and G-men, are all first cousins, or even siblings."

Joseph Romance looks more directly at the meaning of John Kennedy's assassination. For many Americans, the events in Dallas tore a hole in good times that seemed trajected for even better days. The aftermath of the limousine massacre, from this perspective, is a world gone to hell. To understand what happened—and why—might reset the American moral order. Ellroy critiques this view as ridiculous. Nonetheless, how we understand the assassination is still important. Romance puts Ellroy's USA Underworld Trilogy, in particular *American Tabloid*, in dialogue with Don DeLillo's *Libra*. Both books represent an effort to make some kind of sense of that event. For Ellroy, the whole rotten façade demands exposure. The Kennedys, the mob, the CIA, the FBI are all corrupt. Ellroy's version portrays venal human nature clawing for money, power, and dominant glory. DeLillo surmises a different story, where the force of history is a plausible explanation. People may be driven by pressures beyond their control, but they are not essentially bad. Neither author offers solace. Ellroy argues that American innocence never existed and thus could not be killed by bullets aimed into a motorcade. DeLillo reenacts the event as the culmination of such an extraordinary confluence of forces that we may never know what happened—a different, equally depressing conclusion.

Darrell A. Hamlin draws conclusions with his chapter. Hamlin focuses on Ellroy's announced intention to dispel childish belief so that the dark criminal energy of our history gains its due. James Ellroy opens *American Tabloid*—and thus the entire Underworld Trilogy—with a prologue indicating his project to re-tell American political history as a crime story with famous politicians mattering less to the plot than underworld figures. "Our continuing narrative line is blurred past truth and hindsight," Ellroy declares. "Only a reckless verisimilitude can set that line straight." This essay brings James Ellroy's critique of American political life forward toward a post-Trump reality where the white-collar crime tendencies of politicians (bankrolled by dark money) give way to a more purified organized crime structure, *mobsterism* as both the philosophy and the practice of the state. MAGA will live on in political life as a troubling theory of greatness in American history that is closer to the truth than *Camelot,* and that is part of its power. For Ellroy, American history can only be told with a "reckless verisimilitude," demolishing the movie set so that more truthful structures of understanding can be built as monuments to the real greatness of American achievements.

It is our project here to alert both general and academic readers that the encounter with the work of James Ellroy is a challenging, often distressing, perhaps even somehow damaging fall through a looking glass into his dark wonderland, a place he entered himself as a child. Like detectives who arrive first at a horrifying scene, his audience cannot hope to be spared the grisly, criminal aftermath in the facts and fiction of his cultural presence. A mess of gore and implication. Ellroy's art may or may not entertain, because for good or ill, it is the art of wounded, ruthless, informative imagination.

NOTES

1. James Ellroy, *My Dark Places* (New York: Vintage Books, 1996), p. 396.
2. James Ellroy, *The Black Dahlia* (New York: Mysterious Press, 1987).
3. James Ellroy, *American Tabloid* (New York: Knopf, 1995); James Ellroy, *The Cold Six Thousand* (London: Century, 2001); James Ellroy, *Blood's a Rover* (New York: Knopf, 2009).
4. Steven Powell, *Love Me Fierce in Danger* (London: Bloomsbury Publishing, 2023).
5. *My Dark Places*, p. 108.
6. *My Dark Places*, p. 3.
7. *My Dark Places*, p. 122; Jack Webb, *The Badge* (New York: Avalon Edition, 2005), p. vii.
8. James Ellroy, *The Big Nowhere* (New York: Mysterious Press, 1988); James Ellroy, *L.A. Confidential* (New York: Mysterious Press, 1990); James Ellroy, *White Jazz* (New York: Knopf, 1992).
9. James Ellroy, "My Mother's Killer," *Crime Wave: Reportage and Fiction from the Underside of L.A.* (New York: Vintage Books, 1999), pp. 49–62.
10. *American Tabloid*, p. 5.
11. Philip Shenon, *A Cruel and Shocking Act*: The Secret History of the Kennedy Assassination (New York: Henry Holt and Company, 2013), p. 11.

BIBLIOGRAPHY

Ellroy, James. *The Black Dahlia*. New York: Mysterious Press, 1987.
Ellroy, James. *The Big Nowhere*. New York: Mysterious Press, 1988.
Ellroy, James. *L.A. Confidential*. New York: Mysterious Press, 1990.
Ellroy, James. *White Jazz*. New York: Knopf, 1992.
Ellroy, James. *American Tabloid*. New York: Knopf, 1995.
Ellroy, James. *My Dark Places*. New York: Vintage Books, 1996.

Ellroy, James. "My Mother's Killer," *Crime Wave: Reportage and Fiction from the Underside of L.A.* New York: Vintage Books, 1999.
Ellroy, James. *The Cold Six Thousand.* London: Century, 2001.
Ellroy, James. *Blood's a Rover* New York: Knopf, 2009.
Powell, Steven. *Love Me Fierce in Danger.* London: Bloomsbury Publishing, 2023.
Shenon, James. *A Cruel and Shocking Act*: The Secret History of the Kennedy Assassination. New York: Henry Holt and Company, 2013.
Webb, Jack. *The Badge.* New York: Avalon Edition, 2005.

Chapter 1

James Ellroy's California

Susan McWilliams Barndt

California is more than just the backdrop to James Ellroy's fiction. The Golden State is an active presence in his writing. Coming out of Ellroy's pen, California seems to be a living, thinking, willing being, a force more powerful even than the weapons of destruction that his most ambitious human characters wield. When he gets called, as he often does, a California writer, it is not primarily because Ellroy lives in California (which sometimes he does, and sometimes he does not). It is because California is central to the psychology of Ellroy's work.

Ellroy himself has gone so far to suggest that none of his stories would be plausible or even possible without their Californian setting. In the hundreds of grisly crimes he has committed to the page, crimes both actual and imagined, Ellroy has made California complicit. As he recounts telling an acquaintance about his own mother's murder in California's southland, "The region defined the crime," and "the region was the crime," and, indeed, "the region explained it all."

But what does he mean? What about California, and what about Southern California in particular, is Ellroy imagining when he describes the place as "this deus ex machina" that springs his characteristic darkness into motion?[1]

To understand the writing of James Ellroy, it is necessary to understand how James Ellroy understands California. Arriving at some such understanding is the aim of this essay. But be warned at the beginning—this warning being perhaps unnecessary, given the horrors of his writing—Ellroy's understanding of California is dark. And his understanding of California, that place that has trained so many American eyes to see only its glittering lights, goes beyond state lines. James Ellroy's California implies James Ellroy's America, a place where, despite and perhaps because of all those glittering lights, dark things are afoot. It is a place where the promise of reinvention speaks to subterranean self-loathing. It is a place where the possibility of being famous stokes narcissistic fantasies. It is a place where the endless production of cinematic entertainment turns us all into habitual voyeurs. James Ellroy's California is a place that not only cultivates self-hating narcissists and voyeurs but also rewards them. In other words, as Ellroy sees it, California is an incubator of sociopathic criminality.

THE GREAT MIGRATION

California begins for James Ellroy as a destination for migrants. Los Angeles, in particular, is that seemingly paradoxical thing: a home for those who have "migratory tendencies."[2] This is not merely a matter of autobiographical and historical fact, though it is both of those things. California, in Ellroy's telling, is a place that has always "vibed migration," even in its most settled or staid moments.[3] In his account, because California has long been a migratory destination, and because the population of California—especially in the early to mid-twentieth century—consisted mostly of recent migrants, California cannot be understood except as having been built and imagined and experienced in response to migratory longings. As Ellroy explains it, "The people who flocked there flocked there for unconscious reasons that superseded the conscious application of logic and made anything possible." And that unconscious migration "explained every absurd and murderous act that went down there."[4]

Although in that passage Ellroy does not specify the content of this migratory "unconscious" or those migratory longings as he conceives of them, he elsewhere demonstrates what he might have in mind. For one thing, Ellroy follows legions of other thinkers in noting that California has always attracted people who yearn to start their lives over. (He says of his own mother, who for Ellroy is a paradigmatic Californian, "She was a big one for starting over."[5]) California has always traded on the idea, Ellroy writes, that "you can reinvent yourself en route," that you can go there and "assume your desired identity and make attitude count for a thousand times its hometown value."[6] Los Angeles is "where you go when you want to be somebody else."[7]

Of course, as any armchair therapist would tell you: a person who desires to reinvent himself or herself is a person who is to some degree self-loathing. Those people who dream of becoming somebody else can't like themselves all that much; otherwise, they wouldn't dream of leaving their lives and their selves behind. In his writing, Ellroy brings this fact to the fore. Like Danny in *The Big Nowhere*, whose "cross-country journey" Ellroy describes as being rooted in "self-hatred," Ellroy's characters most often become Californians because they do not like themselves.[8] In his way of telling the story, California was built by, and has continued to attract, self-haters. It is a state populated by escape artists in the most literal sense of that term. Californians are people who have devoted their lives to the art of escaping the self.

Given that emphasis, Ellroy makes it easy to explain why the signature industry of California is cinematic entertainment, and the signature ambition of Californians is acting. In his words:

> All actors are fucked up. They *are* their art. Their gift is impersonation. The goal is to become something that you're not. . . . It's a riff on Woody Allen's line: "My one regret is that I'm not someone else."[9]

As Ellroy allows us to see it, the state of California literally has capitalized on its major resource: people who desire to inhabit other lives. California sells fantasy stories in which a select group of Californians live out their dreams by play-acting the lives of other people. We call it "show business," and we call it that so often that it is easy to forget how odd a term—and concept—it is: the attempt to make money through pretense.

And to the extent that the rest of the world buys those stories (in both the economic and emotional senses of that term), California does more than just make money. It doubles down on its escapist identity. It sells another round of its own animating desire, spreads its own foundational gospel:

> The celebrity matrix. Revised and deconstructed for the rube readers of a distinct demographic.
>
> The estranged. The horny. The bereft and aggrieved. The worshipful stargazer ablaze with self-hatred.[10]

And another generation of pubescent self-haters (what Hollywood would have us call "starlets") board buses and planes and hurry themselves to the West Coast, searching for the someone elses they might become and further fueling the dream of what Ellroy calls the "fantasy windfall."[11]

Now, everyone knows that few of those young aspirants will "make it," or truly partake of those riches born of lucking into (or earning) a fantasy life. By any kind of realistic accounting, as Ellroy shows, it is foolish—pathetic, really—to believe that you will succeed in that signature Californian enterprise. Consider Ellroy's account of the two males closest to the murdered Nicole Simpson: "O.J. Simpson wanted to be white. Ron Goldman wanted to be an actor—an equally ridiculous ambition."[12] In other words, to be the kind of person who is emblematic of what it means to be a Californian, you can't merely be self-hating. You also must lack a sense of limits, especially your own. Or, as Ellroy puts it, acting is the quintessential Californian goal, and "the goal entices narcissists."[13]

Put all of this together, and the nature of James Ellroy's California becomes a little clearer. He says to us: California is the land that was built by, and that continues to attract, self-hating narcissists.[14] A very select group of those folks luck out and make a luxurious living at their preferred game of impersonation, a stroke of good fortune that also feeds their most narcissistic desires for attention and control—since their luxurious living comes from the selling of films that showcase their acts of impersonation and the peddling of their own subsequent celebrity. This all means, of course, that the rest of us are feeding the Californian beast by watching (about which I will have more to say later).

That vision of California has two important implications, both of which have to do with criminality. First, as Ellroy illustrates repeatedly: if self-hating and narcissism are the qualities that make for the quintessential Californian, they are also the qualities that underlie certain kinds of violent criminality. An actor aspires to control the perceptions and beliefs of others through disguise and make-believe; many kinds of criminals (and frequently the criminals in Ellroy's fiction) try to do the same. Both actors and criminals regularly seek to transcend the rules and strictures of ordinary life. Both actors and criminals are defined by their capacities for certain kinds of transgression. Both find their own selves somehow wanting; they are, in Ellroy's telling, "soft and self-obsessed men."[15] Notably, both acting and stalking express the desires to inhabit a different life, to stake a claim on a different life, and to have a place in a different life.

Ellroy's account of O. J. Simpson provides one example of this equivalence between the actor and the violent criminal. Says Ellroy, Simpson's "nice-guy impersonation" and his "long-perfected chameleon aplomb" were useful to him in the two activities in which we know for sure he engaged: pursuing celebrity, and "beat[ing] the shit out of [his wife] over the last five years of her life." But in those activities, he was "cracking under the weight of his own emptiness." Simpson, in other words, was that emblematic Californian type: the self-hating narcissist. That made him a star. And it made him a wife-beater. And it probably made him a murderer. The will to fame and the will to violence spring from the same "socopathic" source, as Ellroy calls it. The criminal persona is not an alternative to or a split from the acting persona; the criminal persona and the acting persona are one and the same.[16] As Ellroy tells it, one may even feed the other.

Ellroy provides another example of the linkage between the desire to act and the desire to do violence in the character of Michael Martin Plunkett, the narrator in *Killer on the Road*. Plunkett, against some "oncoming tidal wave of self-loathing," starts to fantasize that he can take on another persona or inhabit other lives. He becomes inspired by a comic-book character named Shroud Shifter who speaks "a retarded version of Nietzsche" and specializes in identity theft. Shroud Shifter is able "to disguise himself without changing costume" by "concentrating so much on the person he want[s] to rob or kill, that he soak[s] up . . . that person's aura." By doing this, Shroud Shifter becomes effectively invisible, with "a carte blanche ticket to take over the world." Plunkett actualizes this fantasy—literally a comic-book fantasy—by studying to be a person he is not and becoming, eventually, a brutal serial murderer. As Plunkett allows us to see, the ambition to escape the self—to render the self "invisible"—can be pursued through what we traditionally think of when we think of acting but also through the studying and stalking of other people, with the intent of slinking into their lives and doing them grievous harm.[17] Plunkett, in fact, does both at the same time; he embodies the indistinguishability of actor and criminal. The man who hates himself but also wants to take over the world—the self-hating narcissist—is a consummate actor, and thus a consummate killer.

Perhaps Ellroy's longest meditation on this theme of self-hating narcissism comes in his meditations on Robert Blake (whom Ellroy calls "Little Sleazer"), the actor most famous for his starring role in the film *In Cold Blood*—and who was later arrested for murdering his second wife (Bonny Lee Bakley, known to Ellroy as "Mail-Sex Mama"). Ellroy first compares Blake to the "real-life rodent Charles Schmid," who "killed teenage girls in the '60s." Says Ellroy, "He was short, dark, and narcisstic. He wanted to be an actor." He elaborates:

> Combine coolness and rage. Merge them maladroit. You get the psycho default mode of bad actors.
>
> Who tend to indulge bad habits. Who tend to disdain inhibition. Who tend to confuse their lives with their roles.

The Mail-Sex Mama's mama on her brief son-in-law:

> "He would be real nasty and sometimes he would be sweet. She liked him when he was sweet. I told her that he's an actor, and how is she going to know when he's acting?"

Or, as Ellroy opines, "The Suspect's an *actor*—oh, shit, we're fucked in L.A."[18] In other words: the particular unconscious orientation that inclines certain people to be actors, that "psycho" orientation rooted in self-hating and self-aggrandizing, also inclines them toward criminality. LA is "fucked"—California is "fucked"—in no small part because it has done nothing but attract and reinforce and promote the kind of self-hating narcissism that feeds its major image and industry. And in doing so, it has fed a particular brand of murderous criminality.

For Ellroy, acting and criminality are inseparable; the movie scene and the crime scene are in too many ways the same kind of place. We all know this on some level; we acknowledge this in our language by calling them both "scenes" and talking about them in terms of "staging." But Ellroy brings the implications of that linguistic acknowledgment to the fore. In indulging self-hating narcissists in one of those venues, he shows us, Southern Californian culture may be indulging much more.

WATCHING THE DETECTIVES

At the same time as it makes stars out of self-haters, the dynamics of the entertainment industry turn the rest of us into voyeurs. Voyeurism is one of the most frequent motifs in Ellroy's fiction, from his earliest to his most recent work.[19] Again, Ellroy is far from the first person to observe that the celebrity culture for which California is itself famous depends on turning the rest of us into eager, passive watchers. But in Ellroy's hands, the category of voyeurism moves into a territory even more disturbing than that which is usually traversed by those who lament, say, our cultural fascination with watching young celebrities implode. And Ellroy's analysis has several interlocking dimensions.

First, Ellroy makes the logical but rarely acknowledged connection between the fact that the powers of Hollywood teach us to love watching—watching movies, watching TV, watching celebrities—and the fact that watching is a consummate skill both for those who want to commit crimes and those who want to solve them. A good criminal and a good detective are both people who are good "watchers," and indeed Ellroy uses that word to describe both the committers and fighters of crime in his fiction. Especially when he describes a character as a talented watcher, that character is often someone—a so-called "bad cop," for instance—who is both a committer *and* a fighter of crime. He associates voyeurism, in other words, both with lives centered on crime and with the blurring of the line between law-breaking and law-enforcing.

In addition, Ellroy suggests that because Hollywood folks want to keep the rest of us watching and watching, they have to feed ever more titillating and violent images up for our eyes. In doing so, they create and feed a hunger for violence in the culture at large; they create, in other words, a voyeuristic hunger for violent crime. We, as an audience, demand ever more dramatic and violent imagery to keep us entertained. We want bigger and more realistic explosions, more life-like violence and bloodshed, more immersive watching experiences. Because of the psychodynamics that pervade California, the state, through Hollywood, encourages all kinds of people to become somewhat obsessed with crime and criminality, no matter whether they are in point of fact criminals. It is no mystery, in Ellroy's way of seeing, why "true crime" is perhaps the most consistently popular genre of entertainment—and by many counts, the fastest-growing genre of entertainment—in the contemporary United States.[20]

Many of the connections that Ellroy makes in these regards come from his own childhood, from what he calls his own voyeuristic "curse." The idea of this voyeuristic curse is central to Ellroy's self-understanding. In fact, the first thing that Ellroy reveals about himself in the autobiographical work *The Hilliker Curse* is that he grew up with a "voyeur's eye," an eye that inclined him both to a fondness for cinema and to a fondness for spying on other people, particularly women.[21] As he told one interviewer, "I love movies, and I'm a voyeur." So "I was going around looking in windows and peeping and perving out here and there."[22] Eventually, Ellroy started breaking into local houses, finding that "burglary was voyeurism multiplied a thousand times," providing the thrill of "other worlds briefly captured."[23]

His voyeuristic criminal pursuits, says Ellroy, owed in no small part to a "tabloid sensibility" that Los Angeles not only enabled but also encouraged.[24] Voyeurism satisfied not only his hunger for watching, a hunger that had been fed by a steady diet of cinema, but also his self-hating and self-aggrandizing hunger to look and fit into other lives—both hungers that, as he tells it, are central to the California experience and the California unconscious. "L.A. looked *gooooood* in 1953," he writes. "I was a peeper, a voyeur, a baby fiend gassed on it all."[25] And what gassed up Ellroy was not just the voyeurism of his own criminality, but the voyeurism of looking at and imagining the crimes of others. "I came to murder as a voyeur," he writes. Watching TV, always watching, Ellroy followed the exploits of every local criminal sensation. And his father, a stereotypical Angeleno, fed the fuels of Ellroy's flame:

> My father co-signed my crime obsession. He never tried to derail my one-track tendency. I could read what I wanted to and watch unlimited TV. He talked to me like a pal. He shot me choice gossip gleaned from his years as a Hollywood bottom-feeder.[26]

The suggestion that Ellroy makes here, and that he makes again and again in his writing, is that California is all about watching and being watched, and that the cultural fascination there with the act of watching other lives (or watching others inhabit lives other still) creates a generally voyeuristic culture. (Tellingly, "voyeur" is one of the words Ellroy uses most repeatedly to describe his characters.)

Again, the act that is central to the success of the entertainment industry—watching others, and most often watching them while you are in the dark—has a criminal counterpart in everyday life. The movie watcher behaves not so differently than the peeping tom (or the "respectable" writer who spends his career writing about peeping toms). On top of that, the constant Hollywood appetite for gossip and intrigue—the more titillating and gruesome, the better to watch—also has a corollary in everyday life: a cultural obsession with criminals and crime. It breeds a market for crime stories, among other things, which is one of the main reasons that Ellroy says that "noir is primarily L.A. based."[27] California breeds the habits of, and the hunger for, crime. That manifests itself in crime stories, crime movies, crime television; it manifests itself in the actual commission of crimes; and it manifests itself in a muddying of the lines between all of those things.

Ellroy illustrates this proposition in more than one of his novels by creating scenarios in which would-be criminals and crime-fighters deliberately ape Hollywood productions about criminals and crime-fighters. Show imitates life imitates show. For instance, in *Clandestine*, the protagonist apes a television star when he is looking for information about a lost woman:

> Through a door a cranky voice called out, "Who is it?"
>
> "Police officer, ma'am," I called out, consciously imitating Jack Webb of "'Dragnet" fame.
>
> Giggles answered my announcement. The door was flung open a moment later, and I was confronted by the adoring gaze of a gasbag matron. I quickly sized her up as a crime buff and took my act from there.[28]

More personally, Ellroy writes about his own intense relationship with the television show *The Fugitive*:

> I watched episodes of *The Fugitive*. They ticked time to the JFK hit. I recall the plotlines and the guest-star women still.
>
> I watched *The Fugitive* and read crime novels. I brain-screened crime fantasies. I eyeballed rich girls and their fortyish moms throughout Hancock Park.
>
> Obsession suited me . . .. The blur heightened.[29]

Hollywood dramas, as Ellroy suggests on more than one occasion, offer a script for real-life criminal activity and investigation. The voyeur watches actors playing in a criminal drama, and then the voyeur imitates the imitation. The line between play-acting and law-breaking muddies. It all becomes a kind of blur.

To take a step back, Ellroy's depictions of voyeurism link watching to a kind of passivity that is not just physical but moral and ethical as well. It is not just that voyeurism links the entertainment industry to the criminal element; it is that voyeurism creates a certain kind of cultural ethos that is chilling at best and probably outright damaging to the human relationships that are the necessary fabric of a healthy society. As Peter Wolfe, one of Ellroy's most thoughtful interpreters, puts it, "Watching both paralyzes action and creates the emotional distance that chills moral response." So in a culture like California, where voyeurism is both obliquely and directly encouraged, "the upshot" is "a society of orphans, loners divided from both each other and a sustaining, nourishing past." Individuals exist in conditions of "bleak detachment," longing to connect with others but unable to do so in ways that are truly interactive, let alone meaningful or fulfilling. Voyeurs are people who are talented at using their eyes, but Ellroy reveals how the watchers are more fundamentally blind.[30] Ellroy's California is a place in which everyone is staring at each other, but nobody knows how to see each other; it is a psychologically and socially damaged and damaging place.

In *Perfidia*, for example, Kay Lake confronts the bad-cop-character William H. Parker and calls him a "goddamn voyeur." She elaborates:

> You knock on women's doors at night and extort them, because you get your kicks that way, because you have a famously bereft marriage, and you're coming out of your skin with boredom and that slimy, itchy *something* that drives brutal men like you.

Parker does not deny the charge, saying, "I won't deny that I tend to watch and stare." He then says that Lake is not actually mad about his watching; she is mad because she hates the fact that she *likes* to be watched. Lake steps toward him, and the moment is sexually charged. ("Their arms brushed. Her body was warm.")

Then Lake says to Parker: "Whatever you do, don't underestimate the fact that *I see you.*" In fact, she says, "recognition is a two-way street." Parker, unnerved, takes a step back.[31] The watcher, for all he has seen, has failed to account for the obvious: that the watcher can be watched, too. He has been blind to his own visibility. Being a voyeur has made Parker feel powerful and in control, but Lake exposes how impotent and vulnerable he really is. In this exchange, there is a major power shift; Lake evens the playing field between herself (a social outsider) and Parker (who is a captain in the Los Angeles Police Department). Lake's account of Parker's voyeurism, we are meant to see, cuts to the truth. For all his watching, he has not really seen.

Ellroy makes a similar case in describing his own "watcher's lifetime": the period of his own obsessive voyeurism, which by his account lasted almost

40 years. He talks about his watching as an act that gave him a false sense of "mastery and an endless ticket to ride." What that false sense of mastery concealed, what was "vaulted and lockboxed" by all that watching, Ellroy writes, was a pervasive and "debilitating hunger" for love and connection, particularly with members of the opposite sex. His watching allowed him to imagine he was in control, in large measure because he was afraid of the degree to which he might actually be helpless, or at least dependent. He had to overcome the lie of his voyeurism—to realize that what he really was out for was "women looking back and up at me"—to even begin to live a conscious life. By Ellroy's account, his voyeurism had almost "proved fatal" in distracting and distancing him from what he really had always wanted.[32] The voyeurism in which he had been schooled, and which he had worked so hard to perfect, was in fact blinding him to himself. And it was preventing him from having real relationships with other people.

It is telling that more than one of Ellroy's criminal characters are also professional photographers. They are individuals who are granted serious professional authority and power in the Californian hierarchy, and they are both watchers themselves and mediums for others to be able to become watchers themselves. Again and again, Ellroy draws pictures of California which are pictures of a culture (or a "mini-culture") of watchers.[33] In that culture, people are always looking and being looked at; seeing and being seen is a primary activity. Taking pictures and having pictures taken of you are considered not just respectable but desirable occupations. Yet that cultural emphasis works to preclude self-knowledge and the mutual recognition that are the necessary supports for any mature human relationship or any flourishing human community. Just as psychologists have noted that voyeurs are in one way or another delusive about their relationships with the people whom they watch, Ellroy suggests that California is a place which is socially delusive, socially stunted, socially dangerous.[34] It is both a reflection of and a contributor to a "shifting and lonely America," in which failures of recognition are the rule, even though everyone is always looking at each other.[35] Although LA and California, with all their sunshine and glitz, don't seem like the "lonely landscapes" that are typical stage for Gothic writing, in Ellroy's telling they are just about the loneliest landscapes on Earth.[36] He says it outright: "L.A. Life is," he writes, "lonely."[37]

CHEAP DATES

For Ellroy, the pervasive loneliness of California helps to explain what is finally, for him, a signal feature of the state: the prevalence of random and often manipulative sexual relationships, many if not most of which involve the victimization of women. In a culture juiced on its own reinvent-your-own-life mythology, filled with self-hating narcissists and lonely watchers, it is not just unsurprising but logical that individuals will pursue superficial and often aggressive sexual agendas. In Ellroy's telling, this fact has always been part of the fabric of California, going back to the times when "white settlers raped Indian squaws" all over the state, and later, when the "Wild West lawmen" who "were psychopaths and drunks" assaulted whatever women came their way. Californians have thrived on their own embrace of some kind of wild-western myth about themselves. But "the Wild West played hell on women—then and now." As such, "Wild West Saturday Nights comprised a myth of their own."[38] (Ellroy, it is worth noting, was talking about a "rape culture" long before self-proclaimed activists were doing the same.)

In Ellroy's telling, the promise of cheap sex has always been part of what attracts lonely and self-hating people to come to California. People have often migrated to California, in Ellroy's telling, because they imagine it as a place where they can satisfy sexual desires that would be outré at home. Tellingly, he describes his own parents' moves to California in those terms:

> My father arrived in the '30s. He was a tall, handsome guy with a gigantic *schvantz* and an inspired line of bullshit . . .. He jumped on every woman who'd let him and firmly believed that every woman who didn't let him was a lesbian . . .. [My mother] got the urge to start over in a sexy, new locale.

If you have a desire to come to Los Angeles, Ellroy says at one point, your submission to the myth of the city "categorizes you as an opportunist with a hidden sexual agenda," as a person who is almost bound to imagine your own desired reinvention in terms of sexual desire itself.[39] People come to California out of a desire and hunger, and in service to desire and hunger. Almost unavoidably, those desires and hungers manifest themselves in outsize or exploitative sexual activity.

Interestingly, the suggestion Ellroy makes here lines up in the psychological sense with his account of California as a destination for self-hating narcissists. Psychoanalytic theory teaches that narcissistic people are not just "attention-seeking and exhibitionistic" but also "are unstable in their sexual involvements." Sexual promiscuity is a common trait of narcissists. And narcissists become promiscuous, in the psychoanalytic account, to satisfy their fantasies of omnipotent control and to engage in a kind of projective identification that precludes real intimacy.[40] It is psychologically unsurprising that in a culture that attracts and coddles self-hating narcissistic behavior, sexual promiscuity and sexual exploitation would be closer to the rule than the exception.

Ellroy's discussions of his own adolescence and early adulthood are illustrative. His own experiences demonstrate how the narcissism and loneliness that are so embedded in California culture collide when it comes to sex, fostering an atmosphere that is predatory at best. As he remembers it, Ellroy spent much of his young adulthood stalking lonely women, knowing that lonely women were everywhere to be found in Southern California. And he knew, he says, that "lonely meant hungry. Hungry meant horny and estranged and accessible." For years, he stalked and spied on those women—ever the voyeur—and when he finally emerged from his "watching" period, he "perfected the art of womanizing": "I once scanned faces for rectitude. I now scanned them for predation." Ellroy describes how the loneliness and self-hating grandiosity that had propelled him into voyeurism later propelled him into shallow and manipulative sexual relationships.[41]

Ellroy describes his own forays as mildly exploitative, but his real fascination is with the crucible that Los Angeles is for extreme and devastating sexual violence. From the moment his mother was murdered (in what he suspected and later learned was a crime that had something to do with sexual desire), Ellroy has focused his attention—and focused his readers' attentions—on California as a site of brutal sexual violence against women. The Black Dahlia, a beautiful young aspiring actress (of course) who was chillingly tortured and killed in Los Angeles in the opening days of 1947, was his first major literary subject.[42] And virtually all of his subsequent novels include some scenario of sexual predation or abuse of women. It is "obsessive male desire, random male desire," born of the idea of Los Angeles itself, that in particular haunts James Ellroy's California, just as it haunts James Ellroy's own life.

CONCLUSION: JAMES ELLROY'S CALIFORNIA, JAMES ELLROY'S AMERICA

Even given all the grisly and gruesome gore that marks James Ellroy's fiction, in some ways the most purely upsetting volume of his work is *My Dark Places*, the autobiographical volume in which he recounts undertaking, thirty-something years after his mother's murder, the mission to find her killer. What is most upsetting about the book comes not from imagining how hard it must be, to be a motherless son, although that is upsetting enough. What is most upsetting is that Ellroy seems to return, again and again, to the futility of trying to find or identify *anyone* in the "ambiguously defined" and "shit-kicker" San Gabriel Valley (which is more or less the area of Los Angeles that stretches out to the city's east).[43] Ellroy describes the area, correctly, as a place cut up with freeways and transients and migrants and movers, as a place without a center of gravity. It was and is a place where the murder of a young mother attracted little attention, the story competing as it did against various celebrity headlines. It was and is a place where so many people were coming and going that nobody would really remember seeing that young woman—or be able to identify the man she was with—on the night of her killing. And it was and is a place that is so atomized that few people would even claim to have known that young mother at all.

Part of the truly tragic undertone to *My Dark Places* is Ellroy's lament that "the region defined the crime," that "the region was the crime," and that "the region explained it all." The greater Los Angeles area has always been and is and may always be a place where, although lots of people are always around and looking at each other, great crimes can go unseen and unsolved. It is a place so sprawling and estranging that satisfying or intimate human relationships are rendered all but impossible, and the idea of community is little more than a Hollywood fantasy. Come to Los Angeles, Ellroy writes, and "you can live in a community of people who came to L.A. to be somebody else."[44] It's a typically haunting phrase, for what kind of community can flourish among people who move centrifugally, trying to pull farther and farther away from any kind of center? Ellroy's writing gives the answer: not any kind of community you'd want to be alone in for too long at night. And yet in his writing, the best Los Angeles seems to be able to offer its inhabitants is the promise of what might happen if you go out alone at night. And so the city and the state contribute to the further debasement of the already debased residents.

When Alexis de Tocqueville visited Saginaw, Michigan, which at the time of his trip to the United States was the western frontier, he was horrified to behold a society of individuals who shared nothing but the fact that they were leaving their old lives behind. In Saginaw, he writes, "Chance, interest or desire had brought together these thirty people in this narrow space. There was no other common link between them, and they were profoundly different."[45] The only thing the residents of the frontier had in common, though they lived together, was the fact of their self-interested desires. On top of that, the residents of Saginaw acted as if they were not a community; they cast only looks of hatred and suspicion on one another. What Tocqueville saw in Saginaw, so reminiscent of what Ellroy sees in his own western frontier, taught him that "equality of condition" could mean something other than the third-grade version of democracy as a condition in which we all love and tolerate each other. Equality of condition, Tocqueville saw, could mean something base and disturbing, an equality among men who cared nothing for each other, who were bound only by their geographical proximity and commitment to advancing their individual self-interests. The worst that Tocqueville imagines for democracy, in *Democracy in America*, is that mass democracy would turn out to be something like an extended version of Saginaw—one that also has all the problems of a complicated and vast society, not to mention great power. It was the thought that would move him, in that book, to emphasize the importance of associations in a liberal democracy, to emphasize a more robust spirit of equality.

It is not a stretch to say that James Ellroy's California is the powerful and complicated Saginaw that Tocqueville most feared. Not only is it a powerful and complicated place, but also it is a place that confounds rather than promotes human association. James Ellroy's California is corrosive to political order in the specific sense of that order, a fact which is underscored by his recurring motif of lawmen who are lawbreakers. But it is also corrosive to political order in the first order, in the sense that Ellroy's California is a place which not only cannot sustain or nurture but actively undermines possibilities for the healthy human relationships that are the bedrock of community and public life.

One of the things that is said most commonly about James Ellroy's writing is that in it, he washes to the surface the hidden parts of California, the seedy underbelly to all that glitz and glamour. But what gives Ellroy's writing special power is that he understands, in a way that perhaps no other Californian writer understands so well, is that the glitz and glamour *is* the seedy underbelly. And the underbelly *is* all that glitz and glamour. The beauty is the beast. When we invite in all that beauty, it is the beast that comes to feed at our table.

California is the destination toward which the American endeavor has pointed, the point west toward which we have exhorted our young men (and women) to go, the physical instantiation of so many American dreams. It's the aspirational American "somewhere," Ellroy tells us, and that should be frightening. Because in the end, California is only a notable "somewhere" because it is "the Big Nowhere."[46]

NOTES

1. James Ellroy. *My Dark Places*. New York: Alfred A. Knopf, 1996. p. 251.
2. James Ellroy. *Crime Wave: Reportage and Fiction from the Underside of L.A.* New York: Vintage, 1999. p. 262.
3. James Ellroy. *Destination: Morgue!: L.A. Tales*. New York: Knopf, 2004. p. 12.
4. Ellroy. *My Dark Places*. p. 251.
5. Steven Powell, ed. *Conversations with James Ellroy*. Jackson, MS: The University Press of Mississippi, 2012. p. 92.
6. Ellroy. *Crime Wave*. p. 261.
7. Ibid. p. 239.
8. James Ellroy. *The Big Nowhere*. New York: Warner Books, 1988. p. 234.
9. Ellroy. *Crime Wave*. p. 165. That sentiment is so important to Ellroy that he repeats it elsewhere. "The actors' psyche as defined by some actor-savant: 'My only regret in life is that I'm not somebody else.'" p. 91.
10. Ellroy. *Destination: Morgue!* p. 171.
11. James Ellroy. *The Hilliker Curse*. New York: Vintage, 2011. p. 15.

12. Ellroy. *Crime Wave*. p. 239.

13. Ibid. p. 165.

14. Psychoanalytic literature suggests that all narcissists are to some degree self-hating—people who are "diagnosably narcissistic" have "a sense of vague falseness, shame, envy, emptiness or incompleteness, ugliness, and inferiority"—and so the description of the "self-hating narcissist" technically may be redundant. I use the term here because I think it helps to explicate Ellroy's thinking. See Nancy McWilliams. *Psychoanalytic Diagnosis, Second Edition: Understanding Personality Structure in the Clinical Process*. New York: Guilford Press, 2011. p. 185.

15. Ellroy. *Crime Wave*. p. 91.

16. Ellroy. *Crime Wave*. pp. 238–241.

17. James Ellroy. *Killer on the Road*. New York: HarperCollins, 1986. p. 18.

18. Ellroy. *Destination: Morgue!* pp. 161; 165–166.

19. See Jim Mancall. *James Ellroy: A Companion to the Mystery Fiction*. Jefferson, NC: McFarland & Company, 2014. p. 200.

20. See, for instance, Carol Memmott, "True-Crime Series Go Gangbusters," *USA Today* (June 26, 2012), 2d; Carlett Spike, "The Pod Squad," *Quill* 110.1 (Spring 2022), 8–13; Emily Steel, "For Cable Network, Crime Certainly Pays," *The New York Times* 164.56 (January 5, 2015), B1–B4.

21. Ellroy. *The Hilliker Curse*. p. 3.

22. Powell. *Conversations with James Ellroy*. p. 156.

23. Ellroy. *My Dark Places*. p. 132.

24. Ibid. p. 106.

25. James Ellroy. *LAPD '53*. New York: Abrams, 2015. p. 3.

26. Ellroy. *My Dark Places*. p. 106; 388.

27. Ellroy. *LAPD '53*. p. 55.

28. James Ellroy. *Clandestine*. New York: HarperCollins, 1982. p. 238.

29. Ellroy. *Destination: Morgue!* pp. 36–37. Elsewhere, Ellroy talks of watching "The Fugitive" and writes, "The title character was my imagined self as a sexual igniter. . . . I fucking lost it and wept every Tuesday night." (Ellroy. *The Hilliker Curse*. p. 26). In another reminiscence, he says:

> I was obsessed with that show in a way I've never been obsessed with any show since. Here's this tormented fifteen-year-old kid, and his stand-in is handsome David Jannsen who's bopping around from one town to the next, all of which look like L.A., cops are in hot pursuit, and the grooviest woman in town falls in love with him wherever he goes. (Powell. *Conversations with James Ellroy*. p. 59)

30. Peter Wolfe. *Like Hot Knives to the Brain: James Ellroy's Search for Himself*. Lanham, MD: Rowman & Littlefield, 2005. p. 186.

31. James Ellroy. *Perfidia*. New York: Knopf, 2014. pp. 127–128.

32. Ellroy. *The HIlliker Curse*. pp. 70-71.

33. Wolfe. *Like Hot Knives to the Brain*. p. 186.

34. Elizabeth L. Jeglic. "Voyeurism." In *Encyclopedia of Psychology and Law*. Edited by Brian L. Cutler. Thousand Oaks, CA: SAGE Publications, 2008. p. 735.

35. Ellroy. *The Hilliker Curse*. p. 26.

36. Wolfe. *Like Hot Knives to the Brain*. p. 242.

37. Ellroy. *LAPD '53.* p. 38.
38. Ellroy. *My Dark Places.* p. 64.
39. Ellroy. *Crime Wave.* pp. 261–262.
40. Otto F. Kernberg. *Aggression in Personality Disorders and Perversions.* Binghamton, NY: Vail-Ballou Press, 1992. p. 63.
41. Ellroy. *The Hilliker Curse.* p. 42.
42. James Ellroy. *The Black Dahlia.* New York: Warner Books, 1987.
43. Ellroy. *My Dark Places.* p. 20.
44. Ellroy. *Crime Wave.* p. 261.
45. Alexis de Tocqueville. "A Fortnight in the Wilderness." *Journey to America.* Edited by J. P. Mayer. New York: Anchor Books, 1971. pp. 391–392, 395.
46. Ellroy. *The Big Nowhere.* Ellroy also uses the phrase "the Big Nowhere" to describe Los Angeles in *The Black Dahlia.* p. 350.

BIBLIOGRAPHY

Ellroy, James, *My Dark Places.* New York: Alfred A. Knopf, 1996
Crime Wave: Reportage and Fiction from the Underside of L.A. New York: Vintage, 1999.
Destination: Morgue!: L.A. Tales. New York: Knopf, 2004.
Destination: Morgue!: L.A. Tales. New York: Knopf, 2004
The Hilliker Curse. New York: Vintage, 2011.
Killer on the Road. New York: HarperCollins, 1986.
Jeglic, Elizabeth L., "Voyeurism." In *Encyclopedia of Psychology and Law.* Edited by Brian L. Cutler. Thousand Oaks, CA: SAGE Publications, 2008.
Kernberg, Otto F., *Aggression in Personality Disorders and Perversions.* Binghamton, NY: Vail-Ballou Press, 1992.
McWilliams, Nancy, *Psychoanalytic Diagnosis, Second Edition: Understanding Personality Structure in the Clinical Process.* New York: Guilford Press, 2011.
Mancall. James, *James Ellroy: A Companion to the Mystery Fiction.* Jefferson, NC: McFarland & Company, 2014.
Memmott, Carol, "True-Crime Series Go Gangbusters," *USA Today,* June 26, 2012.
Powell, Steven, *Conversations with James Ellroy.* Jackson, MS: The University Press of Mississippi, 2012.
Spike, Carlett, "The Pod Squad," *Quill* 110.1, Spring 2022.
Steele, Emily, "For Cable Network, Crime Certainly Pays," *The New York Times* 164.56 January 5, 2015.
Tocqueville, Alexis de, "A Fortnight in the Wilderness." *Journey to America.* Edited by J.P. Mayer. New York: Anchor Books, 1971.
Wolfe, Peter, *Like Hot Knives to the Brain: James Ellroy's Search for Himself.* Lanham, MD: Rowman & Littlefield, 2005

Chapter 2

Through the Eyes of *Les Femmes*

James Ellroy's Gender Politics of "Killing Women to Save Them"

Deirdre M. Condit

This chapter examines the gender politics within James Ellroy's crime fiction by focusing on the fervent, autobiographical preoccupation with his personal relationship to both masculinity and violent crimes against women that permeates his literary body. Throughout his work, Ellroy struggles to reconcile a credible conception of heroic masculinity for himself, and for his male characters, with his own personal history of sexual compulsions and predatory behaviors toward women. While scholars generally agree that Ellroy's particular brand of "nostalgic masculinity" invokes the traditional, hegemonic, and racialized notions of maleness that dominated American political culture in the post–World War II era (Albrecht, 2015; Ashman, 2020), I want to argue that his struggle with masculinity is complicated by the concomitant rise of feminism during and after World War II that increasingly nudges women to refuse to collude in their own self-subordination—an aspect of masculinity theory generally overlooked by Ellrovian scholars. Drawing on the work of feminist theorist Sarah Hoagland, I argue that Ellroy's personal struggle, and the commensurate struggles he writes into the men he invents, derives from a central feature of traditional masculinity that reproduces men as both women's protectors and predators, simultaneously, and which requires, through the system of heterosexualism, that women collude in their own subordination to make the system work (Hoagland S. L., 1995). As post–World War II feminism continues to gain strength, it increasingly empowers women to stop covering for heterosexualism's incoherencies. As a result, masculinity's brutish truths are progressively laid bare. Ellroy's project reflects the rising panic experienced by many men in response to this disturbing exposure.

In keeping with Hoagland's feminist theorizing about heterosexualism and the nature of violence against women, this essay argues that Ellroy's resolution to men's frustration at their increasingly obvious exposure turns out to be to blame women for their own victimization at men's hands—thereby deflecting the fault and absolving men, and Ellroy himself, of the need to square their predator/protector conundrum at all. Across his work, Ellroy routinely relies on the worn-out, crime novel bromide *cherchez la femme*, meaning "look for the woman," thus suggesting that there is always a woman to blame for men's troubles (Chevalier-Karfis, 2020). For Ellroy, this is his guiding truth; as he explains in an essay discussing *The Black Dahlia*, "'Cherchez la femme, Bucky. Remember that.' I do. It's God's great gift to me and my moral bedrock. I will never forsake that pure thought" (Ellroy, "My Mother and the Dahlia," 2006). Ellroy notes elsewhere that his life's work is a "quest for 'atonement in women'" ("James Ellroy on Writing the Hilliker Curse," 2010). As Hoagland's work will make evident, it is only within a system of gender politics like heterosexualism that the idea that women are somehow accountable for their own victimization, in both fact and fiction, could possibly make sense. And yet, giving life to that grotesque idea is precisely what Ellroy has been about since first learning of his mother's brutal, sexualized murder when he was just a boy of ten (Ellroy, *My Dark Places*, 1997, pp. 126–27).

Though Ellroy insists that he really "lives in 1942" and "what happens today is of no interest" to him, this essay concludes by noting that increasingly, because of a progressively more powerful feminist movement, the eyes of *les femmes* have become empowered to stare back at the predators and to speak of what they see. In doing so, *les femmes* are increasingly giving witness to the myriad myths of heterosexualism's "protections" and giving voice to their horrific experiences of predation. As a result, a quarter of the way through the twenty-first century, the ubiquity and brutality of men's predatory behaviors has become ever more evident in American gender politics—much to the discomfort of many men of power. Predictably, the system of heterosexualism is fighting back—trying to reassert the "masculine virtues America needs" (Hawley, 2023). The danger, once again anticipated in Hoagland's prescient theorizing, is that enhanced violence, in many guises, will be the response when women refuse to collude.

While the works of writers like James Ellroy have surely fueled masculinity's historic sense of empowerment and entitlement to both protect and predate upon women, contemporary feminism increasingly empowers women to see the system of their own subordination for what it is. As a result, as more women feel empowered to reject heterosexualism's demand that they collude with the system that protects and empowers those who overwhelmingly commit violence against women, crime fiction works like those of James Ellroy, works that celebrate, relish, or sensationalize women's gruesome deaths, and other forms of violence against women, at the hands of "bad" men, so that "good" men can save them, will increasingly lose their appeal, as well.

PRE–WORLD WAR II MASCULINITY MEETS POST–WORLD WAR II FEMINIST WOMEN

One of the most important contributions of post–World War II feminism is the ongoing reexamination and deconstruction of America's gender politics and our systems of sexual power. Before the war, the basic tenets of American gender politics were essentially dichotomous and stable. "Good" men were women's protectors, and women, "by nature" more fragile and vulnerable, needed men's protection. Good men were women's heroes. "Bad" men, on the other hand, were predators and criminals who threatened good men's women. Born in 1948, Ellroy's life began as America's feminist welling tsunami gained speed with the end of World War II. Radical transformations in women's lives, caused by the war, rapidly undermined America's sex dichotomous ideology when the bulk of the country's men were sucked out to wage war on two foreign fronts. The sudden absence of most young and middle-aged men left women to fill in the countless public and private roles previously occupied almost exclusively by those men. Regardless of the numerous outcries that working women were "unnatural," the "Rosie the Riveter" effect meant that women spent much of the war period learning different lessons than those they had learnt previously through the narrow lens of femininity permitted them in a world that had been defined by a sex dichotomous system. Without men to protect and provide, women had to learn to function independently and self-reliantly in both the public and private realms.[1] Sisters were learning to do it for themselves. As feminist scholarship has amply documented, once learnt, a large portion of these women had no appetite to unlearn those new lessons when the war was through (Kimmel M. S., 2008).

By contrast, the battle lessons learnt by America's manly warriors were exactly the opposite. While America's women were busily deconstructing the sex dichotomous system they had previously accepted as truth, the lived realities of war-making were reinforcing men's understanding of the manly lessons of virtue, strength, dominance, fearlessness, courageousness, and violence, thus hardening masculine ideology even further (Robb & Pattinson, 2018). Men went to war against other men; thus, their battles of manliness spiraled upward. Men's physical might and their courage were what made them men of war. Men went to war to protect the women and children back home. In short, the old masculinity gained tautological heft: war was a manly pursuit (Jarvis, *The Male Body at War: American Masculinity during World War II*, 2004).

Horrifically, millions of men lost their lives, but for those who survived, coming home held the promise of returning to the rewards, privileges, and benefits for which they had been fighting so vociferously: sexual and other access to grateful, pliable, doting sweethearts and all the powers that come to the victors of the world. Men expected to return to the world they had left, a world in which the privileges and power that came with living as America's independent, free controllers of the nation would once again be theirs (Pitt, 2021). In order for this to happen, however, America's new, confident, and independent Rosie the Riveters had to somehow be shoehorned back into their useless high heels, re-aproned at home, and forced off the country's manufacturing floors and out of their new office suites (Kimmel M. S., 2008). Many women resisted. Women, who had been living without a man telling them how to live for many years by the end of the war, liked their newfound freedoms and were not easily persuaded to surrender them again.

Thus, one side of the sex dichotomous system slumped. The "woman" side of the two-bar frequency graph of the sex binary shed its crisp lines of feminine identity. The category of woman morphed into a fluid and diverse shape that defied easy containment across the ensuing decades. Women decided to wear pants. Women bobbed their hair. Women earned paychecks. Women wanted credit in their own names. Women sought contraception and other reproductive health care options to ensure that they became parents only by their choice. Women expressed their own understanding of sexuality. Women no longer needed men in their lives, at least in the ways they had previously, so men had to make themselves somehow newly desirable or risk irrelevance.

By contrast, the "man" side of the sex dichotomy system responded with ever greater rigidity. No longer easily measured against a knowable (and definable) "other," many men grabbed the boundaries of masculinity and wrapped themselves within them even more tightly, avidly trying to shore up their differences from what they had always understood women to be. Masculinity pulled itself in, staking out new attributes that were ostensibly *really* definitive of manliness, such as military power, athletic prowess, elective politics, business, wealth accumulation, and education in elite and exclusive disciplines. Through their pursuits and their actions, men attempted to reinscribe and resolidify the "natural" distinctions between men and women.

Christina Jarvis argues that in the post–World War II era, American culture faced the problem of reabsorbing America's returning warriors; men who had simultaneously been primed for physical violence but whose desires to exercise that violence had been carefully regulated through the hierarchical system of control that marks the American military structure (Jarvis, *The Male Body at War: American Masculinity during World War II*, 2004). America's full-throated pivot toward reconstituting the American nuclear family after the war, through creation of the GI Bill, veterans' mortgage benefits, and a popular culture that willingly colluded by producing endless "family shows like *Leave it to Beaver*" provided a way to channel men's needs for domination and power into the model of paternal control. As Kimmel notes, the social commitment to recreating the nuclear family was also aimed at bringing women back home (2013).

Despite this, over the last three-quarters of a century, since the end of World War II, the speed with which women have been stepping out has only actually increased. Today, women are endlessly renovating their side of the sex dichotomous system of femininity, fragility, and dependence by reinventing their identities and often thereby trampling on the old standards of the idea of discrete sex/gender differences. The resounding financial and cultural success of the 2023 release of *Barbie*, a film about the existential death of women's doll-like existence and the feminist embrace of women choosing to be whatever they want to be in the world, demonstrates the extraordinary reach of feminist empowerment since the end of World War II (Gerwig, 2023).

That is not to say that all women have abandoned the marks of femininity altogether. Change doesn't come that quickly. Many social and political interests within the larger political culture, those still deeply reflective of the history of hegemonic masculinity, continue to work aggressively to get women back where they are thought to belong (Hawley, 2023). Despite these efforts, however, a lopsided dialectic has developed between women, who seek to throw off their feminine subjection, and the historic system of hegemonic masculinity which fervently wants to return women to their former, private, tiny selves. Regardless of the arguments made by (primarily) feminists to the contrary, a good portion of men and masculinity have stubbornly resisted the idea that in the post–World War II world, masculinity, as it had historically been constituted, has increasingly become antiquated.

A FEMINIST CRITIQUE: MASCULINITY UNDER HETEROSEXUALISM

Over the past two hundred years, feminists have offered scores of critiques of the system of masculinity, but Sarah Hoagland's late 1980s work on the morality of masculinity offers important insights into American gender politics, generally, and provides a pointedly useful tool for understanding Ellroy's struggles, in particular. According to Hoagland, masculinity in a heterosexual system is constituted by men through *both* predation and protection, which work in tandem to render women helpless (Hoagland S., 1989). The heroic tale of heterosexualism's masculinity held that there is a clean, bifurcated relationship among types of men within masculinity: men are either predators *or* protectors. Men who predate on women are bad men; men who protect women are good men. But as Hoagland makes evident, heterosexualism is more entwined than that. The gender politics of heterosexualism means that protectors and predators each need the other. Protectors, in order to gain identity, power, and status from their role as protectors, need other men to predate. This is so, Hoagland explains, because the need for protection is predicated on the threat (real or perceived) of danger—danger that is invoked by predation.

Concomitantly, predation is also part of the privilege of masculinity. That is, protective men are entitled to predate on *some* women in order to obtain them: it is the benefit of masculinity—the prize, if you will. The code of masculinity carefully demarcates *which* women, *whose* women, are ripe for predation and which women are "off limits" because they are "someone else's protective property." The key to the system is understanding the code—the rules and mores that guide men, and constrain them appropriately, so they can effectively negotiate the switchback system of protection and predation. This is important, not so as to make women safer but to keep the gender economy of women's bodies clear, among men. Predation takes many forms along a continuum of danger: from "girl watching," to stalking, to sexual harassment, to sexual assault, to isolating and controlling, to capturing and kidnapping, to killing. Both predators and protectors might engage in any or all of these at various times and with various women and often with impunity. As Hoagland points out, "the logic of protection is essentially the same as the logic of predation. Through predation, men do things to women and against women all of which violate women and undermine women's integrity. Yet protection objectifies just as much as predation. To protect women, men do things to women and against women; acting 'for a woman's own good,' they violate her integrity and undermine her agency" (Hoagland S., 1989, p. 176).

Additionally, it is important to note that heterosexualism also depends, in no small measure, on men understanding (though overtly denying) the illusion that men who protect and men who predate are really one and the same men. It is a kind of ignoble lie.

Protectors are supposed to get something for their beneficence—they are promised both sex and love, and, at the end of World War II, this included material and marital benefits of all sorts. Love is the adoration and admiration that becomes communicated through women's bodies as willing sex. Love is sex without resistance. Or, resistance that is really acceptance. This is not a new take on heterosexualism. Rousseau, for example, was celebrated for his poetic writings about the joys and allure of women's resistance to men's sexual aggressions. As he notes in *The Emile*, for example,

> If woman is made to please and to be subjugated, she ought to make herself agreeable to man instead of arousing him. Her own violence is in her charms. It is by these that she ought to constrain him to find his strength and make use of it. The surest art for animating that strength is to make it necessary by resistance. Then amour-propre unites with desire, and the one triumphs in the victory that the other has made him win. From this there arises attack and defense, the

> audacity of one sex and the timidity of the other, and finally the modesty and the shame with which nature armed the weak in order to enslave the strong. (Rousseau J.-J., 1979)

For Rousseau, the *right kind of resistance* makes sex *feel* like predation—but without the moral compromise for the man involved.

Predators, "real" predators, also get sex but generally it is unwilling sex. Or, predators, by definition, get unwilling sex from women, but, according to heterosexualism, *because* they have abandoned the protection of other men, and so, have actually invited it. So the logic of forced sex under predation is the same logic as sex under protection. But it is sex, nonetheless. In both circumstances, the attachment becomes linked to the thrill of resistance; the violence becomes erotic in either case (MacKinnon, 1995, p. 135).

Men cannot sustain this system on their own, however; women must collude in their own subordination if the system is to hold. This is key to understanding how heterosexualism persists. In order to be the objects of protection, women must be in danger, meaning they must be portrayed as and rendered helpless, and therefore, the targets of predation. This requires that women agree to act as their male protector says they should. They must make themselves helpless, appear feminine, and stay home within the boundaries of their protector's zone of control. Failing to do so exposes the myth of protection and thus undermines men's incentives to play the part. Moreover, when women reject or otherwise abandon their prescribed gender role as helpless victim, they become unintelligible within heterosexualism (Hoagland S., 1989, p. 182). In discussing Elizabeth Short's life, the real murdered woman whom he would fictionalize in *The Black Dahlia*, Ellroy describes her as a young woman who had set out to make her life on her own terms, outside of the protections of her Medford, Massachusetts family. Her "play girl life" and her rootless style of living meant to Ellroy that "her life was indecipherable" (Ellroy, *My Dark Places*, 1997, p. 126). Elizabeth Short was just one more woman, like any lone woman hitchhiker; she was perceived as having given up her right to protection and thus she invited her own attack. As Ellroy explains, "She turned herself into a cliché that most men wanted to fuck and a few men wanted to kill. She wanted to get deep dark down and cozy with men. She sent out magnetic signals. She met a man with notions of deep-dark-down-and-cozy cloaked in rage. Her only complicitous act was a common fait accompli. She made herself over for men" (Ellroy, *My Dark Places*, 1997, p. 127). Such women are repugnant to the system; men generally understand them as detestable and immoral. In order to reestablish the system's equilibrium, men respond by amplifying "overt physical violence against them in order to reaffirm women's victim status" (Hoagland S., 1989, pp. 175–176). When women act independently and exercise their freedoms outside of the protective perimeters of men, men must increase their threats against them to get them back in line. Under heterosexualism, such "bad women," who bring on predation by living "outside" of men's protections, also serve as contrasts to the "good women," who remain within the confines of their protector's realm, thus reinforcing the power of protection.

The success of masculinity as a system necessarily, then, also requires controlling women's ability to communicate about their experiences under heterosexualism—to each other and to men. In order for men's system to be protected, women must refrain from speaking the truth about their oppression and they must not call out those who abuse them. Should they dare to speak, their voices must somehow be silenced to keep the myth of masculinity intact. On the one hand, this has meant men literally cultivating a culture of ignoring women's voices; all women to some degree suffer the fate of Cassandra—the mythological daughter of Priam who was given the gift of prophecy but who was also fated to never be heard or believed. On the other hand, when violence is done to women by men, much of it is focused on removing women's ability to speak or to scream. The cover of the Warner paperback edition of Ellroy's bestselling novel *The Black Dahlia* shows a close-up profile of a presumably dead, prone Betty Short, her lifeless, doll-like glassy black eyes staring upward from within her starkly white porcelain face. Her mouth, slashed open from cheekbone to cheekbone, just as was done to the body of the once living Elizabeth Short by her attacker, makes clear her predator's message—she has been rendered mute through the violence done to her (Ellroy, *The Black Dahlia*, 1987). Protectors and predators both ignore or silence women's voices within heterosexualism.

People communicate in many ways beyond speaking; among the most powerful is through their eyes. The system of masculinity is so fragile, however, that men cannot risk women's knowing regard and so they must control women's gaze. One way to do this is to establish the gaze as ubiquitously male in nature, thus keeping the arrow running from men toward the objects they wish to claim (Mulvery, 1990). The other way is to eliminate or control women's capacity to see or to look back and communicate what they see through their eyes. Rousseau, again, notably teaches Sophie to become her own doll, ensuring that when Emile gazes at her, he sees nothing in her delicate, porcelain features, but his own shining image, shining back at himself in her two empty glass orbs, reflecting back nothing but admiration. Rousseau cautions Sophie that should she have the odd stray thought of her own, or the urge to open her dead-doll eyes to actually look, she must avert her eyes demurely, so as not to discomfort Emile, the man for whom she lives (Rousseau J.-J., 1979, p. 367).

When men see the things they do to women under heterosexualism, they experience shame. Empirical psychology tells us the experience of shame causes people to "deny, hide, or escape" and "promotes defensiveness, interpersonal separation, and distance" (Tangney, Stuewig, & Mashek, 2007). Moreover, shame invokes the person to search for "ways to preserve their self-esteem" (Gray, 2018). Indeed, research shows that "shame-prone individuals are more likely to engage in externalization of blame, experience intense anger, and express that anger in destructive ways, including direct physical, verbal, and symbolic aggression, indirect aggression (e.g., harming something important to the target, talking behind the target's back), all manner of displaced aggression, self-directed aggression, and anger held in" (Tangney, Stuewig, & Mashek, 2007, p. 351). Through the pen, Ellroy has spent the six decades since his mother's unsolved murder warding off the possibilities of experiencing his own shame.

Finally, a necessary paradox within the sex dichotomous system is that though stability and success of the system requires careful training and regulation, it must also be understood as entirely natural (Hoagland S. L., 1995). *Men* and *women* really exist, as ontologically distinct types of beings, because nature makes them that way. Thus, it is *natural* (or divine) that men are the protectors and women require protection (Hawley, 2023, pp. 17–28). The resort to essentialism precludes the challenge that something is wrong with the system (Laqueur, 1990). Indeed, it precludes opting out. So that people who do opt out are, by definition, then *un*natural and, therefore, regardless of what they experience, they pose little threat to the natural order of masculine power and domination.

The post–World War II world into which Ellroy was born was the same moment when women's resistance to the demands that they submit willingly to the system of heterosexualism had begun to gather momentum. Women, like his mother, were discovering their voices and seeking economic freedom through the workplace and away from the confines of domestic living. While most scholars look at the structural and other political elements reflected in Ellroy's work for evidence of the impact of the times on his writing, in my reading of his work, the arrow goes the other way. In the Ellroy household, the political was very much personal. Even as a boy-child of ten, at the point of his own mother's death, Ellroy had observed and internalized many of the era's lessons about "appropriate" masculinity and femininity. This is certainly true, at least from the lessons his father tried to teach him about what it meant to "be a man" of his day. Ellroy's library, taken as a piece, can be read as his struggle to negotiate his own identity within the heterosexualism-masculine-predations-and-protection-gender-politics-scheme.

THE MANY STORIES OF JAMES ELLROY THE PREDATOR AND JAMES ELLROY THE PROTECTOR

From the beginning, Ellroy has known he was a predator, but he never quite admits just how much his own predatory behaviors might have in common with the perpetrator who sexually assaulted and killed his mother. Despite his silence on the subject, his discomfort with that possibility is glaringly evident through the "ellipses" in his works (Ellroy, Brown's Requiem, 1981, p. 320). What makes Ellroy unsure is his response to his mother's death. Disoriented by his own pre-adolescent sexual response to seeing her naked as she stepped out of the bath, just a few months before her death, and torn between the emotional demands of his divorced and waring parents, Ellroy tells us he had been nurturing a childish hatred for his mother when he learnt she had been killed. As Ellroy explains it, "I hated her and lusted for her. And then she was dead" (Ellroy, *My Dark Places*, 1997, p. 112). This realization has haunted Ellroy ever since.

Over the subsequent six decades, the James Ellroy story is a tale of a man seeking to understand both his mother's death and the nagging sense of culpability generated by his early sexual obsessions about her (Ellroy, *The Hilliker Curse: My Pursuit of Women*, 2010, p. 36). Much of his personal life has been dedicated to the "pursuit" of women who resemble his red-headed mother, Jean Hilliker. In a series of failed relationships and marriages, as he recounts them across two autobiographies and numerous interviews, Ellroy continues to explore his fixation with her and with her unsolved murder. Through his intensely autobiographical crime fiction writing, he has repeatedly reimagined her death—exploring new endings so the killers are known. He frequently writes himself and his mother's ghost into the characters he invents, recreating and reimagining their relationship and rewriting their ending. He devoted a year of his life to trying, unsuccessfully, to solve her murder himself. Despite his dedication, and his mastery with the pen, Ellroy has yet to find a resolution that will finally allow him to leave her at rest (Ellroy, *My Dark Places*, 1997; Ellroy, *My Mother's Killer*, 2007).

Born in 1948, Ellroy was a child of the fifties and sixties, a period in American political history deeply affected by the dramatic changes in the nation's gender politics. These tectonic cultural changes were evident in Ellroy's childhood home. By his own account, his home was not a happy one. His parents' divorce, not long before his mother was murdered, was angry and filled with cross invectives, traded through the young Ellroy. Though the imaginative fiction writer's early descriptions of his mother are suspect, filtered through the sexual compulsions with which he views her, Ellroy describes Geneva "Jean" Hilliker as a white California woman, typical of the period: vivacious and competent. Like so many women after World War II, his mother worked full-time as a nurse and, because of her professional stability, she was the recognized breadwinner in the family. Across the arc of his life, Ellroy's recollections of his mother soften, but from the time of her death until the publication of his second autobiography, *The Hilliker Curse: My Pursuit of Women*, he writes her with uncomfortable scorn and rebuke

(Ellroy, *The Hilliker Curse: My Pursuit of Women*, 2010). He describes her as a "whore" and obsesses over her sexual activities. And though he readily admits his take on his mother was heavily filtered through his father's lens, Ellroy has spent much of his life grasping to understand who she was as a person (Ellroy, *My Dark Places*, 1997).

A persistent motif in Ellroy's writing is trying to "see inside" what he does not understand or what is otherwise obscured from his vision. He tells us in *My Dark Places* that he discovers and steals a football in the backyard of a home he has planned to break in to. "I stole it and cut it open with a pocket knife to see what was inside" (Ellroy, *My Dark Places*, 1997, p. 121). Later, he describes imagining the evisceration of Elizabeth Short's body by her killer, saying "all I saw was Betty being cut, slashed, poked, probed and dissected" (Ellroy, My Dark Places, 1997, p. 125). In *Brown's Requiem*, Ellroy's protagonist discovers two slaughtered and gutted greyhound puppies near the body of his sadistic villain, Fat Dog (Ellroy, *Brown's Requiem,* 1981, p. 149). Ellroy once again eviscerates dogs, this time Doberman Pinschers, in *White Jazz*, describing their hideous torture and disembowelment in great detail (Ellroy, *White Jazz*, 2001). As a teenager, Ellroy the youth became a peeping tom, breaking into the homes of girls about whom he had become obsessed, but whose lives were opaque to him. "I started prowling backyards and looking in back windows. The prowling was a thrill in itself. Back windows gave me intimate views. Bathroom windows were the best. I saw half-dressed women and women and girls in robes. I like to watch them putter in front of their mirrors (Ellroy, *My Dark Places*, 1997, p. 121). Recently, Ellroy dismissed the importance of these early predations, saying "my youth . . . has become distorted by repetition . . . my breaking and entering into houses and sniffing girls' undergarments and stealing five-dollar bills: Technically it's burglary, but it was craven. It was circumspect. It was very easy to do back then. . . . I did that 15, 16, 17 times over the course of two and a half years and got away with it." Ellroy sees his predation as a sign of his love for the girls whose lives he violated. "It was for the girls at Hancock Park. Those girls live in me: Kathy, Julie, Peggy" (Marchese, 2019).

In contrast to how Ellroy understood his mother, he depicts his father as a failure of a man, whose only claim to manliness was through his sexual predatory successes (Mancall, 2014, p. 85). Though Ellroy credits his father as anatomically exceptionally qualified as manly (Ellroy comments ubiquitously about the size of his father's penis), as a provider and protector, Armand Ellroy was an evident failure (Ellroy, *My Dark Places*, 1997, pp. 103–10). He lived off women, he lied about his status as a war hero, and in the end, he turned to his son, needing the child to stand in for the lost mother and nurse the father. Described as lazy, weak, and ineffectual, Ellroy's father failed at performing the other masculine tasks that were so heralded in post–World War II masculinity.

Ellroy's father died when Ellroy was seventeen, leaving his son orphaned, isolated, and socially adrift throughout his twenties. As a young adult, Ellroy spiraled further away from the civilization in which he lived. He dropped out of school, committed sex crimes involving the violation of the homes and things of young women he fetishized, stole to provide for himself, drank massive quantities of alcohol and abused drugs with abandon, and eventually adapted to the realities of impoverished homelessness. Regardless of how grotesque his life became, Ellroy remained undeterred by the deprivations of street life, the hunger of poverty, or the emotional instability of his fugitive lifestyle. Only when alcohol and drug addiction finally ravaged his body to the point of near death did Ellroy decide to change his behavior and seek sobriety—though, like most addicts it would take him repeated tries. His criminal breaking and entering sexual predations only stopped when his prowling was discovered one night as he entered a backyard of a home he mistakenly thought was empty. Finally thwarted by the threat of hard consequences, levied from the world he lived in but not of, Ellroy found another outlet for both his crime and sexual obsessions; he began to write. Lacking formal education but having developed a thirst for reading crime fiction after his father supplied him with books to read each week, Ellroy set about teaching himself how to write his way out of the pitiable world he had created for himself. Homelessness and poverty hindered his progress but finally, at the age of thirty-six, Ellroy published *Brown's Requiem*, a well-received first novel—one that drew heavily from his own, limited life experiences and from the mountain of crime fiction he had avidly consumed.

Brown's Requiem, a classic detective novel in form, unsurprisingly, draws heavily on Ellroy's own autobiographical history, complete with numerous allusions to his mother and her unsolved murder (Ellroy, *Brown's Requiem*, 1981, p. xi). Ellroy's protagonist, Fritz Brown, follows a string of murders with the hopes of striking it rich when he finds who is responsible. Formerly a cop, now turned "private eye," Fritz falls in love with Jane Baker, the sister of the depraved man who would prove to be one of several monstrous criminals in the tale. A one-night stand with Jane launches Brown toward a fantasy life with her he imagines once he solves the case, investing in her his hope for redemption from the "flawed life" he has built for himself alone (Mancall, 2014, p. 57). This idea, that bad men can be redeemed through the love of a good woman, persists across Ellroy's world; it has become his métier (Luce, 2019). But who is this "good woman" in Ellroy's writing?

Ellroy explores this question in *Brown's Requiem* through three fictional versions of his mother. The first, and most obvious, appearance of Jean Hilliker is in the guise of Jane. Ellroy draws her as the innocent, ideal woman, living under the protection of an older male benefactor, who supports her quixotic desire to play the cello. In the end, horrified by who Brown is and what he has done, Jane rejects Brown's one-sided vision of a married love nest, and, recoiling in horror from his "good man" depravities, retreats back into the sanctity of her benefactor's protections. Redemption for Brown must come at a distance; just her rejection is sufficient to put him on the path to being a better man (Ellroy, *Brown's Requiem*, 1981, pp. 317–21). Ellroy's quest for the healing, "good mother" gets more satisfactory expression in his representation of Sister Kallie, who Brown comes across in his journey for truth (Ellroy, *Brown's Requiem*, 1981, pp. 181–82). Though she rebuffs his entreaties for sex, she allows Brown to rest his head on her breast through the night, thus "restoring" him and "healing him through her mothering" (Mancall, 2014, p. 60). Finally, Ellroy's mother makes a final, if brief, appearance in the character of Louisa Hall, Ellroy's "bad mother," who refuses to nurse her newborn, thus perhaps fating him to a life of crime[2] (Ellroy, *Brown's Requiem*, 1981, p. 283). Ellroy's search for "the good woman" or, as he puts it throughout his many autobiographical means, "HER" eludes both his character, Brown, and Ellroy himself.

In the forty years since Ellroy published *Brown's Requiem*, the now 75-year-old author has produced an impressive library of crime fiction, including eighteen novels, most of which have been generally applauded, numerous short stories, and two edited crime fiction anthologies. But it isn't just fictional violent crime about which Ellroy obsesses; across two autobiographies and scores of interviews, Ellroy makes it clear that he has also spent much of his life constructing, curating, and narrating his own story as the son of a murdered woman about whom he continues to be disturbingly sexually obsessed and as a man who is ruled by his own sexual compulsions. His life and his life's work, in many ways, comprise a disturbing tale about his mother's gruesome, unsolved murder, and his fear that his own sexual obsessions and his inclination toward predation—eventually transmogrified in Ellroy's own telling of the tale into *love and protection* for women—somehow resulted in her death and in the deaths of so many other women (Wolfe, 2005). Even more insidious, however, is that James Ellroy's autobiographies make it clear he wants his readers to believe this, as well.

Ellroy's fervent and repeated denials of his own possible culpability are ubiquitous throughout his work. The message in his novels is clear: James Ellroy does not kill women; James Ellroy writes to *save* them (Ellroy, *The Hilliker Curse: My Pursuit of Women*, 2010, pp. 21–23). His autobiographies repeatedly make clear his LOVE for women, regardless of his personal life of bizarre sexual compulsions. In Ellroy's words, SEX IS LOVE, so surely he does not sexually abuse women. What Ellroy is telling us is that regardless of what he actually does, *he* is not a predator; he is women's protector. Like most boy-children of his age, he fancies himself women's hero. *Cherchez la femme* has become his catchphrase.

And yet, Ellroy *does* kill women. Gruesomely. Routinely. In great detail in his imagination and again through his pen. Ellroy tells us he brings women to God (Ellroy, *The Hilliker Curse: My Pursuit of Women*, 2010, p. 186). He comes to love dead women (Ellroy, *My Dark Places*, 1997, p. 243). And he cannot stop predating on them as a voyeur. How are we to understand a man, who remains haunted by both his sexual obsession with his murdered mother and writing about murdering women, yet claims to be saving them as he does so (Ellroy, *The Hilliker Curse: My Pursuit of Women*, 2010, p. 186)?

Ellroy prides himself on his talents as an imaginative storyteller. He is a master at twisting nuggets of truth (his mother really was murdered; JFK really was assassinated; J. Edgar Hoover really was the Director of America's FBI) and making up the world around those nuggets into stories that Ellroy wants us to think could be true. He learnt this, perhaps, from the fact that his mother's murder went unsolved. Police work often fails. Despite the fact that clues abound, sometimes they just can't "get the guy." Bad guys win and good guys lose. But if one is a writer of crime fiction, one can make the ending come out any way one wants it to. Ellroy "solves" the murder of Betty Short in *The Black Dahlia*; he "solves" his mother's murder in *Brown's Requiem*.

Crime fiction writing is about solving "who done it." In Ellroy's world, the institutions charged with answering that question failed him and so Ellroy does it through the pen. Solving his mother's murder is a consistent motif across several of his books. In addition, his works also routinely resurrect his mother through the women characters he writes. As noted above, all three women in *Brown's Requiem*, for example, are drawn from his mother in some way, as if he is trying to figure out which version of her is the real Jean Hilliker. Moreover, the entire plot of that first novel, not surprisingly perhaps, is glaringly autobiographical, mapping Ellroy's own life in detail and form. But his second novel, *Clandestine*, reanimates his mother and her murder, once again. Ellroy argues that he wrote this second iteration simply as an attempt to get his mother's murder "out of his system." It was not until publication of *The Black Dahlia* that Ellroy's obsession with his mother's murder had full expression, however. Though this work is credited by some with finally resolving his mother's death, at least metaphorically, because in the novel version of her death, Betty Short's murder is solved, that is a misreading of the ending. Ellroy resolves the fictive victim's murder by the end of *The Black Dahlia*, but Ellroy deflects with his ending, opting to write Short's murderer as a woman. But Ellroy knows overwhelmingly it is men who kill women (Ellroy, *My Dark Places*, 1997). Moreover, Ellroy lets the woman perpetrator escape punishment—she is never held accountable. Surely if Betty Short was killed by a woman, then it could not have been Ellroy himself who killed her. Or his mother. Either in real life or in the fictional worlds of his tortured imagination.

Hoagland presents heterosexualism de novo, but Ellroy is a case study in its development. Ellroy claims that his life is dedicated to contradictory goals: both saving and pursuing women. In Hoagland's language, Ellroy positions himself interchangeably as both woman's protector and her predator—and in so doing renders them basically indistinguishable. Ellroy insists that his personal predation is driven by love. So too do the men in Ellroy's crime fiction elide the distinctions between protection and predation. Examining why and how this happens reveals an Ellrovian world in which men's culture of masculinity is predicated on a kind of fluid intermingling of the masculine powers of predators and protectors that then, concomitantly, gain expression through the deployment and enactment upon the bodies of women. Women, who whether alive or dead, bear the burden of men's redemption. Both *Clandestine* and *Blood on the Moon*, for example, feature characters confused over who is the "good guy" and who is the "bad guy." In *Clandestine*, police officer Fred Underhill discovers he has much in common with murder suspect Eddie Engels. As Mancall notes, "throughout the novel, Underhill will confront evil men whose vices exaggerate or resemble his own" (Mancall, 2014, p. 64). The blurring of masculinities is even more pronounced in *Blood on the Moon:*

> Hopkins and Verplanck are matched in their eccentric but opposite genius as well as their desire to protect innocence. As a policeman, Hopkins seeks to punish the criminals who prey on the innocent. Verplanck also sees himself as protecting innocence. He carefully tracks his victims for weeks on end, tracing their movements and studying their private lives. He kills them to 'preserve' their innocence, murdering them before they descend into what he considers vulgar sensuality. (Mancall, 2014, p. 42)

Ellroy's world understands women as existing for men's purposes. As Hoagland makes clear, when women fail to make men's lives as protectors and predators possible, they do so at their own peril. Ellroy recounts a moment when, in response to his declaration that he wanted to live with his father, his mother slapped him, "knocking me off the living room couch. I banged my head on a coffee table. I called her a drunk and a whore. She hit me again. I made up my mind to fight back next time. I could brain her with an ashtray and negate her size advantage. I could scratch her face and ruin her looks so men wouldn't want to fuck her" (Ellroy, *My Dark Places*, 1997, p. 111). Her drunkenness and her anger in that moment rendered her both a bad mother and, in Ellroy's budding young understanding, a bad woman, as well. To the adult Ellroy's grown masculine identity, his mother represented all of the failures of post–World War II women, because they stepped out of men's protection. Not only did Ellroy's mother work outside the home, but she also drank and had sex with men who were not his father (nor Ellroy, it seems).

While she was enacting a life of a post–World War II liberated woman, Ellroy understands her through the lens of pre–World War II masculinity.

The difficulty is that he also saw his father through that same lens. Neither parent measured up. His mother was not the right kind of feminine mother; his father failed at masculinity. Ellroy tells us he hated them both. The sum for him was that the promise of family, a promise that surrounded him, was not available to him. Divorce was uncommon in 1958. His was a failed family. Who does the child Ellroy blame? And then, Ellroy tells us, he experienced his eruption of sexual compulsion. Targeted at, but also in his mind, caused by his mother's unregulated wantonness. She became the sex object men are supposed to get for being men. And she was murdered because of it (Ellroy, *My Dark Places*, 1997, p. 408). The institutions of femininity and masculinity and the family were already failing the young Ellroy, the child. But when his mother is murdered, his experience of institutional failure becomes even more severe. As he tells us in his detailed recollection of her murder investigation, even the cops investigating the crime fail him (Ellroy, *My Dark Places*, 1997).

But cops were not supposed to fail. In the early crime novels he read and the television crime shows he watched, the cops were the good guys and they always won; the bad guys did horrible things but were always held to account (Ellroy, *My Dark Places*, 1997, pp. 122–124). In that world, it was easy to distinguish the "real" protectors and the "real" predators. In his real child's life, however, he was learning more complicated lessons. The good guys failed to solve his mother's murder, and he found himself sexually aroused by her, even in death. He immersed himself in crime fiction in which killing women, often using sexual means, is common. He discovered the story of Elizabeth Short's unsolved murder; she and his mother became indistinguishable. Ellroy knew he was predating on women; his mother in particular. He tells us he became obsessed with imaging what it would be like to have sex with her, to attack her for having sex with him, and maybe, even to kill her. "I rescued Betty Short and became her lover. I saved her from a life of promiscuity. I tracked down her killer and executed him" (Ellroy, *My Dark Places*, 1997, p. 126). It becomes his world. And thus, he sublimates his internal "camera," as he calls it, into his imaginings of women's deaths. As he unravels the story of Elizabeth Short's murder, positioning himself as her savior—because he can solve the unsolvable crime, he realizes that both women, Jean Hilliker and Elizabeth Short, had *made themselves vulnerable* by their choices, their actions, and their lifestyles (Ellroy, *My Dark Places*, 1997, pp. 213–17). With only a handful of clues, filtered through his father's own predatory lens, Ellroy began to understand that though "bad men" had killed each of them, ultimately, both women were to blame for their deaths: Jean Hilliker and Elizabeth Short got themselves killed.

Adult men and women learn to perform their appropriate gender roles in a carefully regulated system (Butler, 1999). Being able to function within this complicated system requires vigilant adherence to the rules and norms of the system. Under heterosexualism, "Boys will be boys" means, learn when and upon whom to predate, when and whom to protect, and how to discern and negotiate the differences. The lessons taught are complex, coded by a complex system that marks women by their behaviors, appearances, and their willingness to submit to and keep close proximity to men's protections. Boys learn to discern which women are the "Madonna's" and which women are the whores (Hunter College Women's Studies Collective, 1995, pp. 32–35). In Ellroy's father's home, because all women were comprehensible only through sex, all women were whores, especially Ellroy's mother. As Ellroy writes, "My father began to systematically poison my mind against my mother. He told me she was a drunk and whore. She was fucking her divorce lawyer" (Ellroy, *My Dark Places*, 1997, p. 105). What if your mother is a whore? How do you make sure? Perhaps you see her naked, coming out of the bath. When she looks at you without shame, you know: "She saw me looking at her breasts. She told me that the tip of her right nipple got infected after my birth and had to be removed. Her tone was in no way provocative. She was a registered nurse explaining a medical fact" (Ellroy, *My Dark Places*, 1997, p. 112). Your father tells you often and repeatedly that she is a whore, and you believe him. Ellroy responded with a sexual obsession for his mother that reconfirms his father's opinion that she was a "Lush and a Whore" (Ellroy, *My Dark Places*, 1997, p. 107).

Learning to perform one's own gender roles well and consistently should lead to the benefits and cultural boons that characterize masculinity, but none of this accrued to the young Ellroy; he continues to seek their rewards as an adult. But there too they elude him because he learnt the wrong lessons, or he learnt the lessons wrong. He had no loving father teaching him which were the "good girls" and which were the "bad girls" and how to behave accordingly. They were all bad to Ellroy's father because they were all prey. So the child Ellroy longs for the safety of the protective family—he pursues it throughout his life, trying to find the right woman who will give him the kind of safety of maternal love that he craves. His pursuit of women is a double entendre – it is Ellroy pursing the protection of the family (which translates to women's emotional safety within the family as well as the patrilineal safety of the father's home, which the father *protects* as his own, and through within the child finds the safe haven) qua the good mother, and it means Ellroy's pursuit and predation of women, so he can finally have sex and love in the same place and resolve his own inner conflict between his endless need for sexual predation on women and his desire to get what protectors want, which is *the woman* as exclusively his prize. As Ellroy opines, "My male characters are looking for women to capitulate to—because they, by dint of their femininity, offer up a world of softness, self-sacrifice and probity that the male world is incapable of delivering. I'm not inured to the depictions of violence—but it is always a sole vehicle to bring men to self-knowledge—and to some stupendous women" (James Ellroy on Writing the Hilliker Curse, 2010).

On some levels, Ellroy understands that his quest for "the woman," as he puts it in *The Hilliker Curse*, is inextricably linked to his own crime-drenched childhood and his personal obsessive sexualization. His defining literary technique of rewriting history (including many famous American crime events like the death of Betty Short and the deaths of John Kennedy or Martin Luther King), together with his intriguing, perpetual rewriting of his own life's story, derives from his unresolved quest to resolve both his and the wider political crisis of masculinity's incommensurable, dual identity as both predator and protector. Ellroy cannot square his own personal commitment to masculinity's duality—to a life enjoyed both as protector and predator. And neither can his endless stream of women partners, perhaps, as well. Ellroy understands that the predator and the protector are one and the same features of a unified masculine ontology.[3] Because he, like so many men, does not want to have to choose, the answer is to sublimate the responsibility to the women themselves.[4]

Solving real crimes takes much the same course. Investigators begin with clues, attempt to connect the dots among the facts they find, and develop a narrative about what led up to the crime, how the crime happened, and what happened to the criminal after the crime happened. Investigators often must fill in the missing blanks with ideas or suppositions. In writing crime fiction, the author wants the reader to do the same: fill in the blanks, with the goal being to misdirect the reader until the author is ready to "reveal" the unseen truth that lies behind the story they have woven. But in the real world, crimes are not always solved; there are often missing clues; there is often no resolution.

There are two characteristics to Ellroy's writing that help us understand his work. His drive to control as the narrator allows him to direct what the reader sees. On the one hand, as the narrator, he gets to tell the story as he wants it to be told. We see the clues he wants us to see. We see the victim, not as the perpetrator sees them but as Ellroy, the controller of the narrative, wants us to see them. For his first several books, he actually leaves victims on the page and describes the violence done to them off the page. After his mother's death, as he began developing a taste for crime fiction, he noted that when reading Mike Hammer, "I could not endure depictions of violence on women. The same held with TV and film fare. *I could not see it*. I had to shut my eyes. I banished hurt women from my purview" (Ellroy, *The Hilliker Curse: My Pursuit of Women*, 2010, p. 19). As the author, he gets to control both the reality and the fiction.

They become indistinguishable in his hands. Though his mother's murder remains, *in fact*, unsolved, he rewrites that truth through his retelling of the murder of Elizabeth Short—whose real murder also remains unsolved. Ellroy "saves" the character, Betty Short, through his narrative prowess by resolving both her murder and the murder of his mother, for whom Elizabeth Short had become his simulacrum. But it also means he gets to fill in the blanks. He makes up what is not known. Because real history is incomplete and fractured, he gives us the evidence and the perpetrators that in real life simply are never held to account. In his role as narrator, he becomes her protector—if only a fictive one. Writing about crime is necessarily about being a voyeur to the worst of human beings but also being able to be the savior.

Ellroy thus uses his fiction writing talents for more than writing crime fiction. The self-proclaimed exhibitionist/narcissist is engaged in the endless production and rewriting of "the story of James Ellroy," as well. It is a project perhaps as important to his life's work as his fiction crime writing has been. Using the same techniques to control the narrative of his own life, he narrates the lives of the women he marries, the lives of the influential men in his world and his relationships with them, and perhaps most critically, the lives and deaths of his own mother and father. He has carefully designed his own public personae—his self-composed "demon dog" identity, woven across his many public interviews and appearances, profusely offered in his ubiquitous confessional mode. Ellroy knows he profits from his mother's death through this endless, public, confessional representations of her life and her death (Ellroy, *White Jazz*, 2001) (Ellroy, *The Hilliker Curse: My Pursuit of Women*, 2010). Whether he continues to reproduce himself and his life in the public square because it boosts his books sales, or because it provides the exhibitionist in him a kind of public confessional therapy, is unclear. Regardless of what Ellroy really believes motivates his life's work, the truth is that he has constructed a world that has *impact* beyond the pages of his books or the interviews he lets. And as much as he wants to control what *we* see in and of him, the attempt at inverting the gaze herein reveals a very different world than the one Ellroy believes he has constructed.

Ellroy believes "God brings women to him." For him to save and for him to love. And for Ellroy, love is sex and sex is love. He loves them when they are dead *because* they are dead. As he says in the Taveira interview,

> cops are just suckers for women. Promiscuous as a breed. They're all very tender. Q: It feels weird to me that you and what I surmise are your cop buddies hang out reading sex murder files. You say that's motivated by tenderness, that it's love? A: Yes, Stephanie Gorman, she's just a heartbreakingly good child. I mean, she's a contemporary of mine; she's just a year younger than me. She died not far from here.

And later,

> Yes, yes, you don't want to, you want your hand on your dick and the pictures in your mind. I would always pass out because I'd drink myself off the amphetamines grasping for some woman's face. You're right; it often starts with visual imagery. I have to tell the story. Stephanie, you're dead. We're never going to the prom. We're never going to make out in your dad's car. We're never going to spend the night together and make love. *You're dead.* If the 17-year-old James Ellroy and the 16-year-old Stephanie Gorman, who matriculated one high school apart, got together, a Christian and a Jew, an upper-middle-class girl and a poor boy who's a dipshit, it never would have happened. That's that. What can I do for you now? I can write a piece about you and honour you and give your spirit to the world. (Taviera, 2012, p. 365)

Despite his protestations to the contrary, in my reading of Ellroy's work through the eyes of a feminist political theorist, and as one who has personal experience with sexual violence, it is difficult to understand his work as a love story for women. Indeed, his novels have relatively few named women characters. For example, less than a fifth of the named characters in the four books that comprise his so-called *LA Quartet* are women. When he does write women into the story, they are likely there as victims, depicted in gruesome ways, murdered, dismembered, and otherwise hacked up, tortured, and raped. As Allamand puts it, Ellroy's "fictional universe is characterized by both an absence of justice and a hyperbolic violence almost always enacted against women's bodies" (Allamand, 2006, p. 350). Unnamed women or minor women characters who survive his pages are usually relegated to lives as prostitutes, madams, or women engaged in deeply disturbing sex acts or pornographic tableaus. Though he has drawn a few women characters who are, themselves, either cops or perpetrators, or, as is typical of his writing of men, sometimes both at the same time, most women, like Jane Baker in *Brown Requiem's,* are intelligible only through their male relationships; they are relevant only as men's lovers, sisters, mothers, girlfriends, or former any of these. Virtually none of his women characters could pass even a generous version of the Bechdel test.

Ellroy's work joins the increasingly gruesome subgenre of crime fiction that emerges in the late twentieth century, showing readers "the physical opening of bodies, the psychological exposure of damaged minds, and the inscription of personal traumas on the bodies of victims" (Horsley, 2005, p. 112). As such, one might dismiss his particularly graphic and grotesque treatments of women's bodies as simply one more in a common, if disturbing, genre of crime fiction. As Horsley notes, "increasingly, the violated body of the victim has come to act as the symbolic focus for the crime narrative" as an "indication of a pervasive fascination with the spectacle of the traumatized body." Horsley concludes that "The idea of the late twentieth century as a 'wound culture' has gained wide currency. In the 1990s in particular, physical wounding and psychological trauma were among our cultural preoccupations and the 'cult of abjection' was a defining feature of the decade's artistic and literary theory" (Horsley, 2005, p. 117). And others have read Ellroy's work through this lens. Mancall argues that

> in its treatment of sexuality, *Blood on the Moon*, in fact, sets a pattern for later Ellroy novels: as the result of childhood trauma, an impulsive sexuality possesses the killer, who can only relieve or express his urges through increasingly grotesque murders. The protagonist also may be compulsive in his sexuality, engaging in voyeurism or liaisons with prostitutes or other forbidden partners. But the killer cannot control his sexuality and, as a result, ends up isolated and hidden. The protagonist, on the other hand, succeeds in tempering or masking his compulsions and is capable of forming lasting social bonds. (Mancall, 2014, p. 42)

And later, that, "the killer and protagonist may be twins, but the protagonist successfully resists the killer's alienated impulses and earns the approval and affirmation of his colleagues. The pattern will play itself out not only in the later L.A. Noir novels, but also in the novels of the L.A. Quartet" (Mancall, 2014, p. 43).

Ellroy's work, then, reflects the dual consciousness of both the perpetrators he seeks and the protector he claims to be. Ellroy knows he is a perpetrator; he is deeply afraid that he could have been *the* perpetrator. Thus, his crime fiction writing allows him to have it both ways: he gets to perpetrate the crimes he imagines or reimagines, on the one hand, and he gets to claim the status of protector of women against whom such crimes are committed, on the other. But Ellroy struggles with the perpetrator facets of his own masculine identity. His father was a perpetrator. He knows he has predated on women. So when he has the chance to write the *Black Dahlia*, he writes the murderer as a woman. But because he knows that historically, and overwhelmingly, women do not commit this kind of violent crime against other women, the woman perpetrator in *The Black Dahlia* is not subjected to the criminal justice system. Though he claims that both his mother and Betty Short get the ending they both deserve, in reality, he replicates the very phenomenon that allows their murders to go unsolved. No one is held to account for the deaths of these women. Ellroy knows this and does it anyway—because he can't help himself, because that's what predators do. They hide their predation under the cloak of protection. In Ellroy's own words, men kill because they can. "Mutilation is language" (or, as Horsley notes, "the production of [the killer's] text on the body of the victim. The killer's text is one that works to implicate the detective who decodes it (and thereby the reader and the literary critic) in his own crimes and cultural attitudes" (Horsley, 2005, p. 141) that screams "I have power over you." Both predation and protection empower men and necessarily victimize and disempower women. "Good" men, however, the men who are the "protectors" of women, have to displace their sex-linked predation because it violates their protective self-image. So inevitably the blame must be displaced onto the victim: What was she wearing? Why was she out at night? Why did she get in that car? Where was her protector?

Perhaps when murders are solved, the dead are allowed to rest. Unsolved murders, in particular, seem to have a grim, endless life of their own, however. Neither Jean Hilliker nor Betty Short, if asked, would want their desecrated bodies and their gruesome murders endlessly exposed and re-exposed in the public square. Ellroy can't help looking at them and he wants us to do so as well. At first, as a young boy and then a young author, Ellroy tells us he had to avoid actually looking at the mutilated bodies of the women he killed. But in time he becomes more comfortable doing so. A photograph of his mother's mutilated body is featured on the first page of *My Dark Places*, under the chapter "The Redhead," for example. But his mother's body is depicted lying face down in the dirt; like the undiscovered killer, Ellroy does not want his victims looking back at him as his pen does the violence to them that spills out onto his pages. He turns his head. He gouges out their eyes. He sees that he sees, but he does not want them to see him as he looks.

Ellroy's particular form of predation is deeply imbricated with his own sexual obsessions. Sex is love, for Ellroy. And by sex, Ellroy means his own sexual animation. He speaks frequently about his endless pursuit of sexual gratification. He understands his mother as his sex object. He first shows her love and then, after she dies, his love turns to hate. He shifts the responsibility for his sexual obsession with his mother to her. She causes his sexual attraction because she was a whore. Whores bring it on themselves. She brought her death on herself because she stayed out. She had sex with men. She was a rover. She rejected the umbrella of male protection; she didn't qualify for it with his father, because she was a whore. And the boy-child, Ellroy, was impotent to provide it. And he hated her for his sexual obsession with her. She had red hair. She was loose. She could not get a champion. She and Betty Short lived and died outside of the heterosexual umbrella of men's protection. They caused their own vulnerability. They caused their own predation. They caused their own deaths. Because, as Ellroy makes amply clear, men kill women (Ellroy, *My Dark Places*, 1997).

But Ellroy cannot keep himself in the protector lane because, as he makes clear in his repeated public confessions, he is also a perpetrator. But that is even more complex in Ellroy's writing, as he, himself, is a kind of sexual predator, one who has, according to his own accounts, limited himself to *looking*, to voyeurism, to "peeping tom" crimes. He recounts in *My Dark*

Places a period in which his looking transformed into more invasive sexual predation, breaking and entering the homes of women about whom he was obsessed, and violating their personal items and clothing. He committed the crimes and then he wrote about doing the crimes. Thus, writing about crimes against women allows one to perpetrate those crimes once again. And Ellroy knows this. Which is why he positions himself as a feminist—a protector of women, in both his fiction and throughout his various self-narratives, expressing revulsion at men's violent abuses of women (James Ellroy on Writing the Hilliker Curse, 2010). Paradoxically, however, Ellroy, the man, and the "bad men" protagonists he invents normalize men's compulsive and often violent use and abuse of women for their own power-seeking and sexual purposes (Ellroy, *The Hilliker Curse: My Pursuit of Women*, 2010, p. 7; Ellroy, *Brown's Requiem*, 1981, p. 296; James Ellroy on Writing the Hilliker Curse, 2010; Luce, 2019). In claiming feminist credentials, Ellroy noted in 2010 that "It's my need to protect women that Jean Hilliker most surely defines. I specifically need to protect women from misogynistic men—which is a big burden to bear" (James Ellroy on Writing the Hilliker Curse, 2010).

In discussing Elaine Scarry's seminal *The Body in Pain*, Frazer and Hutchings note that

> Scarry's analysis of pain brings out that this is an experience that cuts off relations between people, since it is ultimately an experience that cannot be shared. Pain shrinks the world—to one's personal dwelling space, to the room, to the bed or to the chair; "the absence of pain is a presence of world; the presence of pain is the absence of world." (Frazer & Hutchings, 2020, pp. 178–82)

In Scarry's words, "the example of torture sets up the stark distinction between the direct and indirect experience of pain. Precisely because the witness (or perpetrator) cannot feel the pain of someone else's body, the exposure and representation of embodied pain is able to instantiate domination, and the destruction and torture of bodies becomes available for use" (Scarry, 1985, p. 18) (Frazer & Hutchings, 2020, p. 185).

Frazer and Hutchins argue that "a key point about the experience of pain and injury is that it separates the body in pain from the person's own capacities for language, representation and interaction" (179) and that among the many contexts where this can happen, they include political contexts, "where the separateness of embodied pain is easily disavowed by those who are not suffering, and subsumed other some other category. Torture becomes information gathering, the affirmation of the regimes' power; it is even commensurate with crimes committed or the information needed rather than radically asymmetrical" (179–80). Perhaps Ellroy's endless deployment of sexualized violence against women, even his own self-confessed obsession with *real* sexualized violent crimes against women, comes as a result of his need to simultaneously assert the power of masculinity to perpetrate such violence by silencing women, on the one hand, and to take it into himself as if to become the victim to feel what his mother felt, on the other.

> What cannot be doubted, in situations where one person is inflicting injury on another, is the unequal relationship of power. The doubt that others suffer, the erasure of injury by this absence of human connection the "overweening and colossal" presence of the power that accounts for the relative position and relation of individuals and the gulf of sympathy between them. What is not in doubt, in the torture scenario, is the power of the state (or of the criminal network, of the revolutionary party, of the gender order) that brings torturer and tortured together. What cannot be doubted, as soldiers fight wars, is the power in the name of which the actions are conducted, the authority that is obeyed. (Frazer & Hutchings, 2020, p. 181)

Scarry

> suggests that an incapacity to express and represent pain and injury feeds into and sustains a particular kind of political imagination. Within this imagination is not the experience of pain and injury but the relation between perpetrator and victim that anchors the meanings of torture, war and other extremes of political violence. The representation of this relation is entirely in the hands of those not in pain. This does not mean it is in the hands of the torturer or injuring soldier; Scarry suggests rather that it belongs to the state (or other organization or structure) from which permission to inflict pain is derived. (Frazer & Hutchings, 2020, p. 181)

While Ellroy's writing is the instrument through which the delivery of women's pain occurs, as Hoagland makes clear, it is the wider structure of heterosexualism that is really where the power lies.

The problem is a serious one for men, for masculinity, and certainly for Ellroy, at least in his personal life. In one curious moment, articulated in his second autobiographical monograph, Ellroy fleetingly resolves his own identity conflict by writing himself in *as* The Woman. In discussing the fictive child born from his supercop protagonist, Bucky Bleichert and his wife, Kay Lake (the fictional narrative closure at the ending of *The Black Dahlia*), Ellroy says, "The daughter was born in 1950. She's 56 now. She's a sturdy and dutiful woman with narrative gifts. She's Jean and Betty and me. She's a Hilliker assuredly" (Ellroy, *My Mother and the Dahlia*, 2006). It is important to note that in addition to simply claiming the woman as himself, Ellroy reconfirms the identification, making this fictive girl child with "narrative gifts" the same age as he. Thus, Ellroy gives birth to himself, but in the guise of a protected girl-child, raised in the family he never knew, but in doing so, he also becomes all of the women victims about whom he reads, writes, and obsesses. In becoming the women he predates upon in his pages, and in his imaginings, he finally succeeds in taking their voices, averting their gaze, and resolves thc incommensurability of predation and protection that defines a life lived as a 1940s masculine self.

WHERE DOES THIS LEAVE WOMEN?

Feminism has gained breathtaking velocity since the mid-point of the twentieth century; women routinely, now, engage in conversations about what it means to live under heterosexualism and collectively devise strategies to help themselves and each other slip away. Previously, women's voices had gone mostly unnoticed because heterosexualism entitled men to ignore women's voices anyway. Part of the political crisis that America, and much of the world, finds itself in today, over *the gender thing*, is that because of the successes of feminism, the category of woman itself is dissolving—like Ellroy's Jane Baker, women simply no longer have an appetite for their own victimization. The word "woman" has slumped out of knowable shape. Those whom heterosexualism has always defined as "women" increasingly refuse to live the doll's life anymore. Even Barbie has simply walked away. James Ellroy and his characters, seek the familiarities and comforts of the early 1940s, thinking themselves safe from having to deal with the changes in gender politics that postwar feminism has created. They are wrong, of course.

As Hoagland would predict, a hysterical reaction, expressed primarily by men (though their Sophie's are dutifully echoing their men's cries for a return to the familiar), is increasingly evident across the nation today. For the part of our species for whom life was made knowable because they could see themselves reflected in those dead doll eyes, they no longer know what they look like. Or, perhaps, they don't like what they are being forced to see about themselves. Their predictable response has been to try and shut women up—to simply stop them from speaking. To once again take away from women the things that have given women the means and the freedom to escape heterosexualism's "protective" grasp—control over their status as citizens, their ability to live without the vestiges of couverture, and the ability to take control of their reproductive decisions. To smash Barbie's Dream House, as if doing so will scare her back inside where she belongs (Prigge). Their frantic need to reclaim the powers of masculinity reaches in all directions, not just toward women, because once women began to slip their grasp, masculinity's hegemonic position in the broader culture, that nostalgic power and control that is racialized and marked by class and other privileges, also began to slip away, as well. There are frantic attempts to claw back the boundaries of "knowable" masculinity everywhere. It is evident in the looming specter of Trump—the predator, being once again heralded as a candidate to be the nation's most powerful "protector." It is found in the men of Josh Hawley's ilk, feverishly blasting rainbow festooned beer cans; blowing up rockets; ejaculating their autos into outer space, or shoving women back into domestic submission by trying once again to make women's bodies incubate the species; demanding that women produce offspring for the most powerful sex that, nevertheless, is not powerful enough to reproduce itself. It is in the terror of words that moves them to ban books so that children's eyes not see different truths. It is there in the effort to silence black people by end running their spoken vote power or upping the threat of violence by killing them on screen. By literally demanding that people must "not say gay." Arendt warns us that "The problem with violence . . . is that the end to which the violence is directed is always in danger of being overwhelmed by the means it justifies. . . . The most probable change it will bring about is a change to a more violent world" (Frazer & Hutchings, 2020, p. 80). It is a cautionary reminder for this moment in history.

It is so extremely difficult for victims of sex crimes to talk about them. It is this truth that has kept those crimes so frequently unpunished. Not so long ago, fighting back in a rigged system, where the guns and knives and fists, and lifelong training in the cult of masculinity that prizes dominance over everything else, had mostly proven impossible. Valerie Solanas bravely looked masculinity in the eye, saw the predators hiding in the protectors' cloaks, and what she saw drove her to say, "We better take *them* out first" (Solanas, 1971). Lorena Bobbitt didn't die like a good woman, but instead, picked up the knife and fought back (John and Lorena Bobbitt, n.d.). Both women were quickly dispatched to the insane asylums of history. But nurtured and encouraged by a robust and growing feminist community, women, in particular, have continued to find their voices and speak; where they can, taking back control of the sexual violence they have experienced and speaking their truths about those experiences aloud. It is difficult to pinpoint the exact moment when it began. One could perhaps rightly point to that profound historical moment of Anita Hill, sitting calmly before an all-white, all-male, Senate Judiciary Committee in 1991, reclaiming her dignity, and speaking the words of sexual harassment that were spoken to her, that victimized her, in an office space that provided cover for her perpetrator and covered her in shame. Since then, a chorus of women's voices building the #MeToo movement are now shouting back at the perpetrators of a shocking litany of sexual violations perpetrated by men of privilege and power (but not only those men), many of whom have been lauded as America's finest across the past century. In 2018, Christine Blasey Ford found the courage to look up at *another* Senate Judiciary Committee, one once again vetting a would-be lifetime Supreme Court jurist, and she too had the courage to speak her perpetrator's name and to describe his predation upon her. This time, however, Ford's words were bolstered by the women and men of color sitting on one side of the Senate Judiciary Committee, who nodded often in solidarity, many recalling their own experiences with various violations by powerful men—a clear indicator of the progress that followed Anita Hill's 1991 pioneering courage. Ford found herself staring into the eyes of numerous Senators on the other side of the bench, however, who, like Ellroy, opted to shield themselves from her gaze by interposing an outside woman prosecutor for protection. The irony in that moment is priceless. And in the spring of 2023, the shaking but committed voice of 79-year-old E. Jean Carroll, asked a jury of her peers to see her sexual assault as she saw it through her own eyes, not through the eyes of the man *qua* former president. That jury of nine—six men and three women—held Donald Trump liable for assaulting her thirty years earlier in a department store dressing room—a man who had publicly crowed that because of his "celebrity," could assault the bodies of women at will.

This is an extraordinary moment, really. These courageous women make the world look at their experiences, *not* through the eyes of the perpetrators—the men who do the crimes, who fantasize about doing the crimes, who want to do the crimes, who read about doing the crimes, who fetishize such crimes, or who write the crimes—but through the eyes of the women who live with, and perhaps die, because of those crimes. The gaze has shifted; *les femmes* are now looking back and demanding the world see men, masculinity, and violence against women through the eyes of the people who experience it. If Ellroy wants to save women, perhaps it's time he stops killing them in the first place, stops blaming them for their deaths, starts holding himself, and the system of heterosexualism, responsible. *Cherchez les hommes*, Ellroy. Perhaps it's time to remember *that*.

NOTES

1. It is important to note that the sex dichotomous system was always an ideal. Contrary to the vapid images, Hollywood told the nation, for example, the lives of Western women settlers often defied the prescribed sex role behaviors more adamantly adhered to by the more "genteel," mostly white, and generally privileged women of the East during this period. So, too, the truths of enslaved African American women give the lie to the entire system, as Sojourner Truth so pungently made clear. Lesbian and other non-woman identified women, until only very recently, have had to make their lives outside the margins of their generally enforced sex role identities, but living under the threat that discovery of their treachery often resulted in their punishment and death. On the other side of the dichotomy, there have always also been men who spurned their lessons of "appropriate" masculinity, opting for lives outside of

the protector/predator way. While some did so because they understand themselves within what we now identify as the LGBTQI community, others have done so for ethical, religious, or other personally defined reasons. In order for the system to work and be sustained, men defectors from prescribed masculinity have generally been vanquished, denied, murdered, and vilified, in much the same way defecting women have historically been treated under patriarchy's system of sex dichotomous domination.

2. For an excellent analysis of Ellroy's obsession with the good mother/bad mother dichotomy, see Carole Allamand's *A Tooth for a Private Eye: James Ellroy's Detective Fiction*, in which she examines Ellroy's fixation on the maternal breast as the source of his fascination with women's murders, through the lens of Melanie Klein's psychoanalytic work (Allamand, 2006).

3. In describing his reaction to pictures in pornography magazines at one point, Ellroy notes,

> They bored straight into my heart. I was the porno bookstore clerk out to save them from pornography and take his reward in sex. I hoarded their pictures the way Harvey Glatman hoarded pix of his victims. I gave my girls names and prayed for them every night. I sicced (sic) the Dahlia killer on them and saved them as his blade descended. They spread their legs and talked to me while I flew on Benzedrex inhalers. *My Dark Places*, 170.

4. One of the conundrums of heterosexualism is that this masculine choice does *not* extend typically to their relationships with other men, who are themselves enmeshed in the political economy of the hierarchies within heterosexualism.

BIBLIOGRAPHY

Albrecht, M. M. (2015). *Masculinity in Contemporary Quality Television*. London: Routledge.

Allamand, C. (2006). The Tooth for a Private Eye: James Ellroy's Detective Fiction. *The Journal of Popular Culture, 39*(3), 349–364.

Ashman, N. (2020). Nostalgic Masculinity: Homosocial Desire and Homosexual Panic in James Ellroy's This Storm. *Crime Fiction Studies, 1.2*, 221–36. doi:10.3366/cfs.2020.0022

Butler, J. (1999). *Gender Trouble*. New York: Routledge.

Chevalier-Karfis, C. (2020, August 26). 'Cherchez la femme': The Sexist French Expression. *ThoughtCo*. Retrieved from https://www.thoughtco.com/cherchez-la-femme-sexist-french-expression-1368635

Ellroy, J. (2005). *Blood on the Moon*. New York: Vintage Books

Ellroy, J. (1981). *Brown's Requiem*. New York: Vintage Books.

Ellroy, J. (2021). *Clandestine*. New York: Vintage Books

Ellroy, J. (1987). *The Black Dahlia*. New York: Warner Books.

Ellroy, J. (1997). *My Dark Places*. New York: Vintage Books.

Ellroy, J. (2001). *White Jazz*. New York: Vintage Books.

Ellroy, J. (2006, June 19). My Mother and the Dahlia. *Virginia Quarterly Review, 82*(3). Retrieved 2023, from https://www.vqronline.org/essay/my-mother-and-dahlia

Ellroy, J. (2007, July 8). My Mother's Killer. *CQ*. Retrieved from https://www.gq.com/story/james-ellroy-murder

Ellroy, J. (2010). *The Hilliker Curse: My Pursuit of Women.* New York: Vintage.

Frazer, E., & Hutchings, K. (2020). *Violence and Political Theory.* Cambridge: Polity.

Gerwig, G. (Director). (2023). *Barbie* [Motion Picture].

Hawley, J. (2023). *Manhood: The Masculine Virtues America Needs.* Washington, DC: Regnery.

Hoagland, S. (1989). *Lesbian Ethics: Toward New Values.* Institute of Lesbian Studies.

Hoagland, S. L. (1995). Moral Revolution: From Antagonism to Cooperation. In N. Tuana & R. Tong (Eds.), *Feminism & Philosophy* (pp. 175–92). Boulder: Westview.

Horsley, L. (2005). *Twentieth-Century Crime Fiction.* Lancaster: Oxford University Press.

Hunter College Women's Studies Collective (1995). *Women's Realities, Women's Choices.* New York: Oxford University Press.

James Ellroy on Writing the Hilliker Curse. (2010, August 12). *Knopf Doubleday Publishing Group Newsletter.* Retrieved from https://knopfdoubleday.com/2010/08/12/ellroyqa/

Jarvis, C. S. (2004). *The Male Body at War: American Masculinity during World War II.* DeKalb: University of Northern Illinois Press.

John and Lorena Bobbitt. (n.d.). Retrieved from https://en.wikipedia.org/wiki/John_and_Lorena_Bobbitt

Kimmel, M. S. (2008). *The Gendered Society* (3rd ed.). New York and Oxford: Oxford University Press.

Kimmel, M. S. (2013). *The Gendered Society.* New York: Oxford University Press.

Laqueur, T. (1990). *Making Sex: Body and Gender from the Greeks to Freud.* Cambridge: Harvard University Press.

Luce, E. (2019, May 31). James Ellroy on His Dark Places. *Financial Times*, pp. 1–7. Retrieved February 5, 2023, from https://www.ft.com/content/8849ea5a-8136-11e9-b592-5fe435b57a3b

MacKinnon, C. A. (1995). Sexuality, Pornography, and Method: "Pleasure Under Patriarchy." In N. Tuana & R. Tong (Eds.), *Feminism & Philosophy* (pp. 134–61). Boulder: Westview.

Mancall, J. (2014). *James Ellroy: A Companion to the Mystery Fiction.* Jefferson, North Carolina: McFarland & Company.

Marchese, D. (2019, August 19). James Ellroy on His Life in Crime, His Imaginary Dog and the Need to Provoke. *New York Times*. Retrieved May 7, 2023, from https://www.nytimes.com/interactive/2019/08/19/magazine/james-ellroy-interview.html

Mulvery, L. (1990). Visual Pleasure and Narrative Cinema. In P. Erens (Ed.), *Issues in Feminist Film Criticism* (pp. 28–40). Bloomington: Indiana University Press.

Pitt, J. (2021, July 23). *American Masculinity After World War II*. Retrieved 2023, from https://www.nationalww2museum.org/war/articles/american-masculinity-after-world-war-ii

Prigge, M. (n.d.). A Pro-Trump Pastor Destroyed A Barbie Dream House With A Bible Wrapped Around A Baseball Bat Because Sure, Why Not. *Uproxx*. Retrieved August 30, 2023, from https://uproxx.com/viral/trump-pastor-destroyed-barbie-house-baseball-bat-bible/

Robb, L., & Pattinson, J. (2018). *Men, Masculinities and Male Culture in the Second World War*. London: Palgrave MacMillan.

Rousseau, J.-J. (1979). *Emile or On Education* (A. Bloom, Ed.). New York: Basic Books.

Scarry, E. (1985). *The Body in Pain*. New York: Oxford University Press.

Solanas, V. (1971). *The S.C.U.M. Manifesto*. London: Olympia Press.

Tangney, J. P., Stuewig, J., & Mashek, D. J. (2007). Moral Emotions and Moral Behavior. *Annual Review of Pyschology, 58*, 345–72.

Taviera, R. (2012). Interview with James Ellroy. *Comparative American Studies, 10*(4), 362–375. doi:10.1179/1477570012Z.00000000026

Wolfe, P. (2005). *Like Hot Knives to the Brain*. Lanham: Lexington Books.

Chapter 3

Black Dahlia and Aesthetic Crimes

Erik Anderson

In *Ornament and Crime*, Adolf Loos famously rails against ornamentation of all types as crimes against humanity.[1] Even tattoos, he says, are aesthetic crimes, enjoyable only for latent criminals and degenerate aristocrats. But the notion of an aesthetic crime needn't be confined to the alleged excesses Loos saw in body art and Art Nouveaux. A case might be made for the claim that late twentieth-century urban and suburban planning in the United States, which resulted in seemingly endless boulevards flanked on both sides by hideous utilitarian strip malls, is, or has at least resulted in, equally clear cases of aesthetic crimes. An altogether different kind of aesthetic crime involves the notorious 1947 Black Dahlia murder in Los Angeles in which the mutilated body of a young female murder victim is artfully staged in an abandoned lot in a housing development. The murder serves as the basis for James Ellroy's 1987 novel *The Black Dahlia*, and unsympathetic readers might cite Ellroy's cheesy dialog and sensationalistic depictions of a criminal underworld as aesthetic crimes of yet another sort. In this chapter, I explore some of these varieties of aesthetic crimes, focusing on part one of Ellroy's *L.A. Quartet*.

In order to approach the question about aesthetic crimes in *The Black Dahlia*, I will first flesh out the general notion of an aesthetic crime by drawing on ordinary intuitions and working with examples. This will put us in the position to ask how we should understand the proper relations between aesthetic and moral values. I will then briefly survey the current theoretical landscape and identify a position known as *immoralism*, which, I will argue, best serves to foster an understanding and appreciation of the aesthetic crimes in Ellroy's work. I go on to put *immoralism* to work, arguing that *Black Dahlia* is aesthetically better not despite but rather because of its crimes.

AESTHETIC CRIMES

To begin with an example, one kind of aesthetic crime might involve the callous waste of resources involved in the conspicuous consumption and ostentatious displays of wealth that concerned Loos: excessive ornamentation, marble walls, towering glass, intricately carved gargoyles, heavy teak furniture, and all variety of architecturally and otherwise functionless, profligate decoration. Gilding toilets with gold and diamonds harvested by slave labor from environmentally catastrophic mines in Central African rainforests involves another layer of moral violation to this kind of aesthetic crime. In such cases, whatever aesthetic value the ornament and decoration might have is moderated by the negative moral value due to the egregious levels of waste, pretention, and vulgarity. In such cases, it is difficult to disentangle the moral and aesthetic values. Copious quantities of gold are both gorgeous and gaudy, and imply both virtue and vice.

Loos was concerned with the kinds of ostentatious displays of wealth that took the form of gaudy, structurally nonfunctional ornamentation that exemplified a long architectural history of European buildings for and by the spectacularly wealthy. Such crimes are not unfamiliar in the United States. today. Billionaire Row just south of Central Park in Manhattan is a contemporary example. Consider too the new neighbor who moves into a modest neighborhood, scrapes off the tidy 2,000 square foot ranch home, and replaces it with a 6,000 square foot trophy home constructed in the style of an Italian Renaissance estate mansion that seems to have been miraculously transported from Tuscany.

Offensively wasteful scale and decoration comprise just one sort of case. There are others. Consider, as we witness in the 1955 noir classic *Rififi*, an artfully planned, executed, and untraceable robbery carried out with such masterful skill and elegant technique as to count as an aesthetic success on its own terms, regardless of criminality or morality: a beautiful crime. Stealing art is obviously another kind of aesthetic crime, but is not very interesting conceptually. It is also probably not what most people would understand by the term.

Instead, what might ordinarily come to mind upon hearing the term "aesthetic crime" is perhaps something so hideous and offensive to the senses—so aesthetically awful—that it amounts to a crime. Such things are obviously a matter of taste, but surely, there are relatively straightforward examples.

Every municipality of a certain size has a miles-long boulevard, lined almost exclusively by strip malls fronted by parking lots and ugly signage, divided into a grid of traffic lanes and traffic lights, teeming with cars and trucks filling the air with noxious fumes and the ceaseless din of road noise.

Cases of environmental degradation and destruction can be considered aesthetic crimes of a similar sort. For instance, the damage done to the Passaic River, with its lower 15 miles from Great Falls to Newark being designated as a Superfund site, seems like another case of aesthetic malfeasance.

Once we have the concept, examples are easy to come by: a particularly badly rendered drawing, the turquoise and purple house that everyone in the neighborhood loathes, overuse of peacock feathers in almost any context, spectacularly mismatched Christmas decorations, award show red carpet misfires, and so on. An "aesthetic crime" in this sense involves things profoundly ugly, poorly executed, and inappropriate to the extent of being cringe-worthy.

Consider now a totally different kind of example. If Ellroy's *Black Dahlia* had been available for purchase only on paper made from the pulp of an endangered sub-species of Sequoias, printed using ink made from the blood of orphans, and bound in leather made from the skins of baby sea turtles, it would be an aesthetic crime of yet another variety. Although this kind of case mixes aesthetic beauty with a moral beast, it seems relatively easy to disentangle the two kinds of value. But other examples of aesthetic crimes make this more difficult.

An example closer to what I have in mind involves the kind of norm-breaking and shocking contraventions that characterize much of early Modern Art. Famously, Marcel Duchamp's provocative and mischievous "readymades" were intended to and succeeded in shocking artworld establishment figures. Most famously, Duchamp signed and dated an ordinary urinal and entered it into the 1917 exhibition of The Society for Independent Artists in New York City with the provocative title *The Fountain*. Although he was a member of the Society's board, *The Fountain* was rejected, as Duchamp knew it would be.

Following his friend's lead, American Surrealist Man Ray constructed his own mystique and notoriety on a similar foundation of transgression. Working alongside Marcel Duchamp, Ray pushed the boundaries of art beyond previously accepted cultural norms and conceptual limits. Appealing to a growing interest in the largely unexplored human psyche, especially the subliminal layers just below consciousness, he worked to produce provocative and disturbing, yet slyly aesthetically appealing Surrealist masterpieces. The only traces remaining of many of these works are photographs—which are themselves now part of the Surrealist canon.

Ray describes his creative process and its outputs as the workings and products of a criminal mind:

> I deliberately dodged all the rules . . . . I mixed the most insane products together, I used film way past its use-by date, I committed heinous crimes against chemistry and photography, and you can't see any of it.[2]

Thought of in this way, many art historians might want to characterize the history of art as an ongoing process of criminal activity of the aesthetic variety: the history of aesthetic crimes, as it were. This is certainly the way twentieth-century Art History is described by Robert Hughes in his influential *The Shock of the New*.[3]

In the next section, I explore some relations between the aesthetic and the moral values. My aim is to arrive at some understanding of how assessments in one realm of value interact with those in another. This, I hope, will shed some light on and help us to appreciate the aesthetic crimes committed in Ellroy's *Black Dahlia*.

MORAL VALUE AND AESTHETIC VALUES

We try not to conflate kinds of values: economic, intellectual, pragmatic, political, and so forth. In particular, we try especially hard to avoid conflating aesthetic and moral values. For example, we admonish one another for drawing conclusions about a person's character based just on their appearance. No one claims that the class of the virtuous comprises all and only the beautiful. If your dog gets into my trash, pointing out that he is an exemplary instance of his breed doesn't get him off the hook. Despite our best efforts to draw them apart, there remains a vexing question about the relation between moral and aesthetic values.

Autonomism in philosophical aesthetics, also known as aestheticism, is the view that moral and aesthetic value are two distinct kinds of value that have no systematic dependence on one another. Advocates of autonomism hold that the moral value of a work of art should have no bearing on its aesthetic value and *vice versa*. A work of art can be considered aesthetically valuable regardless of whether it is morally good or bad.

Autonomists such as Oscar Wilde hold that neither the moral excellence nor the moral flaws of a work have any bearing on its aesthetic value. Morality is one thing and aesthetics is a completely different thing. Thus, Wilde held that art is, strictly speaking, "useless" and that its value lies solely in its ability to provide aesthetic pleasure. According to Wilde, art should be appreciated for its own sake, without reference to any moral or social purpose. Art should be autonomous, he believed, separate from any moral or practical considerations.

> There is no such thing as a moral or an immoral book. Books are well written, or badly written. That is all.[4]

Thus, radical autonomists hold that moral value is never relevant to aesthetic value. A work of art can be aesthetically pleasing even if it is morally flawed because the aesthetic value of artworks is independent of their moral value. Aesthetic value stands alone.

On the opposite side of the spectrum from autonomism is radical moralism. This view, attributed to Leo Tolstoy, is the view according to which aesthetic value is a function of moral value and varies directly with it.[5] Art should express moral values and should make people and societies better. Thus, according to Tolstoy, morally excellent art is also aesthetically excellent, while morally flawed art is also aesthetically flawed. He thought that bad art should be eliminated, and even went so far as to include his own famous masterpieces, *War and Peace* and *Anna Karenina*, among the morally and aesthetically deficient works that should be banished.

According to the moralist, aesthetic value is a species of moral value. Not all moral flaws are relevant to aesthetic assessment, but moral flaws are often aesthetic flaws. If a work of art has a moral flaw that is significant to the overall meaning or aesthetic impact of the work, it should be considered an aesthetic flaw. For example, if a novel has a racist or sexist message, this would be considered a moral flaw that would also by consequence be an aesthetic one.

Neither radical moralism nor radical autonomism seem defensible in any real sense. There is a relatively clear and intuitive distinction between moral value and aesthetic value, just as there is between economic value and aesthetic value. Some aesthetically valuable works of art convey a moral or ethical message; others do not. Some artifacts that convey a valuable moral message are also aesthetically valuable; others are not.

Yet, despite the relative clarity of the distinction, there is also an equally clear and intuitive sense in which the two kinds of value are not fully autonomous. Matthew Kieran points out that serious art should be concerned with communicating deep responses and an understanding of human life.[6] Although great art need not convey moral content at all, when art does depict the ethical nature of human experience, it should do so adequately. And in such cases, artworks should invoke in us responses appropriate to the human experiences depicted in them.

Morally repugnant artworks such as "snuff" films, child pornography, racist propaganda and the like suffer aesthetically because of their moral bankruptcy. Body art can at some point turn into self-mutilation. Similarly, the moral content of some works of art is enhanced and augmented by its high level of aesthetic value. Think, Cathedral at Chartres. These sorts of considerations seem to count against both of the radical positions lying at the two ends of the spectrum. Thus, a moderate position is necessary: one that acknowledges the distinction between moral and aesthetic value while also recognizing their interdependence in numerous ways, even if they are not systematically or inherently related. In the following section, will discuss two leading moderate positions, Noel Carroll's "moderate moralism" and Berys Gaut's "ethicism."

MODERATE MORALISM

Aesthetic experience and assessment involve a complex cognitive-affective response that can be appropriate or inappropriate to what is depicted in the work. In the case of expressive art, part of appreciation involves grasping its "emotional profile." In the case of *morally* expressive art, some of the emotions necessary for understanding a work have an essentially moral character. For example, to watch *All Quiet on the Western Front* without a sense of the horror of war is simply to misunderstand that work and what it depicts.

Thus, artworks can be part of moral education by providing audiences the occasion to practice their emotional responses. In this way, Carroll's view neatly accommodates Aristotle's insight that the cathartic function of dramatic tragedies was part of their didactic value.[7]

According to Carroll,

> it is vastly improbable that there could be any substantial narrative of human affairs, especially a narrative artwork that did not rely upon activating the moral powers of readers, viewers, and listeners.[8]

A moral flaw in a work of art can but need not be an aesthetic one and a moral virtue of a work of art can but need not be an aesthetic one.

The moral character of artworks resides in the extent to which the moral assessments or evaluations prescribed by those works are successfully aroused in a receptive audience. Works that fail in these purposes are to that extent aesthetic failures and works that succeed in these purposes are to that extent aesthetically successful.

There are two problems with this position. First, the specific moral character of artworks appears to be largely irrelevant to the account. What matters primarily, according to Carroll, is a kind of successful communication between artist and audience, the moral content of which is secondary. But this seems wrong. My failure to engage emotionally with a work in the way appropriate to the moral message conveyed by it may have more to do with a mismatch between the artist's and my psychological dispositions, rather than any moral failing ascribable to the work itself. A second worry is that a work might fail to convey its moral message but end up being all the better for it.

This might be what happens in cases of works whose didactic aims misalign with a more complex or subtle response elicited in the audience. A preachy message may end up being an amusingly enjoyable bit of cheesiness instead.

ETHICISM

On Gaut's account, the aesthetic value of an artwork is in part a function of the values presumed, expressed, or manifested by it. If, for example, an artwork endorses a particular ethical response to a situation depicted in the work, and an audience deems that this response merited, the artwork succeeds aesthetically. If by contrast, the artwork endorses an ethical assessment or evaluation that the audience deems unmerited, then that failure counts as an aesthetic flaw. Successfully communicating and eliciting appropriate ethical attitudes in a work of art counts as an aesthetic success.

For example, an aesthetic success of the film *Philadelphia* involves its successful eliciting from audiences a sense of empathy and humanity directed toward the members of the homosexual community suffering from HIV infection as depicted in the film. That the attitude elicited in audiences by the film matches the one prescribed by it counts as an aesthetic success. More generally, the aesthetic value of a work is in part a function of the extent to which the prescribed ethical response aligns with the merited one. The many awards *Philadelphia* won the year of its release serve as evidence for this.

Conversely, negative aesthetic value can arise when there is a mismatch between the prescribed response and the merited response. A moral flaw like this can diminish the aesthetic value of an artwork even if it does not diminish that value to zero. Leni Riefenstahl's notorious Nazi propaganda film, *Triumph of the Will,* provides a good illustration of how this works. *Triumph* documents the 1934 Nuremberg National Socialist rallies with stunning cinematic mastery. Hitler is portrayed as a brilliant, visionary Germanic folk hero, loved by his people and whose passionate leadership and dedication to the righteous cause will return glory and respect to a previously humiliated nation. Riefenstahl's combination of exquisitely beautiful images and forceful symbols displayed with undeniable cinematic mastery nevertheless cannot overcome the demerits of its repugnant immoral message. It thus fails aesthetically to that extent.

Gaut's ethicism manages to avoid one problem that faced Carroll's position, viz., that a work might fail to elicit an intended cognitive-affective response in an audience and to that extent be an aesthetic failure. Ethicism sidesteps this problem by focusing on merited response rather than intended and actual response.

Both moderate moralism and ethicism provide insights about ways aesthetic value can vary in proportion with moral value. And this comports with common sense. Nevertheless, must these two types of value always vary proportionately? Why can't there be cases in which the *immorality* of a work contributes positively to its aesthetic value? In the next section, I explore a different kind of moderate position designed to accommodate such cases.

IMMORALISM

Not all moderate theories are committed to the claim that moral and aesthetic values vary proportionally. Immoralists suggest that moral flaws in works of art can actually contribute positively to their aesthetic value even if the correlation is not systematic.

Immoralism has received a lot of attention recently and has been defended by a number of philosophers.[9] According to immoralists, moral defects can contribute positively to aesthetic value when they create, for example, a sense of complexity, ambiguity, or depth in a work of art. As such, works of art that are morally flawed can be more interesting and engaging than those that are morally perfect, as they prompt us to reflect on the moral issues they raise. Thus, in their view, the moral flaws can be seen as aesthetic strengths and the negative moral value of the work of art can contribute to its aesthetic value.

In contrast with immoralism, the common sense case for moralism is strong. Intuitively, the positive moral value of an artwork adds to its aesthetic value. The sense of elevation conveyed by works with a strong and carefully crafted moral message surely contributes to its proper aesthetic value. Similarly, intuitively, the negative moral value of an artwork subtracts from its aesthetic value. The sense of moral decadence induced by works with an immoral message surely takes away from its overall aesthetic value. Autonomists of course will deny these intuitions and will insist that there is no such systematic dependence. Moralists of course will take these intuitions as prima facie evidence in support of their position, which is admittedly compelling.

Couldn't the immorality of an artwork sometimes contribute *positively* to its aesthetic value? The immoralist says, yes. The immoralist thesis is not merely that a work's immorality *need not undermine* its claims to aesthetic or artistic merit. It is instead the much more counterintuitive claim that a work's immorality *can sometimes enhance* its aesthetic value. Some artworks are aesthetically better in virtue of their immorality. The central immoralist claim is highly counterintuitive. How could it be defended?

One way might be to provide the audience with an opportunity for moral evaluation and education. Works that feature depictions of vicious behavior such as torture, cannibalism, or murder might do so in ways that are morally disapproving, morally neutral, or morally approving of those behaviors. In this way, even uncontroversially immoral artworks can serve a morally didactic purpose.

A. W. Eaton suggests a similar line of defense. She argues that just as we can learn from the morality depicted in artworks, so too we can learn from their immorality. The mental work required of the audience in such cases provides the basis of an appropriate aesthetic response:

> [T]he capacity to make an audience feel and desire things inimical to their considered views and deeply held principles is for this very reason and to this extent an aesthetic achievement. In this way, moral flaws of a particular kind can make a significant contribution to a work's aesthetic value.[10]

The didactic function served by mixing aesthetic and moral values might be what brings together otherwise disparate values.

Eileen John defends what she calls an "opportunist" version of immoralism. John's view proceeds from the insight that "art is in some sense opportunist: it seizes on whatever it can in order to make itself matter to us in [a] larger way."[11] Her view achieves a kind of *via media*: she denies *both* that moral and aesthetic values are wholly autonomous *and* that there is a systematic dependence of one on the other. Instead, John holds that while there is no internal relation between the two kinds of values, nevertheless value of one kind might put people in a psychologically receptive state necessary for discovering and appreciating the value of the other kind. Put overly simplistically, a happy moral message might incline readers, listeners, or viewers to be more attentive aesthetically. *Vice versa*, the aesthetically positive nature of a work might incline audiences to be more receptive to the moral message. A spectrum of artworks from children's books to war propaganda might serve to illustrate this point.

Eaton's and John's approaches are open to the charge that they fail to explain what really needs to be explained, viz., that in one case we might judge that the immoral character of a work contributes to making it less aesthetically valuable, but in another case, we might make the opposite judgment. It seems like there should be some theoretical explanation that can head off the charge of arbitrariness.

Taking up this challenge, Matthew Kieran argues that the morally problematic aspects of a work of art can nevertheless have cognitive merit and can thereby play an important role in its evaluation.[12] Cognitive interests expressed in attitudes such as curiosity, fascination, sympathy, and compassion, when directed at morally defective elements of artworks, can, he argues, enhance our discriminatory capacities or perspectives and thereby enhance the aesthetic experience of and aesthetic value of those works. He thus advocates, "experiencing the bad to understand the good."[13] If part of the aesthetic value of a work of art is contributed by cognition, and if a work of art increases our moral understanding, then, *ceteris paribus*, that work of art has an increased aesthetic value.[14]

With the immoralist insight into how moral flaws might turn out to be aesthetic virtues, I turn now to see how the immoralist view might serve as a guide appreciation of aesthetic crimes in Ellroy's *Black Dahlia*.

BLACK DAHLIA AND IMMORALISM

Black Dahlia follows the investigation into the murder of Elizabeth Short, known as the "Black Dahlia," in 1947 Los Angeles. The book explores the dark underbelly of the city and its corrupt police force, as two detectives try to solve the brutal murder case. The plot is filled with twists and turns, as the detectives delve into the victim's past and uncover a web of secrets, lies, and scandal.

Ellroy's writing is highly stylized in a way that perfectly fits the seedy settings, sordid happenings, and desperate lives of the sketchy characters who populate the sordid underworld of 1940s LA. Events are told in Ellroy's trademark idiom, complete with staccato dialog infused with mandatory "cops and crims" lingo. A comprehensive survey of many of the worst of human failings, the novel is steeped in moral failure, moral compromise, weakness of the will, sadism, murder, betrayal, deception, and the spectrum of vice from petty to pathological.

Character, plot, style, you name it: *Black Dahlia* offers a potential treasure trove of questions about aesthetic crimes. Is the gruesome murder depicted in the novel an aesthetic crime? Is the depiction itself an aesthetic crime whether or not the murder depicted is one? Is *Black Dahlia* an aesthetic crime? I think there is a plausible case to be made for an affirmative answer to each of these questions.

The general case for the immoralist reading is straightforward. Art does not have a moral obligation to be positive or morally uplifting. Indeed, some of the most celebrated works of art throughout history have dealt with negative or controversial subject matter. By exploring the darker aspects of human nature, *Black Dahlia* may be offering a more honest and realistic portrayal of the world. For the immoralist, as we have seen, this same point can be marshaled to support the argument that a work is better *not despite but because of* its realistic portrayal of the darker side of human being.

Additionally, to apply the point advanced by Kieran and John earlier, the negative moral value of *Black Dahlia* may be precisely what makes it a compelling and thought-provoking work of art. By delving into the depravity and corruption of the characters, the novel may be challenging readers to confront their own assumptions and biases about the world. Again, the work produces a kind of value feedback loop in which the negative moral value produces positive aesthetic value, which in turn produces a net redemptive overall value.

Pressing the point further, the novel's negative moral value may well be integral to its aesthetic value. The bleak and unsettling tone of the novel creates its haunting and memorable atmosphere. The themes of violence and decay are more effectively conveyed through its negative moral value than if it had a more optimistic message. Surely, a similar exploration of the dark corners of the human psyche drives the aesthetic allure of works from Sophocles to Poe.

If this is right, then *Black Dahlia*'s negative moral value is not a flaw, but rather a deliberate artistic choice that adds to its aesthetic merit. By confronting readers with uncomfortable truths about human nature, the novel may be challenging them to reexamine their beliefs and assumptions, ultimately leading to a deeper and more meaningful engagement with the text.

I will now attempt to provide further support for the thesis that Ellroy's *Black Dahlia* is aesthetically better not despite but rather because of its negative moral value.

MARKETING/PACKAGING

Consider the printed paperback itself. Even before opening it, the artwork already serves to aestheticize the murder. The cover showcases a picture of a young woman who is presumably the victim of the murder case upon which the book is based. The photo has been cropped to only show her head and face. She appears to be lying face-up on the ground, with her head resting on a pillow made of dahlias. Her green eyes are staring straight up in a vacant gaze, and her lips are coated in a blood-red gloss. A vertical line of red runs vertically down from the corner of her mouth deep into her cheek, hinting at a sinister smile carved into her face by the killer. The title of the book, "Black Dahlia," is displayed boldly in black-shading-into-red letters that overlap the image. We are about to have some fun with the gruesome murder of a sexy young woman! A "terrible beauty."

DIALOG

Ellroy's trademark gritty and rapid-fire dialog is intended, presumably, to mirror and stylize the hardscrabble and morally sketchy lives of the characters.

The language is rife with casual use of racial epithets and sexist observations both explicit and implicit. We've barely opened the book when we get "nigger knocker" on page 5. Two pages later, still in the prologue, Bucky and Lee are attempting to break up a riot. As he places the cuffs on Don Santos, Blanchard says, "He's dead meat. Manslaughter Two's a gas chamber jolt for spics. Hepcat here's about six weeks away from the Big Adios."[15] We know early on what we're going to get in this book.

Yet, perhaps the cheesy and morally suspect language is just an artistic move in Ellroy's game, designed to entertain, jar, and jolt for maximum aesthetic effect. Sure, the dialog is cheesy and offensive, but these provide ways to enjoy it, rather than dismiss it. As they say, "You can't yuck that yum."

Consider the scene of destruction when Bucky confronts Madeleine and Emmet at the Sprague estate and ends up destroying a roomful of art masterpieces after finding his love interest and (who he thinks is) her father in bed together.

> I shot the Picasso first. The silencer went "Pffft" and the .45 hollow point blew the canvas in half. The two Mings were next, crockery fragments exploding all over the room. I missed the gargoyle with my first shot—a gold-bordered mirror the consolation prize. Daddy and darling daughter huddled on the bed; I took sight on Rembrandt or Titian or whoever the fuck it was. My bull's-eye blew a dandy hole out of it, along with a chunk of the all. The frame toppled and hit Emmett's shoulder; the heat of the weapon singed my hand. I held on to it anyway, one round still in the chamber to get me my story.[16]

This is a rich passage and serves to illustrate the world of aesthetic crimes that the reader is invited to enter into and enjoy. The fantasy itself—shooting up a sexy room with a sexy gun with a sexy silencer mounted on a sexy barrel—fits perfectly the cheesy language used to describe a sordid scene. Surely, the cheesy dialog is itself part of the fun and not simply an unfortunate and distracting cliché. An otherwise aesthetic defect can morph into an aesthetic virtue.

In many cases, the cheesy language is impossible to appreciate, except as a joke. But in Ellroy's dark fictional worlds, the language fits with and drives our appreciation. Thus, although we might criticize Ellroy for his cartoonish dialog, exaggerated speech patterns, and a high degree of vulgarity, as noted above, he employs these stylistic tropes in order to create a sense of heightened reality and to emphasize the gritty, violent nature of the world the characters inhabit. This provides the reader with a path to appreciating rather than dismissing that world.

It must be said, however, that after 300 pages it can begin to sound less like style and more like shtick.[17] That in itself is probably an aesthetic flaw, albeit not one that gives rise to a moral one. But the problem is exacerbated when the shtick involves the seemingly gratuitous use of numerous and vile epithets to describe the victim and other female characters. Ellroy has been criticized elsewhere for the depth and breadth of the racism depicted in his novels. He has both advocates and detractors on this matter.[18]

The prologue to Black Dahlia is a well-known and representative sample of the kind of racist language Ellroy likes to sprinkle in his dialog. The broader *L.A. Quartet*, as well as more recent works, such as *Perfida* and *This Storm*, are also full of racial invective, slurs, and epithets. Such can seem gratuitous in ways that similar language does not when employed by David Simon or Spike Lee or even Quentin Tarantino. Ellroy has consistently maintained that the casual racism of his characters is an accidental feature of them rather than a defining one. The use of racist tropes is not simply gratuitous; rather, they are appropriate to the settings and the characters and add a layer of complexity that forces readers to confront uncomfortable realities.

> I write characters who are the good guys and who also occasionally drop the racial slur, the anti-homosexual remark, but with these characters racial animus is never a defining characteristic. It's a casual attribute. I like the idea of race as anecdote. I live by anecdote. I live to the exclusion of epigram. Those who think that all people who would express racial animus do that because of a deep-seated hatred boiling within them don't understand that at a certain time and place it was the common linguistic coin of the realm.[19]

Ellory admits relishing the fact that the ambiguity triggers left-leaning, self-appointed language-police-types who are diligently on the lookout for the politically incorrect. He doesn't care about being politically incorrect.

> Critics want racism, and secondarily homophobia, to be portrayed as a defining characteristic, rather than a casual attribute. Racist language uttered by sympathetic characters confuses hidebound liberals. Who gives a shit.[20]

This is not the place to adjudicate the issue of whether or not Ellroy's work is racist. Our question instead is whether the immorality of the characters and/or the work itself adds or detracts from the aesthetic value. The worry is that Ellroy employs the offensive language merely for entertainment purposes. Rather than enriching the characters, the use of racist language instead fetishizes their racism. I think this diminishes the work by indulging rather than confronting our darker tendencies. Nevertheless, this doesn't mean that there is not much of positive aesthetic value elsewhere to appreciate. It just means that only some and not all immorality has positive aesthetic consequences.

EMBRACE OF THE DARK SIDE

Not merely the style employed in describing its sordid world but also the implied attitude of moral approval directed toward that world serve to enhance the aesthetic value of *The Black Dahlia*. Consider again the scene at the Sprague estate discussed above. The reader is encouraged to find it delicious when Bucky opens fire on the roomful of priceless masterpieces. And we do. This peek at our darker impulses through a somewhat comical lens allows us to accept and embrace them at an aesthetic or "psychical" distance, even though we know it is wrong.

Recall the emotional manipulation employed by Madeleine Sprague who uses Blanchard to advance her own agenda. Madeleine looks like Elizabeth Short and knew her in life, which allows her to take advantage of Bucky's irrational obsession with the *Black Dahlia*. She becomes involved with Bucky in exchange for him keeping her name out of the investigation. Their treatment of each other as mutual means is depicted in the most casual way, one that Ellroy's narrative appears to endorse as just part and parcel of human life.

If it failed to convey this attitude of moral approval toward things that we find morally offensive, *Black Dahlia* would simply not be the work that it is, aesthetically speaking. But that needn't make the work aesthetically worse. Indeed, it is intrinsic to the overall positive aesthetic affect it generates in the reader.

THE EXQUISITE CORPSE

According to newspaper reports from the time, Elizabeth Short was last seen alive on January 9, 1947, in the company of several men at a bar in Los Angeles. Her body, found a week later on January 15 in a vacant lot, had been cut in half at the waist, drained of blood, and then staged in a manner that suggested the killer intended to shock and disgust those who discovered her.

> The killer had left his mark on the body in many ways. He had removed geometric sections of flesh from the woman's breasts, and left leg and had positioned the body in a very particular and unusual way. Police and reporters at the scene said that she looked like a disassembled mannequin or a discarded marionette.[21]

The upper half of the body was situated above and to the left of the lower half, the arms extended above the head in a "goalpost" formation, and the legs spread apart. Although the internal organs were largely intact, the body, having been drained of blood, had a pale, "ivory white" appearance like that of a mannequin. Horrific cuts extended the edges of the mouth high into the cheeks creating a macabre "Joker" smile.

In their book *Exquisite Corpse*, Nelson and Bayliss offer a thorough reexamination and analysis of the murder, situating it in the context of the LA art scene, focusing in particular on the widespread interest in and indeed fascination with Surrealism prevalent at the time. The book includes numerous reproductions of Surrealist paintings and sculptures that depict women in dismembered and mutilated forms, some of which closely resemble the condition and positioning of Elizabeth Short's body.[22]

The implication of the book is that the murder scene was an overt reference to Surrealism in general and to the work of the American Surrealist Man Ray in particular. Most importantly Nelson and Bayliss, the corpse was posed in a manner that strikingly resembled Ray's infamous black-and-white photo *The Minotaur*.[23]

The photograph depicts the body of a slender young woman and alludes to classical mythology. The contours of her body resemble a bull's head, with her breasts representing eyes, her upturned arms mimicking horns, and her stomach, shadowed under the ribs, resembling a mouth.

Nelson and Bayliss discuss dozens of other works by Ray and his Surrealist friends and colleagues, including Marcel Duchamp, and suggest that the positioning of the body with the upper and lower halves offset by some distance was possibly intended to reference the Surrealist game of Exquisite Corpse.

The authors venture a kind of dual hypothesis: the murder was both inspired by and in turn, inspired Surrealist art. First, the authors imply that the murderer had intended to produce a Surrealist work of art out of the corpse of a murdered human being. Second, they suggest that the murder served as inspiration or at least point of reference for a notorious later work by Duchamp. As evidence for the latter, the authors point to the suspiciously similar positioning of Short's discarded body and that of the nude in Duchamp's infamous *Etant Donnes*.[24]

In addition to the suggestion that Duchamp's work makes direct reference to the murder, Nelson and Bayliss go on to discuss further circumstantial evidence, including an extensive network of mutual acquaintances among various LA art world figures, the prime suspects in the case, and the LAPD.

We are now in a position to return to our discussion of immoralism. Does appreciating the mutilated body of Elizabeth Short as a kind of Surrealist artwork—an Exquisite Corpse—provide a way to understand the murder as something aesthetically valuable? It does seem that if we were psychologically capable of bracketing off our sense of moral repugnance in order to focus on a purely aesthetic object, we might thereby enter into some kind of "psychically distanced"[25] and purely aesthetic state of appreciation. And that state might be an experience valuable for its own sake. If so, the positive aesthetic experience or value would arise *despite* the negative moral experience or value. Surely this is possible even for ordinary folks. But this would seem to require a considerable amount of mental effort—and not the kind of mental effort that would contribute positively to the overall value of the experience. It seems more likely that this sort of radical "psychical distancing" is possible only for the psychologically and/or morally deviant. Perhaps one might be able, with full knowledge of what one is witnessing, to set all of that knowledge aside and simply enjoy *Black Dahlia* as a literary achievement. I do not want to claim that such manner of aesthetic appreciation is impossible.

More interesting for aesthetic immoralism are cases in which positive aesthetic value arises not *in virtue of* negative moral value rather than despite it. In an influential paper, Carolyn Korsmeyer discusses "the perplexing phenomenon of [. . .] *terrible beauty*, that is, beauty that is bound up with the arousal of discomforting emotions." Terrible beauties are cases in which "art can be beautiful not despite its painful import, but because of it." A "terrible beauty" would help to advance the case for the aesthetic immoralist by showing how "an aversion such as disgust might find some quarter in beautiful art."[26]

Korsmeyer provides compelling examples of "aesthetic disgust" that can result, somewhat paradoxically, in a positive aesthetic experience. Poets from John Donne to Emily Dickenson invoke images of insects and other vermin that feed off human flesh; Caravaggio depicts Doubting Thomas quite literally inserting his hand into the wound in Jesus' side; Robert Stone's *A Flag for Sunrise* includes a harrowing description of the sickening effects of torture, beating, and electric shock. Such cases involve a "mingling of negative and positive affect" into "one dense and complex phenomenon" in which "even disgust itself becomes an experience of beauty."[27]

Perhaps we can understand the Black Dahlia murder on the model of Korsmeyer's "terrible beauties." Does skillfully posing Elizabeth Short's artfully mutilated body in way that invokes or resembles Man Ray's *Minotaur* turn the murderer into an artist and the corpse into an artwork aesthetically appreciable for its own sake? Surely the answer is no. The murder, mutilation, and posing of Elizabeth Short's body are plausibly examples of aesthetic crimes, possibly even artistic crimes—but not crimes that result in or comprise works of art. The crime itself is so morally heinous and so intrinsically bound up in the aesthetic properties of the crime as to make it impossible to redeem any positive aesthetic value. Anything can be a work of art, but this does not mean that everything is.

But what about artistic *depictions* of heinous crimes and morally repugnant acts? Is Ellroy's *Black Dahlia* an aesthetic crime as well? I will argue in the following section that although the work is not itself an aesthetic crime, the aesthetic crimes it contains, including its immorality, contribute to its overall positive aesthetic value in the way supported by aesthetic immoralists.

BODY ART?

Is the Black Dahlia murder an extreme case of body art? This seems to be, or could at least be derived from, the thesis that Nelson and Bayliss embrace in

Exquisite Corpse. They base their case on a theory about the murder espoused by Steve Hodel in *Black Dahlia Avenger*.[28]

Hodel, a former LAPD detective, advances the theory that his own father, George Hodel, was responsible for the murder. According to Hodel, his father had both the motive and the opportunity to commit the murder. He was a known sexual predator and had a history of sexually abusing his own daughter, Tamar Hodel. Moreover, he argues, George Hodel was involved in other criminal activities, such as illegal abortions and drug trafficking, which could have led to a conflict with Elizabeth Short. The father was a trained surgeon and had access to medical equipment that would have been necessary to make the precision cuts and neat dissections found on Short's body. Witness testimony and Hodel's own behavior after the murder suggest that he was involved in the crime. Hodel identifies several witnesses who he believes saw his father with Elizabeth Short in the days leading up to the murder. He cites witnesses who claim to have seen George Hodel's car near the crime scene on the night of the murder. Finally, Hodel suggests that his father's personality traits and behavior are consistent with the type of person who would commit such a crime. He describes his father as a narcissistic and sociopathic individual who had a long history of sexual predation and other criminal activities.

As discussed earlier, Nelson and Bayliss add to Hodel's theory the fascinating and provocative twist that the most likely explanation of the murder is that it was inspired by art-theoretical principles of Surrealism. In defending their thesis, they provide a detailed study of George Hodel's numerous and substantial connections to the 1040s Los Angeles art scene, paying particular attention to his personal acquaintance with Man Ray. The authors go on to catalog his wide-ranging associations with other figures in the Surrealist Art movement prevalent at the time, including, Salvador Dali, Max Ernst, Dorothea Tanning, Rene Magritte, and Marcel Duchamp. The authors also explore the social circles surrounding George Hodel, including filmmakers John Huston and Henry Miller, Surrealist art patrons Louise and Walter Arensberg, artist and art dealer William Copley, filmmaker and Surrealist patron Albert Lewin, collectors and actors Vincent Price, Edward G. Robinson, and Fanny Brice.

Does all of this historical and forensic evidence help to advance the theory that the corpse of Elizabeth Short is a work of body art? On the face of it, this thesis is indefensible. This claim would be not only morally inappropriate but also a conceptual mistake. Body art, one might argue, necessarily involves modifying or decorating the body, such as through tattoos, piercings, or performance art. It is a consensual and voluntary act, intended to be an expression of creativity or personal identity. The Black Dahlia murder, on the other hand, was a violent and nonconsensual act of homicide. It was not intended to be an expression of creativity or personal identity but was instead a brutal and senseless act of violence. Treating a horrific murder and mutilation not as senseless violence but as a creative work of art trivializes and glorifies it.

Nevertheless, perhaps this is where the immoralist about artistic and aesthetic value might again put their theory to work. An immoralist can argue first that there is a way of classifying artifacts as artworks that distinguishes them from otherwise commonplace or ordinary things. An immoralist can then go on to argue that a work's negative moral value contributes to its overall positive aesthetic or artistic value in an ineliminable way. If so, then the Black Dahlia murder might after all be a valuable artwork.

One way to defend this thesis is to appeal to theories of art explicitly designed to accommodate difficult and challenging, perhaps even ugly, anti-aesthetic, or morally repugnant artifacts. So-called "institutional theories of art" have been defended most notably by George Dickie and Arthur Danto.[29] Both authors provide theoretical means of understanding arthood as something achieved by way of social practices of classification rather than by way of strictly formal or aesthetic measures or merit. According to Dickie,

> A work of art in the classificatory sense is 1) an artifact 2) upon which some person or persons acting on behalf of a certain social institution (the artworld) has conferred the status of appreciation.[30]

According to Danto, the distinction between artworks and "mere real things" is that the former but not the latter demand *interpretation* within an art world setting.

> To see something as art at all demands nothing less than this, an atmosphere of artistic theory, a knowledge of the history of art . . . which is so powerful a thing as to detach objects from the real world and make them part of a different world, an *art* world, a world of *interpreted* things. [T]he question of when is a thing an artwork becomes one with the question of when is an interpretation of a thing an *artistic* interpretation.[31]

How does the institutional theory work in practice? Here is the classical case: In 1917, Rene Duchamp took an everyday urinal and transformed it into a celebrated artwork known as *The Fountain*. This was achieved through his actions as a representative of the art world and amidst a backdrop of artistic theory. He signed the urinal and submitted it for inclusion in an exhibition hosted by the Society for Independent Artists, thereby creating one of the most significant art pieces of the twentieth century.

Given the art-theoretical atmosphere in which Elizabeth Short and George Hodel were immersed, Hodel was positioned to act on behalf of the art world and according to Surrealist principles to produce a work of Surrealist body

art. In referencing the Minotaur of classical Greece, the murderer tapped into the power of the unconscious mind to express deep and hidden human fantasies and desires.

Mining these dark places, the murderer advanced the Surrealist project of subverting through disorientation and destabilization of traditional concepts of reality and morality. Paradoxically, the corpse itself, an otherwise "mere real thing" comes to have a life of its own, and to express its own semantic, symbolic, and metaphorical content. The corpse is a self-referential "found object" that announces its own status as art object. The mutilated body becomes itself a work of body art. Moreover, the posing of the body itself—nude, bisected, eerily smiling—exemplifies or instantiates the further Surrealist themes of forbidden desire, fetishism, eroticism, and uncanniness. Finally, the posing of the corpse might serve the Surrealists' political purpose of expressing a profound but otherwise unarticulable anarchistic challenge to ordinary moral, social, and political norms.

CONCLUSION

James Ellroy's *Black Dahlia* both depicts and instantiates a variety of aesthetic crimes. Ordinarily, the dark and depressing content, cheesy and offensive language, and seeming endorsement of moral depravity would tend to count heavily against its aesthetic merit. But the immoralist account of the relationship between aesthetic and moral value helps us to understand how some aesthetic crimes might nevertheless result in aesthetic triumphs.

NOTES

1. Loos, *Ornament and Crime*.
2. Sanchez, "Man Ray: Rayographs & Solarization."
3. Hughes, *The Shock of the New*.
4. Wilde, Preface to *A Picture of Dorian Gray*.
5. Tolstoy, *What Is Art?*
6. See Kieran, "Forbidden Knowledge."
7. Aristotle, "On Tragedy."
8. Carroll, "Moderate Moralism," 228.
9. Eaton, "Robust Immoralism;" Jacobson, "Ethical Criticism;" John, "Artistic Value;" and Kieran, "Art and Morality."
10. Eaton, "Robust Immoralism," 281.
11. John, "Artistic Value and Opportunistic Moralism, 340.
12. Kieran, "Art and Morality," 463–64.
13. Kieran, "Forbidden Knowledge," 63.

14. See Sauchelli, "Ethicism and Immoral Cognitivism," 110.
15. Ellroy, *Black Dahlia*, 7.
16. Ellroy, *Black Dahlia*, 320.
17. Power, "Ellroy's Monuments."
18. For a representative sample, see Power, "Ellroy's Monuments," Rich, "Art of Fiction," and Vasquez, "Dark, Twisted."
19. Marchese, "James Ellroy on His Life in Crime."
20. Rich, "The Art of Fiction."
21. Nelson and Bayliss, *Exquisite Corpse*, 9.
22. For more, see Groves, *The Bedlam Files*.
23. Ray, *The Minotaur*.
24. Duchamps, Marcel. *Etant Donnes*.
25. Bullough famously coined the term "psychical distance."
26. Korsmeyer, "Terrible Beauties," 52.
27. Korsmeyer, "Terrible Beauties," 62–63.
28. Hodel, *Black Dahlia Avenger*.
29. Danto, *Transfiguration*. Dickie, "Art as Institution."
30. Dickie, "Art as Institution," 492.
31. Danto, *Transfiguration*, 135.

BIBLIOGRAPHY

Aristotle, "On Tragedy." In *Aesthetics: A Reader in Philosophy of the Arts*, edited by David Goldblatt and Lee B. Brown, 325–26. Upper Saddle River, NJ: Pearson, 2005.

Bell, Clive. *Art*. London: Charro and Windus, 1914.

Bullough, Edward. "'Psychical Distance'" as a Factor in Art and as an Aesthetic Principle," *British Journal of Psychology* 5 (1912): 87–117.

Carroll, Noel. "Moderate Moralism," *British Journal of Aesthetics* 36 (1993): 223–38.

Danto, Arthur. *Transfiguration of the Commonplace*. Cambridge: Harvard University Press, 1981.

Dickie, George, "Art as a Social Institution." In *Aesthetics: A Reader in Philosophy of the Arts*, edited by David Goldblatt and Lee B. Brown, 490–94. Upper Saddle River, NJ: Pearson, 2005.

Duchamps, Marcel. Etant Donnes. Philadelphia Museum of Art. https://philamuseum.org/collection/object/65633.

Eaton, A.W. "Robust Immoralism," *Journal of Aesthetics and Art Criticism* 70 (2012): 281–92.

Ellroy, James. *Black Dahlia*. New York: Hatchette, 1997.

Groves, Adam. 'Review of *Exquisite Corpse*," *The Bedlam Files*. 2023. https://thebedlamfiles.com/nonfiction/exquisite-corpse-surrealism-and-the-black-dahlia-murder. Accessed 2/21/2023.

Hodel, Steve. *Black Dahlia Avenger*. Harper Collins, 2006.

Hughes, Robert. *The Shock of the New*. New York: Knopf, 1991.

Jacobson, Daniel. "Ethical Criticism and the Vice of Moderation," In *Contemporary Debates in Aesthetics and the Philosophy of Art*, edited by Matthew Kieran, 342–55. Malden, MA: Blackwell, 2006.

John, Eileen. "Artistic Value and Opportunistic Moralism." In *Contemporary Debates in Aesthetics and the Philosophy of Art*, edited by Matthew Kieran, 331–41. Malden, MA: Blackwell, 2006.

Kieran, Matthew. "Art and Morality," *The Oxford Handbook of Aesthetics*, edited by Jerrold Levinson, 451–70. New York: Oxford University Press, 2003.

Kieran, Matthew. "Forbidden Knowledge." In *Art and Morality*, edited by Jose Bermudez and Sebastian Gardner, 56–73. London: Routledge, 2003.

Korsmeyer, Carolyn. "Terrible Beauties." In *Contemporary Debates in Aesthetics and the Philosophy of Art*, edited by Matthew Kieran, 51–63. Malden, MA: Blackwell, 2006.

Loos, Adolf. *Ornament and Crime*. New York: Penguin Classics, 2019.

Marchese, David. "James Ellroy on His Life in Crime, His Imaginary Dog and the Need to Provoke," *The New York Times Magazine*, August 20, 2019. https://www.nytimes.com/interactive/2019/08/19/magazine/james-ellroy-interview.html

Nelson, Mark, and Sarah Hudson Bayliss. *Exquisite Corpse: Surrealism and the Black Dahlia Murder*. New York: Bulfinch Press, 2006.

Power, Chris. "James Ellroy's Monuments to Bigoted Men," *The New Statesman*, June 5, 2019. https://www.newstatesman.com/culture/2019/06/james-ellroys-monuments-to-bigoted-men. Accessed 2/21/2023.

Ray, Man. *The Minotaur*. WikiArt. https://www.wikiart.org/en/man-ray/minotaur-1934. Accessed 2/15/2023.

Rich, Nathaniel. "James Ellroy, The Art of Fiction No. 201," *The Paris Review* 190 (2009): 37–69.

Sanchez, Gabriel H. "Man Ray: Rayographs & Solarizations," *In The In-Between*, July 5, 2014. https://www.inthein-between.com/man-ray-before-digital/

Sauchelli, Andrea. "Ethicism and Immoral Cognitivism: Gaut versus Kieran on Art and Morality," *Journal of Art and Art Criticism* 46 (2012): 107–18.

Tolstoy, Leo. *What Is Art?* Translated by Aylmer Maude. Oxford: Oxford University Press, 1930.

Vasquez, Zach. "James Ellroy, David Milch and a Dark, Twisted Vision of History," *Crime Reads*, June 4, 2019. https://crimereads.com/james-ellroy-david-milch-and-a-dark-twisted-vision-of-history. Accessed 2/21/2023.

Wilde, Oscar. "Preface," *The Picture of Dorian Gray*. Penguin Classics, 2007.

Chapter 4

Dark Mirror

The Resisting Reader and the Crime Writing of James Ellroy

Lexey A. Bartlett

James Ellroy's novels and life writing act as readings of his experiences, attempts to understand his feelings surrounding his mother and her murder by writing about the Black Dahlia case and his mother's murder in both veiled and direct ways.[1] Time, place, and childhood experiences intertwined Geneva/Jean Hilliker's and Elizabeth Short's murders for Ellroy, connections he explains most fully in the memoir *My Dark Places* (1996). Although *Clandestine* (1982) includes Short's case in the background,[2] *The Black Dahlia* (1987) centers on a thoroughly fictionalized investigation of and solution to Short's murder. In the novel, Ellroy and his law enforcement characters pore over the case's minutiae, simultaneously presented for the reader's delectation, whether the reader likes it or not. We all understand the power of the text to transform us, whether for better or worse. The question arises, then, of how, not whether, a work like Ellroy's *The Black Dahlia*, and the larger genre of noir, affects us as readers. This question encompasses many kinds of readers, from a writer like Ellroy reading his own experience through the process of composition, to the readers thematically introduced in his text (the detectives and murderers), and finally to actual readers. Reading transforms the reader, sometimes in dark and dangerous ways, but the reader reciprocates, as these competing perspectives exemplify how reading transforms the text itself, in a mutual reflection. Yet readers also can resist such transformations, if they have the will; as Judith Fetterley explains the act she figures as resistance,

> It is based on the premise that we read and that what we read affects us—drenches us, to use [Adrienne] Rich's language, in its assumptions, and that to avoid drowning in this drench of assumptions we must learn to reread. [3]

Thus, following Fetterley, I will argue that the reader must reread against this text's assumptions and must resist or even refuse this text to avoid being erased.

In Ellroy's 2006 essay after *The Black Dahlia* film's production, Ellroy describes his initial motivation for writing the novel as "[m]isogynistic fury codified," which he explains is "[t]he reason why Betty Short was killed and why I tell redemption tales aimed at women."[4] Ellroy attempts to apologize for his initial motivations, yet misogyny permeates the work without redemption, since the representation of Short and his mother by proxy veers from reviled object to object of desire with little effort to imagine their subjectivity. Language repeatedly reframes Elizabeth Short's identity, partially through her many nicknames but primarily through the stories told of her by those trying to "read" her in order to solve her murder or to exploit her to their own ends—by the media influenced by the District Attorny's office to represent her as a virginal victim, by witnesses or suspects bargaining with their knowledge, by her friends or associates with varied motives, and most importantly by the detective protagonist Dwight "Bucky" Bleichert creating his own vision of her for a profusion of reasons.[5] Bucky wants to solve Short's murder as a solution to his emotional problems, rather than as the real woman she was, so even that desire erases her by recreating her as a false idol. Ellroy's feelings about his mother inflect his imagination of Short's character with a level of promiscuity and seediness bearing little relation to reality,[6] intermixing his own sexual feeling toward both women[7] and his father's castigation of Hilliker after their divorce,[8] so Ellroy's representation of Short feels like a further act of violence, a character assassination, rather than a redemption. Likewise, as Katherine Farrimond argues regarding the film and later burlesque presentations based on Short's murder, an apolitical approach that simply repeats these images fails as "a critique of misogynistic violence," instead perpetuating it by re-presenting it for the audience to consume.[9] Ellroy spins his own reading of these women into a work that creates all readers in his own image, as desiring to consume Elizabeth Short and other women with obsessive intensity, whether they be the detectives, murderers, or the implied reader.

The act of reading, if viewed as an all-consuming desire to know, appears linked by analogy to voyeurism and the act of detection, especially in Ellroy's work. Jim Mancall correlates the sensationalist aspects of reading pornography and detective fiction while casting doubt on some detective novelists' efforts to distance themselves from sensationalism by drawing distinctions between highbrow writing and works of the most lurid variety.[10] Mancall argues that Ellroy uses pornography thematically in his stories to "confront the reader with the voyeuristic pleasures of detective fiction."[11] While Mancall focuses on *White Jazz*, his conclusion that the text "depict[s] the acts of reading and viewing as potentially destabilizing"[12] can be applied generally to Ellroy's work and to the act of reading certain kinds of texts. Mancall claims these works are compelling because "both detective fiction and pornography make explicit that which is normally hidden,"[13] and he concludes that in contrast to the readers of detective fiction imagined by other writers like Gladys Mitchell, "Ellroy's reader is the addict, irrationally, compulsively, drawn to illicit scenes. Ellroy's reader is the voyeur, horrified, but at the same time, 'hungry to watch.'"[14] Like many critics, Mancall views Ellroy's motivation as high-minded and supports this impulse in the name of art,[15] but since the experiences of actual readers may differ from those of readers constructed by the text, many readers will not share the proposed hunger to consume the illicit scenes presented under the pretext of the permission granted by claims to artistic merit. Indeed, as Fetterley points out, the veneration of art and the supposedly universal truths it espouses, especially about American identity, which she shows is by definition male, presents this apolitical veneer over the systems that rely on patriarchal power, which prevents any real critique of that power.[16] We can only expose these hegemonic assumptions by acting as "resisting rather than" "assenting reader[s] and, by this refusal to assent, to begin the process of exorcizing" the ingrained misogynistic patterns of thinking that we have all been taught to read through.[17] Many texts encourage us to adopt these points of view, however, including Ellroy's, making our resistance to them continually necessary.

Nathan Ashman offers some resistance, approaching Ellroy's pervasive theme of voyeurism with a theoretical framework moderated by feminist objections to the voyeuristic gaze by critics like Laura Mulvey, but that also expands the conception of voyeurism from sexual prurience into a generalized "culture of voyeurism"[18] indicated by the dissolution of barriers separating the private from the public through media such as reality television. Thus, while Ashman aligns Ellroy's depictions of detection with the voyeuristic desire to read the hidden, he notes that he will not disregard how *The Black Dahlia* reveals that "the desire to possess the elusive 'feminine object' is still integral to Ellroy's magnification of the voyeuristic potentialities of narrative."[19] Ashman also characterizes voyeurism as "a peculiarly masculine anxiety in Ellroy's texts, [. . .] bound up with the primordial search for truth at the very core of viewing."[20] These observations, combined with Mancall's description of the reader constructed by Ellroy, connect this obsessive desire for hidden knowledge to the feminine object observed by the masculine viewer, and the fact that women rarely feature as this kind of voyeur in Ellroy's texts underscores the gendered construction of this activity and of Ellroy's implied reader. Women are the spied upon, not the spies, in Ellroy's world. While Ashman makes the case that "Ellroy's novels *themselves* are voyeuristic, implicating the reader in these broader narrative patterns of both visual and epistemophilic obsession,"[21] I will argue that the actual reader can and should resist being implicated in this way.

READING AND WRITING, CONSUMING AND BEING CONSUMED

The detective's drive for knowledge links investigation with the act of reading. Using narratological theories, Joshua Meyer connects the detective's activity to how a narrative's reader pieces together the underlying events (the "*fable*") from traces presented in the narration (the "*subject*"), just as the detective fits clues together into a theory of what occurred despite missing information.[22] The detective reads a wide variety of texts, from material evidence to images, interviews with all their textual and subtextual information, observations of activity, and more, as we see in Dwight "Bucky" Bleichert's path to reconstructing the crime. However, to achieve that reconstruction, the detective must perform a close reading, often repeatedly consuming the disturbing traces of the crime, and that consumption will affect the consumer in increasingly disturbing ways.

The search for clues somewhat justifies the detective's voyeurism, sanctioning the perusal of illicit material through the purpose of justice, but as Mancall argues, readers borrowing this justification vicariously must acknowledge their prurient curiosity. The conversation surrounding the consumption of crime literature, whether cozy mysteries or true crime, raises concerns about the ethics of consuming crime merely for entertainment, but readers can have other purposes for reading crime fiction that do not rely on such prurience. Mancall discounts arguments that readers of detective fiction are engaged in the puzzle and seek intellectual or emotional "closure,"[23] an aspect of crime writing and real-life justice that Ellroy himself explicitly rejects.[24] But readers do not read merely to resolve puzzles, although some may. Many of us read such texts wanting to see a semblance of justice restored, through judicial processes, if possible, or if it is not restored, to expose systemic injustices realistically. Such readers are not looking for mere repetitions of truisms that we are all aware of, such as current or historic misogyny, racism, or homophobia in crimes or their policing, and ever more sensational or grotesque depictions of them. We prefer seeing the creative imagination deployed in proposing solutions to these problems, rather than a desperate vision of a world in which nothing changes, an endless *noir* cycle of hopelessness. However, Ellroy also rejects the image of a white knight kind of detective or even ones as marginally ethical as those of Chandler and Hammett.[25] He seems unable to imagine a detective who follows an ethical code and operates with the aim of justice, at least before the experiences related in *My Dark Places*, as it is clear the detectives who worked his mother's case put in serious effort, and Bill Stoner reveals himself to be a similarly dedicated and ethical officer. Where Ellroy does include such a character, like Captain Ray Millard in *The Black Dahlia*, he is limited to the sidelines and ultimately is dragged into the morass Bucky Bleichert creates by suppressing evidence. Carole Allamand explains how Ellroy's own guilt over his mother's murder makes it impossible for him to identify the guilty, as he can only project his guilt onto others, implicating him in a further cycle of guilt.[26] This guilty projection accounts for his construction of detectives and readers that share his own prurient obsessions, as perhaps he is unable to conceive of any other kind of reader.

The way scholars characterize Ellroy's representation of voyeurism and the reader should not come as any surprise, given Ellroy's own ideas about the readership of the genre he writes, his foundational experiences as a reader of true crime, and his personal history of voyeuristic activity. These aspects of Ellroy's writing and experience align with Wolfgang Iser's conception of the reading process with the role that he refers to as the "implied reader," a "construct" in the text itself, which the actual reader may inhabit.[27] Iser posits that the reader constructs multiple doublings of reality by serving as a nexus that brings texts together and produces representations of reality in that process. Iser refers to this concept as "the doubling structure of fictionality, produced by the fictionalizing acts of the literary text."[28] The writer selects elements from reality, recombining and transforming them through writing,[29] but the selection differentiates the text from the real, which lies outside our capacity to capture it in language, and the writer's inherent limitations and biases shape the selection. In this conception, the writer is a reader who produces a complicated new text from those sources, and as Iser writes, "The more one text incorporates other texts, the more intensified will be the process of doubling induced by the act of selection."[30] This intertextual doubling and redoubling appears so prominently in Ellroy's writing because he combines his reading of texts about the Black Dahlia murder with his experience of his mother's murder and countless other texts, including his own. Ellroy's revisiting of these topics in more than one text and his later reassessments of those texts constitute additional readings and writings, additional doublings.

Iser also theorizes reading's reciprocal act of making, as the reader's mind produces this world from the text.[31] The reader completes the process, creating a world by reading, thus highlighting the reader's active role. However, Iser also suggests that the reader may be taken over in the process of reading the text:

> In this respect the required activity of the recipient resembles that of an actor, who in order to perform his role must use his thoughts, his feelings, and even his

> body as an analogue for representing something he is not. In order to produce the determinate form of an unreal character, the actor must allow his own reality to fade out.[32]

While we generally avoid discussions of authorial intention in literary scholarship, Ellroy repeatedly inserts himself into the conversation through his writing in and about his texts, as well as his public comments. He is much more assertive than many writers about how he wants to direct the reader's experience. Ellroy clearly expects his reader to be taken over in the way Iser describes, which explains his admiring statements about De Palma's film and the perspective it forces on the viewer: "You forfeit control and see only what he wants you to see. . . . The filmgoer needs to succumb. . . . He controls response firmly."[33] Ellroy identifies the film's forced perspective with the novel's by noting that the filmmaker "brilliantly followed [his lead],"[34] in fact so well that the film erases Elizabeth Short even more fully than the novel, as Farrimond argues,[35] even as it would erase the viewer's volition in accord with Ellroy's wishes.

I accept Iser's conception of the reading process, but it includes a paradox between the creative power of the reader and the suggestion that actual readers let their reality be subsumed by the implied reader. What happens when the stakes are too high to allow this takeover to occur? When one does not consent to being used in this way? When the body rejects this reading role? This expulsion has been my experience of reading *The Black Dahlia*, a strangely dysphoric experience of not being able to inhabit the implied reader, especially in the character of the voyeur that has been suggested. It is my experience of this refusal and how it emerges in the text's efforts to lure readers to a dark performance of the self that I am interrogating in this essay.

THROUGH THE DARK LOOKING GLASS

As a way of collecting and imagining these understandings of reading and its effects on readers of and in a text like *The Black Dahlia*, I propose the metaphor of a dark mirror, one that reflects but also enacts a dark transmogrification of the reflected. Like the mirror in Lewis Carroll's *Through the Looking Glass*, this dark mirror is also permeable, and the gazer runs the risk of passing through its surface into the dark world on the other side, a world where logic turns upside down and those entering it struggle to retain the orientation of the world left behind. Carroll plays on the child's fancy that mirrors are windows onto another world, the imaginative possibility that we could pass through the mirror and inhabit that alternative space, but Alice finds a distorted and disturbing logic when she crosses the boundary of the mirror's surface to the world beyond. Through experience, we eventually realize that mirrors are surfaces rather than windows, but the uncanny impression of their permeability remains to some degree, along with their clear reversal of our world.

This impression of the relationship between the surface and what lies beyond it connects to ways of looking at detective fiction. Meyer explains the narratological understanding of the detective genre through a spatial metaphor opposing "surface and depth."[36] The detective navigates the surface collecting evidence in order to delve into its deeper significance and unfold the crime's hidden series of events. In this model, the surface is permeable. If we combine this concept of the detective story with reading's multiple acts of creation, new worlds and iterations of reader and text emerge. The detective's act of reading the surface constructs the depth, or the events in the order they occurred that have left the marks being read, and in that process the detective creates themselves as the detective through the activity performed. These processes map onto Meyer's discussion of "the *subject* and the *fable*," with the surface being the subject where the traces of the depth or fable are left to be read and used to reconstruct the prenarrative events.[37] The detective is not untouched in the process, but instead is also transformed by the act of reading, by consuming the traces of violence. The reader of the detective story doubles this activity, becoming the detective by proxy, reviewing the same surface covered by the detective character and constructing meaning as well as a new analogue self or selves in the process. Thus, detectives and readers, through their acts of perception, pass through surfaces into worlds of their creation, transformed by the process.

Depending on the material consumed, varying degrees of darkness shade these iterations of the self and world. D. S. Neff's schizoanalysis of *The Black Dahlia* follows Bucky Bleichert's progression toward psychosis, a key feature of which is his use of "paleologic,"[38] or "thinking in non-Aristotelian, 'psychotic,' schizophrenic ways."[39] Neff asserts that Bucky's distorted thought processes ultimately allow him to solve the crime.[40] As the novel progresses, Bucky crosses a series of boundaries, spatial and mental, that transform him into this darker version of the self, capable of entering into the criminal mindset, but in the process he also becomes a criminal and edges toward increasingly dangerous behavior. This result raises the question of whether the allure of the dark mirror world creates its own gravitational field, such that we must beware of getting too close to its boundary lest we be pulled through. Through his shaping of the reader's viewpoint, Ellroy seems to want to force this process.

When a reader is pulled into the crime novel's dark world, it often is through a connection to the characters there that the reader sees as a reflection of the self, willing or not, in a kind of doubling. The nature of the crime novel thematizes doubles because of the pairings of criminals, victims, and detectives around the crime, especially when all the characters' activities dip into the illicit.[41] Ellroy's novels are rife with doubles, as Cohen, Mancall, and Peter Messent note, identifying characters in them that reflect, mirror, or double one another.[42] Indeed, Messent sees *The Black Dahlia* as "constructed around" a series of characters who are "dark doubles"[43] of each other: Elizabeth Short and Geneva Hilliker, Lee and Bucky, Lee's sister Laurie and Short, Lee and Short, Madeleine Sprague and Short, and more.[44] He also touches on the blurred lines between the police and the criminals they pursue.[45] However, less attention lands on how these characters develop into their own dark reflections, which I argue is through the process of reading or consuming texts that generate these darker selves, often signaled by a concurrent spatial transition; and while critics have considered specific tableaux in the novel and the topography of LA in Ellroy's writing,[46] there is no specific discussion of the spaces where the most dramatic transformations occur, spaces that darkly mirror the normal habitations of these characters. Crossing boundaries yields these transformations into the dark self, and the moments when characters cross into the darker versions of their originating spaces signal those transformations, as the rules that operate in their origins are also thrown into disarray or cast into doubt. Thus, I will argue that through either metaphorical or literal processes of reading, readers, including Ellroy, his characters, and the readers of his work, are drawn through a dark mirror to be transformed into dark versions of themselves in the dark spaces on the other side, a process that should be resisted.

ELLROY: READER, WRITER, VOYEUR, TRESPASSER

Several scholars address Ellroy's propensity to read his own work through his later writing, especially where he feels some need to revise earlier representations. Allamand examines Ellroy's reconsideration of his mother as a murder victim in *My Dark Places* as a contrasting presentation to Elizabeth Short's in *The Black Dahlia*, but she ultimately concludes that Ellroy is still avoiding his own sense of guilt over his mother, preventing him from treating her murder objectively, despite his claims about how the later book is an attempt to redress his misogyny in the first.[47] Mancall cites Chapter 13 of *My Dark Places* where Ellroy runs through Bill Stoner's growing understanding of "men and the cheap excuses they make for violence against women" as evidence of Ellroy's efforts to redress his earlier misogyny, as well as the effort he makes to gain a fuller understanding of his mother, particularly as a twin soul.[48] However, Mancall notes that Ellroy rejects this latter aspect of *My Dark Places* in his second memoir, *The Hilliker Curse*, as a false writerly ploy to make the story cohere,[49] a feature of *My Dark Places* that Katrina Beal also draws out. Ellroy's own assessment supports Mancall's claim that in *My Dark Places* Ellroy begins to question how he commodifies his mother's murder, while simultaneously pointing a finger at the readers who made him do it because of their rapacious desire for the kind of exploitative writing he produces.[50] These examples reveal Ellroy's tendency to situate himself as a reader of his own work while also illuminating the way Ellroy projects himself as a reader in his own writing.

In the act of writing, the writer constructs an implied reader in the text, and Ellroy has specified his idea of the *noir* reader in interviews and his own writing. In Ellroy's introduction to *The Best American Noir of the Century*, he characterizes the *noir* reader as one seeking to experience "the rush of moral forfeit and the abandonment to titillation" as it "makes doom fun,"[51] which certainly accounts for the themes in his own writing and his encouragement to the reader to "Exercise your skeevy curiosity" and be "repulsed and titillated."[52] He defines *noir* by claiming that it "indicts the other subgenres of the hardboiled school as sissified, and canonizes the inherent human urge toward self-destruction."[53] Thus, reading *noir* cements one's identity as the epitome of masculinity, to avoid the accusation of any failing to live up to a specifically defined version of manhood. In Lee Horsley's argument that Ellroy's writing fits into the "classic *noir* cycle . . . concerned with the primacy of male identity, psychic stability and male inheritance," he cites Ellroy's view "that the thriller is an essentially male genre,"[54] with Ellroy saying, "At bottom, for me, it's about male angst. Men perpetrate it, and men read it."[55] The chosen word here, perpetrate, is instructive as Ellroy frames writing in this genre as an illicit act, which aligns with his self-proclaimed pose as "the Demon Dog of American Crime Fiction."[56] This statement further reveals Ellroy's conception of his implied reader as male, and one concerned with a certain kind of male identity. Ellroy conceives of his reader, then, as one who aims to assert a masculine gaze on illicit scenes, usually rife with violence, often sexualized or drawing on racism or homophobia, for the purpose of being disgusted or aroused. While we might judge art effective if it elicits a reaction, we still might question how art benefits us if the primary emotions it produces are disgust or arousal without any suggestion in the work of how to use those emotions. What is the audience to do with those feelings? Ellroy appears satisfied to leave the reader with them.

Ellroy also knows that readers look for an analogue in the text to sympathize with, usually a protagonist with good traits. Yet, as he has commented in interviews, he explicitly wants to refuse the reader that possibility, instead offering protagonists who represent the worst human impulses, committing violent acts often fueled by racism, sexism, homophobia, and other repugnant beliefs.[57] However, Ellroy's approval of *noir*'s canonization of dark impulses connects to Powell's assertion that although Ellroy avoids the romanticized hero of earlier hard-boiled writing, he falls into the trap of romanticizing the darker side of the *noir* protagonist.[58] Ellroy appears to believe that readers will find themselves identifying with these characters anyway, only to realize that they have been immersed in such thinking,[59] problematically exploiting how reading works. Judging by the general critical apologia for his writing, assuming this identification is justified, although it is hard not to notice also that the majority of scholars writing on Ellroy are male, and perhaps fit more comfortably into the mold of Ellroy's implied reader. For example, while Messent calls *The Black Dahlia* "a searing indictment of the worst (though not the only!) side of white American patriarchy and power,"[60] he primarily refers to the economic power and political influence that Emmett Sprague exploits and situates the violence against Short in that context, reducing her death to a mere symptom of political and economic corruption, never explaining how simply presenting these terrible actions condemns them, especially if the reader vicariously delights in them as Ellroy wishes. Cohen focuses on the text's egregious misogyny but reads it as symptomatic of a crisis in masculinity and masculine trauma,[61] and yet if misogyny is the symptom, masculinity has always already been in crisis. We might also ask why no one speaks of a crisis of femininity, which, judging by the history of misogyny and misogynistic violence, has simply been the state of femininity and so not worth mentioning. Some readers, myself included, are repulsed by Ellroy's writing not merely because of the content but also because his implied reader does not make space for us in the text. As Fetterley observes in much American writing, "[the female reader] is asked to identify with a selfhood that defines itself in opposition to her; she is required to identify against herself,"[62] and Ellroy's implied reader certainly feels antagonistic to female identity. Readers are accustomed to the page as a permeable boundary to the world created by the act of reading, but the boundary is harder to cross when the passageway does not accommodate the reader or requires adopting a role that does not sit right. I find no entry in Ellroy's writing.

Ellroy's readerly perspective may arise from the voyeuristic gaze in his work so fully analyzed by Ashman, which of course has its analogue in Ellroy's life. A considerable section of *My Dark Places* details Ellroy's origin story and draws connections between his mother's murder, his early reading of true crime, and his own criminal career. Living with his father after his mother's murder, he is allowed to roam his neighborhood freely at all hours, peering through windows in backyards to get glimpses of women in the kind of domestic intimacy he was accustomed to with his mother, including in states of partial undress,[63] which also figures in the sexual fascination with his mother that he describes throughout the book.[64] He receives Jack Webb's *The Badge* as an eleventh birthday present and becomes obsessed with its stories, particularly that of Elizabeth Short's murder, reading it repeatedly.[65]

The timing of this reading helps link Short's murder with his mother's, and he describes how sexualized images of torture and murder filled his imagination, to the point that he sees them as "God's punishment for my voyeur prowls and thievery," which he stops, hoping to stave off the darker visions.[66] That Ellroy's father gives him material to read that would not be considered appropriate for an eleven-year-old today, especially one whose mother had been murdered, signals a failure of parenting, but it was likely in the range of mid-century ideas of masculine childhood. However, Ellroy's experience shows how such darkness can lure one in, and he comes close to the boundary, only to pull back when fear stops him, at least for the moment; but he continues reading crime writing voraciously and his fantasies continue featuring mixtures of crime and sex.[67]

Ellroy eventually embarks on a years-long campaign of stalking girls he knows,[68] progressing from peeping through their windows to burglarizing their houses, fantasizing about them as he rifles their bedrooms and steals lingerie.[69] He describes fantasizing that these girls are being stalked by the Black Dahlia killer[70] and that he saves Elizabeth Short from her killer,[71] figuring himself as a hero. Since he acknowledges that these fantasies mix sex and crime, he likely imagines that acting the hero will get him access to the sex he craves, a common play on the misguided belief inculcated in many men that sex is a reward or prize for certain behaviors. This belief can lead to misogynistic violence when it is foiled. Ellroy's actual behavior still violates the sanctity of these women's homes, and although he does not perpetrate acts of violence on them, he steps uncomfortably close to that boundary. Having crossed one set of boundaries—the windows, the thresholds—brings the next boundary into reach and makes it that much more permeable. Although Ellroy's criminal career progresses to generic burglary and escalating drug use rather than sex or other person crimes, the first stages of his career uncomfortably echo those of Joseph DeAngelo, the Golden State Killer, who began as a prowler and petty burglar before progressing to serial sexual assault and murder. Why one person goes to the extreme and the other stops is unclear,[72] although it is a common trope in crime writing that boundaries are easier to cross the more frequently they are transgressed, if we think of such classic texts as Stevenson's *The Strange Case of Dr. Jekyll and Mr. Hyde* or Agatha Christie's appropriately titled *Murder Is Easy*, where the murderer notes that subsequent murders come more easily than the first. *The Black Dahlia* also features repeated transgressions of myriad boundaries by its characters.

These preoccupations enter Ellroy's writing through his representations and reproductions of voyeurism, including the symbolic use of windows. As Ashman explains, for Ellroy "windows" are "magnetic 'beacons'" that "signif[y] a convergence between 'voyeurism, secrets and illicit sexuality,'" and "illicit gazing becomes irrevocably intertwined with the search for sex, secrets and the invasion of private space."[73] For most people, windows represent hard spatial boundaries just as mirrors do, but for Ellroy and the person willing to enter into illicit activity, windows can be passed through into the forbidden space on the other side; that passage represents a transformation in the person who crosses through. The literal and metaphorical trespassing of Ellroy's passage from outside a window to the space on its other side echoes the passage of Alice through the looking glass into the world beyond that operates on different rules. These activities become possible after Ellroy begins living with his father after his mother's murder. Ellroy hates the community where he lives with her, but he enjoys roaming the Los Angeles neighborhood where he lives with his father, apparently without the restrictions on his movements or behavior that his mother imposed. Passing from one space to the other precipitates his descent into taboo behavior, although the simultaneous passage from childhood to adolescence might also account for some of that transformation, including his leap as a reader from the Hardy Boys to true crime published for adults, and his introduction to the Black Dahlia murder.

PEOPLE AND PLACES: DARK REFLECTIONS IN *THE BLACK DAHLIA*

Ellroy's acts of reading and rereading his experiences through his writing reflect both the temptation of the images in the dark mirror and the dangers of being pulled through to the other side. These acts are thematized and redoubled in the literal and symbolic acts of reading and constructing identities and narratives and in spatial dislocations in *The Black Dahlia* that lead to characters passing through the dark mirror and being transformed into dark versions of themselves or others, including Lee Blanchard, Madeleine Sprague, Ramona Sprague, and Dwight "Bucky" Bleichert.

When the novel first introduces the murder of Elizabeth Short, Lee and Bucky are working on another case and stumble on the crime scene when they see the other police gathered around her body. The crime immediately captivates Lee, who wants to work the case out of a desire springing from his guilt over the disappearance and probable murder of his sister Laurie. At first, this impulse appears noble, but as Bucky investigates, it emerges that Lee reads the clues connecting Elizabeth Short and the Sprague family and uses that knowledge to blackmail Emmett Sprague, a wealthy property developer. Lee transforms from a victim advocate and representative of the criminal justice system to a victimizer and a criminal. Madeleine Sprague, to protect her father, lures Lee to Mexico and murders him there. Lee has already committed multiple corrupt acts, including framing Bobby De Witt for the bank robbery Lee orchestrated, but the coverup of Short's murderers in exchange for money drops him to a new low, as it betrays his ostensible distress over the similarity of Short's fate and his sister's. When Lee crosses the border into Mexico, he passes into a space where the rules protecting him as a citizen and police officer in the United States, where he knows how to work the system and has some power, evaporate, and he is a nonentity. There, Madeleine Sprague can murder him with impunity, turning him into a darker version of himself—from victimizer to victim. When Bucky follows Lee into Mexico, although not yet knowing why Lee was there, we see his own transformation from a figure of power to one of powerlessness, as he is at the mercy of the Mexican police and the familiar rules he plays by have turned upside down. We find out later that Madeleine Sprague, using an assumed identity, lays the trail of clues Bucky follows to Mexico, putting his life in danger. When Bucky discovers Lee's body, he also finds the grotesque irony of the similarity of Lee's dead face and Elizabeth Short's,[74] and thus Lee becomes a dark reflection not only of himself but of Elizabeth Short, the victim he tried to exploit for his own gain.

Madeleine Sprague has also been playing with the temptations of her own dark reflections, quite literally in the case of Elizabeth Short, whose style of dressing in black she studies and then borrows to tempt Short into a meeting and liaison with her. Maddy acknowledges to Bucky her curiosity about a physical encounter with her spurious double, one that ultimately destroys Short, unaware of the dangers of a relationship with Maddy as her dark reflection. Short's relative naivety draws Madeleine into her darkest actions: her luring of Short to what turns out to be her death, the subsequent murder of Lee Blanchard to hide Short's murder, and the ongoing deception of Bucky. Bucky learns about the two women's relationship, but he covers it up for Maddy in exchange for sex, as Maddy also seduces him in her Black Dahlia guise, given his infatuation with the dead woman. Lee likely follows the same clues to the Spragues' involvement with Short, although he hides his discovery from Bucky as well as the official investigation. Lee's deception enables Maddy to toy with Bucky, as she keeps tabs on the investigation and manipulates him by planting false trails for him to follow. Thus, Maddy acts as both a reader and writer, constructing narratives with Elizabeth Short, Lee, and Bucky that allow her to control their behavior for her own ends. Bucky in turn uses Maddy to fuel his obsession with Elizabeth Short, and although his crime in hiding the evidence of her connection means that he cannot later reveal the whole truth, it does help him figure out the solution. However, in this dance with Maddy, who pretends to be a murder victim but turns out to be a murderer, Bucky nearly dies too, and he fuels the fantasies that bring him dangerously close to passing through the dark mirror himself.

Bucky's obsession ultimately allows him to read the clues to the murderers' identities, although he often discovers them by accident. He sees the production credit for Emmett Sprague in a Keystone Kops short filmed on the same set as Short's pornographic film,[75] which helps him connect Short to Emmett Sprague and follow a trail of clues to Georgie Tilden and finally to Ramona Sprague. His conversation with the widow Jane Chambers about the Spragues' peculiar behavior and the painting she owns based on Victor Hugo's novel *The Man Who Laughs* helps Bucky recognize the remaining clues he needs to read and reconstruct the story of Short's murder. As Neff points out, by the time Bucky gains the capacity to connect these clues, he is dangerously close to losing himself as well,[76] which we see nearly happens in the events around his discovery of the murder scene.

Bucky's continuing work and discoveries in the case foreground the thematization of the effects of reading dark material, both for him and for the murderer, Ramona Sprague, who uses ideas from her reading to reconstruct sadistic scenes with Elizabeth Short. The suicide of Eldridge Chambers opens a new lead for Bucky a little over two years after Short's murder, taking him back into the orbit of the Spragues. He had distanced himself from Maddy after marrying Kay Lake, but the Chamberses turn out to be neighbors of the Spragues, and Jane Chambers, Eldridge's widow, ends up providing multiple clues that Bucky will later connect.

Bucky's own research first turns up a real estate business connection between Eldridge and Emmett Sprague. Jane Chambers confirms that Eldridge helped Emmett Sprague enter into the real estate business community, only to get him removed from the real estate board later because of the scandal around his shoddy homes destroyed by the earthquake.[77] The second clue lies in the strange behavior of Ramona Sprague and her daughters, which led to Jane prohibiting her daughters from playing with the Sprague girls as children. Ramona, with Georgie Tilden's help, would dress the girls up to act out violent episodes of Georgie and Emmett's service in WWI, eventually spiraling downward to a point when Georgie covers one of the Chambers girls in blood and takes pictures of her pretending to be dead.[78] These grotesque pageants are aimed at Emmett Sprague, whose acts of cowardice in the war are reenacted in them,[79] allowing Ramona to write his shame publicly in order to read his reaction and revel in it. Jane says that "Ramona wasn't really responsible for her actions,"[80] so she yells at Georgie, whom she later feels sorry for because of his menial work as a property caretaker for Emmett. It is not clear here why Jane absolves Ramona of responsibility, although Cohen suggests that she "has been forced by her position within the economy of the family to internalize the crisis of her husband's masculinity,"[81] a doubly misogynistic view of her as a weak receptacle of others' concerns and as the ultimate female monster. A mindset framed by traditional gender roles may also form Jane's belief that Ramona's mental instability is a typically feminine weakness. The third piece of the puzzle comes when Bucky regards for a second time the "scar mouth clown painting" in the Chamberses' hallway.[82] When he first reported to Eldridge's death scene, he had initially been struck by the painting "of a clown, a young boy done up in court jester's garb from long, long ago" who "wore a stuporous ear-to-ear smile that looked like one continuous deep scar" and immediately connected it with the pictures of Short's body—"the more I stared the more the two blended."[83] Jane mentions that her husband bought this hated picture for her forty-ninth birthday, and she is fifty-one, a mathematical clue to the timing of the purchase that Bucky does not put together just yet. Much later, Bucky remarks on the painting a third time,[84] and Jane tells him the story behind it, including its inspiration by the character Gwynplain in the Victor Hugo novel *The Man Who Laughs*, a copy of which Bucky has found sprayed with blood at Short's murder scene.[85] He now can connect the painting's inspiration by the book to Short's murder, and the fourth and final piece falls into place when Jane tells him that her husband bought the painting from Ramona.[86]

The use of reading in detection and the influence of reading on the reader come together when Bucky demands to see the receipt for the painting.[87] He then sees the connection: "It was purple stationery, covered with incongruously masculine block printing," and signed by Ramona.[88] He recognizes the handwriting on it as that in the diary describing Short's torture that he found in Georgie Tilden's home, surrounded by evidence of his obsession with death, like body parts in jars, including Short's missing tattoo.[89] Bucky first assumes Georgie wrote the diary and thus that he murdered Short, given his strange behavior, his father's anatomical research that may have cast its shadow on his psyche, and his attacking Bucky when he finds him in his home, which leads to Bucky killing him. The spatial connection with Georgie's belongings misleads him temporarily, but the hand behind the writing, behind the killing, shows itself irrefutably to be Ramona's. It is Ramona who reads Hugo's disturbing novel and recreates its violence, writing it across the body of Elizabeth Short, pushing her too across a dark boundary to death, transforming her into a victim, the dark reflection of the once-living girl.

It is worth noting that the handwriting is "masculine," which also contributes to the false trail Bucky initially follows, but, given Ellroy's conception of writing in the *noir* thriller genre as "perpetrated by men,"[90] that is not the surprise; it is the revelation that the murderer is a woman. Given the unlikelihood of this solution, as women commit far fewer murders than men and sexually sadistic murder of women by women, even with partners, is even rarer,[91] blaming the novel's most grotesque violence played out on the body of a woman on another woman crowns the misogyny of the novel as a whole, but that misogyny in Ellroy's treatment of Short's murder is not a surprise either. From an artistic perspective, the solution's increasingly baroque details strain the bounds of credibility if Ellroy claims to represent the truth, which he does when it comes to the most odious racist and homophobic aspects of his works since that is his alibi for including them; he makes an exception, apparently, for working out a realistic solution to the murder. And, from an ethical perspective, presenting such a fantastical solution to a real unsolved murder case raises myriad questions, in addition to the representation of Elizabeth Short herself and the repeated leering over her body, both dead and alive, that permeates the text and constitutes its most egregious misogyny.

Bucky's investigation centers both on his obsessive consumption of the case material and its reciprocal consumption of him. From the instant he sees Elizabeth Short at the scene, he looks with a double gaze at this body as evidence and as sexual object. He simultaneously notes the marks on her body that might be clues while experiencing signs of arousal, which happens repeatedly when he views and reviews the images from the case or when other bodies re-enact Elizabeth Short—with Madeleine's costume play, with the corpse in the slaughterhouse brought in to test the false confessors, with Lorraine in the El Nido room, to name a few. The novel's opening section links violence and sex, repeatedly referencing girls "given" to Bucky after fights; he finds himself unable to picture their faces, signaling their total objectification. While one subplot focuses on Fritz Vogel's hiring a woman to have sex with his son, whose virginity is treated as a subject for shame and ridicule, Bucky's experiences seem little different, as does Bucky's father's penchant for "girlie magazines," which Bucky views with disgust. These anxieties around sexual prowess certainly constitute part of the crisis of masculinity so frequently discussed in scholarship on Ellroy's work and its context,[92] along with the characters' preoccupation with avoiding cowardice, which appears in Bucky's memory of betraying his Japanese friends, in his and Lee's desertion of the fighting in the Zoot Suit Riots, and in Ramona's war pageants aimed at Emmett. These two masculine obsessions painfully contrast with what the investigation uncovers about Elizabeth Short's activities, given that she does not have to struggle to find sexual partners, but her fantasies of war heroes indicate how women can become complicit in masculine modes of thought. Her blind friend Tommy in Medford explains her obsession with the two servicemen who came to her defense when she was raped, and that sad story also sets up the paradox of men as both victimizers and heroes, an echo of Ellroy's adolescent crimes and fantasies. This contradictory ideology pits men's need to prove masculinity through sex regardless of the cost against the suffering enacted on women because of it, both through this story of assault and the many instances of exploitation of and violence against women revealed throughout the novel.

Bucky's own fascination with the case arises through the sex-violence connection and his projection onto Elizabeth Short of his own desire to find some value in himself. He is attracted to this idea of Short as a fellow seeker, but she primarily exists in his fantasies as an object of desire who will satisfy his various needs. Madeleine Sprague reads this need in him and exploits it by constructing a fantasy for him, for reasons Bucky only realizes later. His interactions with her do him no good, only feeding his obsession and drawing him into wrongdoing as he conceals Maddy's connection to Betty in exchange for sex. His downward spiral shows in the decline of his relationship with Kay, which cannot compete with the dark allure of the Black Dahlia and the dark Sprague daughter. With Madeleine, he flirts with both murdered and murderer, just as he flirts with his own dark side by re-entering spaces where order is disrupted.

DARK WORLDS THROUGH THE DARK MIRROR

Just as the characters all have their own dark reflections, so do the spaces they inhabit. Some overlap, like the Spragues' mansion, which contains clues to the twisted life of its inhabitants to be read by the informed eye, as Meyer reveals.[93] Others emerge over the story, even acting as reflections within reflections of each other. When Lee creates the alternative investigation headquarters at the El Nido for Short's case, he initiates one such space. This ostensibly positive action provides a focused space for the detectives' work, but it also lets Lee conceal evidence from the others. Because of that deception, the El Nido room doubles the house shared by Lee and Kay, and later Kay and Bucky, also revealed eventually to be the corrupt proceeds of crime—the Bobby De Witt framing and the later blackmail of the Spragues. While Kay never enters the El Nido room, her participation in Lee's schemes makes her a fitting inhabitant for the family home that is no longer the clean domestic space it once appeared. She asks Bucky to avoid the El Nido, to "bury that—dead girl,"[94] but he starts to bring images of Betty to their home instead, now spreading the darkness of the El Nido room into what had seemed to be a bright space. Bucky, as an inhabitant of that space, embarks on a trajectory to its even darker versions, progressively enmeshing himself in darkness. Bucky's failing relationship with Kay leads him to spending more and more time at the El Nido, where he is fueled by that space and its contents. Surrounded by pictures of Short both alive and dead that permeate his mind, he reads and rereads the case materials. This activity helps him develop leads and eventually to come to a solution when he picks up additional clues as he orbits the Spragues—from Jane Chambers and fellow detective Harry Sears, who directs him to what turns out to be the scene of the crime—but it contributes to his breakdown.

Bucky rushes to the outbuilding of a condemned house owned by Sprague under the Hollywoodland sign on Sears' tip that they found blood there,[95] and on entering the room, he passes through the looking glass, into a dark mirroring of the detective's room at the El Nido, which we can now see reflects the murder scene. The earlier scene with the sex worker Lorraine foreshadows this passage, when Bucky terrifies her by trying to make her look like Short and then ripping down the blankets covering the photos on the walls. Lorraine reasonably assumes Bucky is the Black Dahlia killer and screams, and Bucky reacts by strangling her to silence her, nearly becoming a murderer himself.[96] These two spaces mirror each other, and so do those who inhabit them, or nearly so, as Bucky turns into the darkest version of himself when he enters the crime scene. Like the image-covered walls at the El Nido, those in the crime scene "are papered with pornographic photographs of crippled and disfigured women" and "tacked-on color photos that looked like they were torn from anatomy texts: close-up shots of diseased organs oozing blood and pus."[97] These images are accompanied by a copy of "*Gray's Advanced Anatomy* and Victor Hugo's *The Man Who Laughs*," both sprayed with blood.[98] These texts and images mirror those in the El Nido, which reflect the murder in texts, and these textual reflections provide a further repeating chain. Texts are written, read by the murderers, written across the body of Elizabeth Short, read by the detectives, written about by the detectives, read by them, and then nearly re-written on another woman's body. This endlessly repeating process raises the question of whether any intervention can occur, but Bucky will not be the one to do it. Instead, he engages in another iteration of the cycle, telling Sears that he will "do a forensic here."[99]

However, Sears hesitates in the face of this disturbed version of Bucky, saying, "kid, you don't look too healthy to me right—."[100] Bucky yells at him, and he departs, leaving Bucky to complete his dark transit. Rather than the objective and systematic investigation we would envision from responsible police work, Bucky says, "Then I opened up my kit and raped the nightmare crib for evidence."[101] This wording not only reflects Bucky's loss of control, but it also shows the illicit nature of this collection. Too upset after tentatively matching some fingerprints to Short's to manage correctly processing them, Bucky "hack[s] a four-digit spread off the door with [his] knife and wrap[s] it in tissue—forensic amateur night."[102] Failing to collect the evidence correctly could undermine the case, thus erasing the only marks that Elizabeth Short left, her own attempt perhaps to write the story of what happened to her, as some crime victims have done, hoping that investigators would find their traces. In any event, Bucky's earlier actions in covering up the evidence of the Spragues' involvement preclude using any evidence he collects because he is tainted, a further erasure of the potential for Short's story to emerge.

The next murky reflection of these spaces comes in Georgie's home, after a stop at the Sprague mansion. Bucky matches some prints from the murder scene to Georgie, and he confronts Madeleine and Emmett in an apparently incestuous moment, which they claim is not incestuous because Georgie is Madeleine's real father.[103] Bucky begins shooting their valuable artworks to force them to talk, turning this former symbol of economic success and rising social status into a carnivalesque scene of destruction, and one that clearly will not yield legal evidence. The Spragues' story provides another link to Short's murder, although Bucky will not get all the facts until his later conversation with Ramona. Georgie's facial disfigurement prefigures that of Elizabeth Short, since Emmett slashes his face as revenge for his affair with Ramona that results in Madeleine, and the resemblance of Madeleine and Short triggers Georgie's desire for Short, which itself triggers Ramona's furious, jealous assault on Short, ending in her facial disfigurement and its ultimate connections to Hugo's novel and the painting of Gwynplain. Bucky's ability to read this chaotic polysemic circle relies on his regression to the associative paleologic that Neff describes, just like the similar trail Bucky has followed to find Georgie and the final clue that will lead him to Ramona as well.

The Spragues also describe Georgie's history, including the influence of his anatomist father whose dissections, they claim, have given Georgie a taste for dead bodies and organs.[104] They also remind Bucky of the leverage they hold over him because of the evidence he has already withheld, dooming his career and the investigation.[105] Georgie's home presents just the image the Spragues painted: specimen jars with preserved body parts and furnishings coated with bodily fluids, crowned by a recognizable tattoo cut from Short's body.[106] However, the centerpiece of this collection for Bucky is the notebook describing Short's torture, written in "neat masculine printing"[107]—printing that he later recognizes as Ramona's after seeing the painting receipt. Georgie comes home while Bucky is reeling from these new insights, and they come together in a fight to the death.

Bucky, whose fascination with and fantasies about Short are pale reflections of Georgie's desire for her and of Ramona's sadistic acts, comes up against the dark mirror, confronting his own shadow self. He kills Georgie—through the eye, a symbol of the voyeuristic gaze—but this shocking confrontation snaps him out of the darker path he is treading.[108] In short order, Bucky finds out about Lee's early knowledge of the Spragues' and Georgie Tilden's involvement in the murder and that Kay also knew about it; preparing to hit her, "a flash of Georgie Tilden stop[s] [him]."[109] It appears that this dark specter turns him back, especially since in this moment, he still thinks that Georgie is the sole torturer and murderer. The complicated question of what stops some criminals from escalating behavior will continue to haunt us, but it appears that in Bucky's case, the shocking vision of what he might become when he confronts Georgie halts him, just as in Ellroy's own case, the frightening temporary loss of mental capacity pushes him to sobriety once he regains his health.[110] But then Bucky sees the painting receipt, and he must confront the other dark form looming just out of sight all this time.

A final trip to the Sprague mansion brings Bucky face to face with Ramona. He makes her tell him the story, and she confirms what he has uncovered, the apparent *fable* of the *subject*, in Meyer's narratological reading, or as close to an orderly telling of all the significant events as we ever get in a text. We cannot mistake this summary of "what really happened" for the *fable* since it is only another version of the *subject*, but such summations commonly stand in for "the truth" in detective fiction, compared to the more diffuse narratives leading up to them. Bucky's first-person narration switches to third-person indirect discourse to report Ramona's story in a compressed version. The most striking part of Ramona's story is the continuous interaction of reading and writing in it. She tells Bucky about becoming embroiled with Georgie, to the extent of poisoning animals as gifts for him—the first instance of her boundary crossing.[111] However, Georgie, now marked by Emmett, rejects her, and she consoles herself by obsessing over Hugo's novel. Ramona "was moved by both the Comprachicos and their disfigured victims," including the boy Gwynplain, depicted in the painting.[112] She hides the painting and communes with it as replacement for Georgie. This repeated consumption of the book and its imagery inspires her to reproduce the Comprachicos' tortures on Short, the target of her jealous rage. The loop of reading and writing, re-enacting and enacting that traps Ramona echoes Bucky's spiraling inward to the solution as he investigates, and so Ramona stands as a cautionary figure to him, a dark double he does not want to become.

Each of these spaces, from the El Nido, to the murder site, to Georgie's home, and back and forth to the Sprague mansion, opens onto the next more wildly nightmarish one, an endless series of progressively darkening worlds through the looking glass. A final echo of the El Nido room appears in *My Dark Places*, when Ellroy sets up corkboards in his rented apartment to organize the investigation information and surrounds himself with his mother's crime scene photos.[113] Ellroy notes the retired detective Ward Hallinen's unspoken question about how he can look at photos of his mother's body, inspired by the assumption that most people would not be able to look at their beloved in such circumstances, a question Ellroy never answers.[114] He uses this space to connect with his mother through fantasy as well, before abandoning it to return home and later search for his mother elsewhere, but it is an eerie after-image of the dark spaces of obsession that nearly lured his fictional detective to his destruction. In his post-film essay, Ellroy links himself definitively to Bucky as a detective, reader, and creator:

"Bucky Bleichert is a fictional cop and a *doppelganger*/writer-filmmaker. He's the man writing out the great adventure of his life and the voyeur viewing sex with a camera. Bleichert is me. Bleichert is De Palma."[115] And, ultimately, Ellroy himself fails to escape this limiting perspective. While he concludes *My Dark Places* with a fuller picture of his mother's life gained from family recollections and her nursing school and work friends, he insists on his obsessive ownership of her to the end. And while he claims he tells "redemption tales aimed at women" inspired by his "[m]isogynistic fury,"[116] he never manages to stop blaming Elizabeth Short and his mother for their own deaths. Twice in the 2006 essay, he ascribes their deaths to their enjoyment of socializing, first when he says that the "misalignment" of Jean Hilliker's "Midwest Calvinist rectitude and Saturday night cut-loose-girl" sides "engendered a desperate unhappiness and killed her"[117] and later when he suggests a similarity between his mother and Short: "They could have been Saturday night cut-loose girls together, before Saturday nights cut them down."[118] This abstraction erases the real cause of their murders: misogyny, likely embodied by men who took it out on these two women. In the report from the criminal profiler Ellroy and Stoner hired, the victimology section states, "On the date of [Geneva Hilliker's] death her risk level was further elevated by her personal circumstances: a woman alone in a car with a man."[119] That such a statement can pass without comment shows the level of acceptance of misogynistic violence in our culture, when an ordinary activity poses an increased risk of death, merely because of the presence of a man. And Ellroy simply perpetuates it by continuing to blame his mother and Short for succumbing to that risk, still unable to read the truth before him, despite his claim that he is going "to redress imbalances in [his] previous writings about them."[120]

Readers' projections and constructions of texts differ as widely as readers themselves. Some readers will find their entry into the text based on what they project, or alternatively see themselves reflected in the text in different ways. These projections or reflections may determine whether the reader permeates the boundary of the text or stays outside its surface, whether or not the reader is consumed in turn, and how thoroughly. While Ramona becomes completely consumed in the dark world she constructs with her reading, Bucky manages to pull back in time, if barely; and so it seems does Ellroy, too. However, the risks produced by some texts raise the question of whether they should be consumed, if not also whether they should be produced or reproduced. Ellroy writes in 2006 that the film will garner even wider attention for his book,[121] giving him an opportunity to reconsider the ethical implications of creating more readers for a text that he acknowledges does a disservice to Elizabeth Short and by extension to his mother, but he opts to ignore this opportunity and lets his work be amplified, despite the harm it might do to perpetuate reproductions of misogyny, racism, and homophobia that are not balanced by any useful direction to amelioration.

MY DARK REFLECTION

My focus on reading in this essay arises from a personal place. Like many academics, reading has been a lifelong passion for me, initially sparked by the nearly magical ability of text to transport me to another place or time and to allow me to inhabit the lives of people both like and unlike myself, an experience reflected in reader response theory. Writers are also theorists of reading, and Ellroy has shown himself to be no exception, given his comments about refusing the reader a good protagonist to identify with, or about wanting readers to find themselves inhabiting repulsive mindsets, or about men being the "perpetrators" and the readers of the *noir* thriller.

Thus, I am not surprised that Ellroy's writing presents insuperable barriers for me. I cannot enter the mindsets of any of his characters. However, I do see my own dark reflection in *The Black Dahlia*. From the opening of the novel, the first time I see a body like mine, it has been butchered and displayed. I am then expected to ride along with a narrator who finds a sexual allure in that image, regardless of the efforts made to redeem him. After the socialization women receive to understand what happens to us at the hands of men, I am also expected to accept that the violence enacted here is at the hands of another woman, protected by a conspiracy perpetrated by yet other women (Madeleine and Kay), and inspired by jealousy of another woman, a sadly misogynistic trope. My power to suspend disbelief is strong, but I must confess it failed here. While I certainly can imagine women participating in or initiating crimes, and doing so at the expense of less privileged women, as we see in multiple places in the novel and in the world, the kind of sexualized violence inflicted on Elizabeth Short almost never occurs at the hands of women, and to suggest so as the solution to a real unsolved crime seems to me to be a disservice to this real victim and her family, not to mention the way her life and activities are portrayed in ways that depart from reality, which even Ellroy acknowledges.[122]

I have also found a lack of acknowledgment of these aspects of the text in the scholarship on Ellroy, with the exception of strong statements by Allamand and Farrimond, and a handful of brief comments about Ellroy's misogyny by other writers before they move on to other topics (a lack that I believe is being addressed by my colleagues in this collection, however). Although Farrimond primarily focuses on De Palma's film, she explains most clearly how the sexualization of the violence against women is so commonplace in our society that it passes nearly unremarked, since as she argues, it is displaced in the film by other sexualized images and has a disturbing afterlife in the burlesque glamorization of Short's murder.[123] But no representation, however artistic, can erase my recognition of the misogynistic violence it contains, and when any representation fails to acknowledge that, I will find no way into it.

The fact that I can find a way into other texts representing violence against women or its aftermath means that we can address these facts of life while providing some path forward. Many writers tell stories containing violence against women without reproducing it for mere entertainment, but Ellroy's novel continually reenacts it through Bucky's sexualization of Elizabeth Short in fantasies that include the visible marks of her torture and murder. While Bucky works to find her killer, his actions preclude any publication of the truth, and the truth he finds represents an avoidance of the real threats that women face, including the threat Ellroy's mother faced, which was a sadly typical example of the way men murder women. I do not claim that Bucky prevents Short's killer from being brought to justice because I know that justice is elusive, and to expect the outcome of a crime novel to provide an easy solution to the problem of justice in the real world is naïve, but many writers manage to present such situations in ways that raise awareness of systemic corruption or injustice in realistic ways that direct our attention to the real problems that need to be addressed. In fact, Ellroy himself offers a chilling indictment of casual misogynistic violence in *My Dark Places* where he enumerates Bill Stoner's understanding of why men kill women. However, even when Ellroy tries to redress his treatment of Short and his mother in his writing in his 2006 essay, he still blames them for their own murders, rather than stating directly that men killed them. The attitude that the text encourages the reader to adopt matters, too; rather than a perverse lingering over violence, focalization can convey sorrow, horror, or one of any other more humane responses that might move readers to positive action.

Despite centuries of crime writing, we are only beginning to address the ethics of writing about crime. What are the ethical implications of such writing and its effects, including such issues as respect for victims, survivors, and the truth? It seems to me that continually ruminating on the traces of crime, lingering over them, and using them for titillation without respect for the suffering they connote, falls on the wrong side of the ethical divide, and judging by the examples of the consumers of these images in *The Black Dahlia*, such ruminations dissolve ethical boundaries and push those consumers into dark versions of themselves. These characters provide cautionary reflections of ourselves as readers, and rather than allowing those reflections to beckon us through the looking glass, we need to resist our darker impulses and find better selves to be on this side of the mirror.

NOTES

1. Carole Allamand, "A Tooth for a Private Eye: James Ellroy's Detective Fiction," *The Journal of Popular Culture* 39, no. 3 (June 2006): 349–64, https://doi.org/10.1111/j.1540-5931.2006.00253.x; Peter Wolfe, *Like Hot Knives to the Brain: James Ellroy's Search for Himself* (Lanham: Lexington Books, 2005); James Ellroy, "My Mother and the Dahlia," *Virginia Quarterly Review: A National Journal of Literature and Discussion* 82, no. 3 (Summer 2006): 217–18; and Steven Powell, *James Ellroy: Demon Dog of Crime Fiction*, Crime Files Series (Basingstoke, UK: Palgrave Macmillan, 2016), 91–93. See Carole Allamand's incisive psychoanalytic reading of *The Black Dahlia* and *My Dark Places* and Peter Wolfe's psychologically inflected readings of Ellroy's novels, as well as Ellroy's own comments on the topic and Steven Powell's detailed discussioned of where the case appears in Ellroy's novels and short stories.

2. Powell, *James Ellroy: Demon Dog of Crime Fiction*, 97.

3. Judith Fetterley, *The Resisting Reader: A Feminist Approach to American Fiction* (Bloomington: Indiana University Press, 1978), viii.

4. Ellroy, "My Mother and the Dahlia," 221.

5. Josh Cohen, "James Ellroy, Los Angeles and the Spectacular Crisis of Masculinity," *Women* 7, no. 1 (1996): 1–15; Joshua Meyer, "Haunted Subjects: Fragments of the 'Sexual Mosaic' in James Ellroy's Los Angeles," *Philament* 13 (December 2008): 57–79.

6. Ellroy, "My Mother and the Dahlia," 221.

7. Powell, *James Ellroy: Demon Dog of Crime Fiction*, 111–13.

8. James Ellroy, *My Dark Places: An L. A. Crime Memoir* (New York: Vintage Books, 1997), 105–7.

9. Katherine Farrimond, "Postfeminist Noir: Brutality and Retro Aesthetics in *The Black Dahlia*," *Film & History: An Interdisciplinary Journal of Film and Television* 43, no. 2 (Fall 2013): 45.

10. Jim Mancall, "'You're a Watcher, Lad': Detective Fiction, Pornography, and Ellroy's L. A. Quartet," *Clues* 24, no. 4 (Summer 2006): 5–7.

11. Mancall, 7.

12. Mancall, 8.

13. Mancall, 9.

14. Mancall, 12.

15. Mancall, 12–13.

16. Fetterley, *The Resisting Reader: A Feminist Approach to American Fiction*, xi–xiii.

17. Fetterley, xxii.

18. Nathan Ashman, *James Ellroy and Voyeur Fiction* (Lanham: Lexington Books, 2018), xiv.

19. Ashman, xxiv.

20. Ashman, xxiv.

21. Ashman, xxiv.

22. Joshua Meyer, "Fables of the Material World in James Ellroy's Los Angeles," *Western American Literature* 51, no. 3 (Fall 2016): 337–38.

23. Mancall, "'You're a Watcher, Lad': Detective Fiction, Pornography, and Ellroy's L. A. Quartet," 5, 8–9.

24. Ellroy, *My Dark Places: An L. A. Crime Memoir*, 389. After the guilty verdict against Beckett in the Tracy Stewart murder case, Ellroy writes, "The non-cops and non-DAs thought that meant closure. I wanted to find the fool who invented closure and shove a big closure plaque up his ass."

25. Peter Schmidt-Nowara, "Finding God in a World of 'Leg Breakers' and 'Racist-Shitbirds': James Ellroy and the Contemporary L. A. Crime Novel," *Western American Literature* 36, no. 2 (Summer 2001): 120.

26. Allamand, "A Tooth for a Private Eye: James Ellroy's Detective Fiction," 362; Ellroy, *My Dark Places*, 402. This aspect of Ellroy's reaction to his trauma that Allamand remarks is apparently clear to the trained but casual observer, since he includes this note in the list of responses to the *Unsolved Mysteries* episode featuring his mother's murder: "A woman from Tucson, Arizona, called. She said she was a psychologist. She said James Ellroy was very angry. He relived his mother's death to punish himself. He wasn't there for her. He felt guilty. He needed treatment." However, he buries it in the list of sometimes wacky responses, perhaps as a way to discredit this view.

27. Wolfgang Iser, *The Act of Reading: A Theory of Aesthetic Response* (Baltimore: The Johns Hopkins University Press, 1980), 34–35.

28. Wolfgang Iser, "Representation: A Performative Act," in *Prospecting: From Reader Response to Literary Anthropology* (Baltimore: The Johns Hopkins University Press, 1989), 236.

29. Iser, 237.

30. Iser, 238.

31. Iser, 243.

32. Iser, 244.

33. Ellroy, "My Mother and the Dahlia," 220.

34. Ellroy, 219.

35. Farrimond, "Postfeminist Noir: Brutality and Retro Aesthetics in *The Black Dahlia*," 37–39.

36. Meyer, "Fables of the Material World in James Ellroy's Los Angeles," 337.

37. Meyer, 336.

38. D. S. Neff, "Anoedipal Fiction: Schizoanalysis and *The Black Dahlia*," *Poetics Today* 18, no. 3 (Fall 1997): 327, https://doi.org/10.2307/1773129.

39. Neff, 325.

40. Neff, 326.

41. Jim Mancall, *James Ellroy: A Companion to the Mystery Fiction*, McFarland Companions to Mystery Fiction 6 (Jefferson, NC: McFarland & Company, Inc., Publishers, 2014), 81.

42. Mancall, 81–83; Peter Messent, *The Crime Fiction Handbook* (Newark: John Wiley & Sons, Incorporated, 2012), 190–94; Meyer, "Haunted Subjects: Fragments of the 'Sexual Mosaic' in James Ellroy's Los Angeles."

43. Messent, *The Crime Fiction Handbook*, 190.

44. Messent, 190–94.

45. Messent, 196.

46. Cohen, "James Ellroy, Los Angeles and the Spectacular Crisis of Masculinity"; Meyer, "Haunted Subjects: Fragments of the 'Sexual Mosaic' in James Ellroy's Los Angeles"; Meyer, "Fables of the Material World in James Ellroy's Los Angeles."

47. Allamand, "A Tooth for a Private Eye: James Ellroy's Detective Fiction," 361–62.

48. Mancall, *James Ellroy: A Companion to the Mystery Fiction*, 153.

49. Mancall, 153.

50. Mancall, 153.

51. James Ellroy, introduction to *The Best American Noir of the Century*, eds. James Ellroy and Otto Penzler (Boston: Houghton Mifflin Harcourt, 2011), xiii.

52. Ellroy, xiv.

53. Ellroy, xiii.

54. Lee Horsley, "Founding Fathers: 'Genealogies of Violence' in James Ellroy's L.A. Quartet," *Clues* 19, no. 1 (1998): 149.

55. Ellroy quoted in Arthur Salm, "Books," *The San Diego Tribune,* on June 29, 1990, quoted in Horsley, 149.

56. Powell, *James Ellroy: Demon Dog of Crime Fiction*, 2.

57. Schmidt-Nowara, "Finding God in a World of 'Leg Breakers' and 'Racist-Shitbirds': James Ellroy and the Contemporary L. A. Crime Novel," 120.

58. Powell, *James Ellroy: Demon Dog of Crime Fiction*, 4.

59. Schmidt-Nowara, "Finding God in a World of 'Leg Breakers' and 'Racist-Shitbirds': James Ellroy and the Contemporary L. A. Crime Novel," 121. Schmidt-Nowara quotes Ellroy from Charles L. P. Silet, "Mad Dog and Glory: A Conversation with James Ellroy," *The Armchair Detective* 28.4 (1995): 236–44 (241), saying, "I want my readers to say, 'Man, what a blast it would be to go back to 1952 and beat up faggots.' Then I want them to realize, '*Oh*, am I *really* thinking that?'"

60. Messent, *The Crime Fiction Handbook*, 197.

61. Cohen, "James Ellroy, Los Angeles and the Spectacular Crisis of Masculinity."

62. Fetterley, *The Resisting Reader: A Feminist Approach to American Fiction*, xii.

63. Ellroy, *My Dark Places: An L. A. Crime Memoir*, 121.

64. See Ellroy, 134, for an example.

65. Ellroy, 122–24.

66. Ellroy, 125.

67. Ellroy, 134, 139.

68. Ellroy, 143.

69. Ellroy, 158–61.

70. Ellroy, 139.

71. Ellroy, 134.

72. Katrina Beal, "Love, Death and the Photographic Image: James Ellroy's Dark Places through Roland Barthes' *Camera Lucida*," *Literature & Aesthetics* 10 (2000): 75–103. Beal's reading is interesting in this context—it marks Ellroy's voyeurism as a passive response, which might be the difference between those who go on to greater transgressions and those who do not.

73. Ashman, *James Ellroy and Voyeur Fiction*, xi.

74. James Ellroy, *The Black Dahlia* (New York: Hachette, 2006), 226. Bucky describes what he sees: "Then Lee was smiling like the Dahlia, with worms creeping out of his mouth and the holes where his eyes used to be."

75. Ellroy, 283.

76. Neff, "Anoedipal Fiction: Schizoanalysis and *The Black Dahlia*."

77. Ellroy, *The Black Dahlia*, 240–41.

78. Ellroy, 243.

79. Ellroy, 311.

80. Ellroy, 243.

81. Cohen, "James Ellroy, Los Angeles and the Spectacular Crisis of Masculinity," 6.

82. Ellroy, *The Black Dahlia*, 243.

83. Ellroy, 239.

84. Ellroy, 307.

85. Ellroy, 285.

86. Ellroy, 307.

87. Ellroy, 308.

88. Ellroy, 308.

89. Ellroy, 297.

90. Ellroy quoted in Arthur Salm, "Books," *The San Diego Tribune*, on June 29, 1990, quoted in Horsley, "Founding Fathers: 'Genealogies of Violence' in James Ellroy's L.A. Quartet," 149.

91. Heng Choon (Oliver) Chan, Kathleen M. Heide, and Eric Beauregard, "Male and Female Single-Victim Sexual Homicide Offenders: Distinguishing the Types of Weapons Used in Killing Their Victims," *Sexual Abuse* 31, no. 2 (March 2019): 136, https://doi.org/10.1177/1079063217724765. According to this study, fewer than 5 percent of sexual homicides in the United States from 1976 to 2012 were committed by women, and only 11.3 percent of their victims were female; Sara Skott, Eric Beauregard, and Rajan Darjee, "Female Sexual Homicide Offenders: A Descriptive and Comparative Study," *Journal of Forensic Sciences* 64, no. 1 (January 2019): 158, https://doi.org/10.1111/1556-4029.13807. As Skott, Beauregard, and Darjee show, five out of seven female offenders in their study had a male partner in the crime, but the sample size is small. This scenario supports Ellroy's vision of a mixed pair of murderers, but the unlikelihood of such a murder to begin with is supported by Chan, Heide, and Beauregard.

92. Fetterley, *The Resisting Reader: A Feminist Approach to American Fiction*, viii.

93. Meyer, "Fables of the Material World in James Ellroy's Los Angeles."

94. Ellroy, *The Black Dahlia*, 236.

95. Ellroy, 284.

96. Ellroy, 262.

97. Ellroy, 285.

98. Ellroy, 285.

99. Ellroy, 285.

100. Ellroy, 285.
101. Ellroy, 285.
102. Ellroy, 286.
103. Ellroy, 289–90.
104. Ellroy, 291–92.
105. Ellroy, 292.
106. Ellroy, 296–97.
107. Ellroy, 296.
108. Ellroy, 298.
109. Ellroy, 304.
110. Ellroy, *My Dark Places: An L. A. Crime Memoir*, 178–81.
111. Ellroy, *The Black Dahlia*, 310–11.
112. Ellroy, 311.
113. Ellroy, *My Dark Places: An L. A. Crime Memoir*, 265, 292–93.
114. Ellroy, 305.
115. Ellroy, "My Mother and the Dahlia," 221.
116. Ellroy, 221.
117. Ellroy, 216–17.
118. Ellroy, 222.
119. Ellroy, *My Dark Places: An L. A. Crime Memoir*, 341.
120. Ellroy, "My Mother and the Dahlia," 215.
121. Ellroy, 215.
122. Ellroy, 215.
123. Farrimond, "Postfeminist Noir: Brutality and Retro Aesthetics in *The Black Dahlia*," 42.

BIBLIOGRAPHY

Allamand, Carole. "A Tooth for a Private Eye: James Ellroy's Detective Fiction." *The Journal of Popular Culture* 39, no. 3 (June 2006): 349–64. https://doi.org/10.1111/j.1540-5931.2006.00253.x.

Ashman, Nathan. *James Ellroy and Voyeur Fiction*. Lanham: Lexington Books, 2018.

Beal, Katrina. "Love, Death and the Photographic Image: James Ellroy's Dark Places through Roland Barthes' *Camera Lucida*." *Literature & Aesthetics* 10 (2000): 75–103.

Chan, Heng Choon (Oliver), Kathleen M. Heide, and Eric Beauregard. "Male and Female Single-Victim Sexual Homicide Offenders: Distinguishing the Types of Weapons Used in Killing Their Victims." *Sexual Abuse* 31, no. 2 (March 2019): 127–50. https://doi.org/10.1177/1079063217724765.

Cohen, Josh. "James Ellroy, Los Angeles and the Spectacular Crisis of Masculinity." *Women* 7, no. 1 (1996): 1–15.

Ellroy, James. Introduction to *The Best American Noir of the Century, xiii-xiv*. Edited by James Ellroy and Otto Penzler. Boston: Houghton Mifflin Harcourt, 2011.

My Dark Places: An L. A. Crime Memoir. New York: Vintage Books, 1997.

"My Mother and the Dahlia." *Virginia Quarterly Review: A National Journal of Literature and Discussion* 82, no. 3 (Summer 2006): 214–22.

The Black Dahlia. New York: Hachette, 2006.

Farrimond, Katherine. "Postfeminist Noir: Brutality and Retro Aesthetics in *The Black Dahlia*." *Film & History: An Interdisciplinary Journal of Film and Television* 43, no. 2 (Fall 2013): 34–49.

Fetterley, Judith. *The Resisting Reader: A Feminist Approach to American Fiction*. Bloomington: Indiana University Press, 1978.

Horsley, Lee. "Founding Fathers: 'Genealogies of Violence' in James Ellroy's L.A. Quartet." *Clues* 19, no. 1 (1998): 139–61.

Iser, Wolfgang. "Representation: A Performative Act." In *Prospecting: From Reader Response to Literary Anthropology*, 236–48. Baltimore: The Johns Hopkins University Press, 1989.

The Act of Reading: A Theory of Aesthetic Response. Baltimore: The Johns Hopkins University Press, 1980.

Mancall, Jim. *James Ellroy: A Companion to the Mystery Fiction*. McFarland Companions to Mystery Fiction 6. Jefferson, NC: McFarland & Company, Inc., Publishers, 2014.

"'You're a Watcher, Lad': Detective Fiction, Pornography, and Ellroy's L. A. Quartet." *Clues* 24, no. 4 (Summer 2006): 3–14.

Messent, Peter. *The Crime Fiction Handbook*. Newark: John Wiley & Sons, Incorporated, 2012.

Meyer, Joshua. "Fables of the Material World in James Ellroy's Los Angeles." *Western American Literature* 51, no. 3 (Fall 2016): 335–57.

"Haunted Subjects: Fragments of the 'Sexual Mosaic' in James Ellroy's Los Angeles." *Philament* 13 (December 2008): 57–79.

Neff, D. S. "Anoedipal Fiction: Schizoanalysis and The Black Dahlia." *Poetics Today* 18, no. 3 (Fall 1997): 301–42. https://doi.org/10.2307/1773129.

Powell, Steven. *James Ellroy: Demon Dog of Crime Fiction*. Crime Files Series. Basingstoke, England: Palgrave Macmillan, 2016.

Schmidt-Nowara, Peter. "Finding God in a World of 'Leg Breakers' and 'Racist-Shitbirds': James Ellroy and the Contemporary L. A. Crime Novel." *Western American Literature* 36, no. 2 (Summer 2001): 117–33.

Skott, Sara, Eric Beauregard, and Rajan Darjee. "Female Sexual Homicide Offenders: A Descriptive and Comparative Study." *Journal of Forensic Sciences* 64, no. 1 (January 2019): 154–62. https://doi.org/10.1111/1556-4029.13807.

Wolfe, Peter. *Like Hot Knives to the Brain: James Ellroy's Search for Himself*. Lanham: Lexington Books, 2005.

Chapter 5

There Is No Honor in LA

Ellroy's L.A. Confidential, *the Violent Detective, and Systems of Harm*

Caitlin B. Coulter

Who or what is a detective? Ever since Dupin, Holmes, Marple, and Poirot, scholars and aficionados of the genre have debated the criteria of the "true" detective. The schism between British and American detective fiction often provides a measure to hold newer authors to, but even under the national umbrellas, there is no clear and consistent consensus. Most scholars of American detective fiction look to Dashiell Hammett as the author who introduced the genre to the States and to Raymond Chandler as the writer responsible for codifying the hard-boiled icon in his novels and his cornerstone essay "The Simple Art of Murder." In this essay, Chandler lays out for his reader a succinct image of his ideal detective and describes a man of limited relationships and self-conscious exclusion from those around him. He depicts a man who rejects police camaraderie and criminal halls alike, understands his status as a lonely man and private detective, and uses this liminality to follow his code of ethics and obtain the information he needs to solve a case. More specifically, the Chandlerian detective is a man motivated by contract, walled in by personal morals, and kept in check by his outsider status in the social circles he must transverse. The tensions between his homosocial desires, moral code, and despairing belief in the status quo of corruption culminate in the infamous "mean streets" and the only detective suited to walk them. However, American detective fiction has come to encompass a more extensive cast of characters than the oeuvre of Chandler and Hammett, and the genre has moved forward into the twenty-first century and its treasure trove of crime and corruption to depict. The divisive semantics of crime fiction, detective fiction, and true crime are not critical to delineate cleanly in order to investigate the shape of the contemporary field productively; arguably, a more inclusive definition of the genre and detective figure allows for more dynamic engagement with the conversations that these novels produce. The pursuit of truth by the only individual uniquely suited or inclined to do so is the underlying tale of the detective, and this thread helps connect the canon of hard-boiled and noir fiction to the burgeoning library of the twenty-first century.

Chandler codified the ideal detective by painting an image of the conflicting characteristics that allow the man who is "everything" to be *of* the world he is in and still *above* it, *outside* it. As a foundational text, "The Simple Art of Murder" has been read, dissected, reread, and unread by scholars for three-quarters of a century, tracing the ways these traits are played on, pulled out, and pushed to interact with the shifting literary landscape. In the same way, the moves made by contemporary novels and authors both deepen and shift the nature of the American detective by stretching and resisting these components of Chandler's ideal detective. I argue that a three-pronged spectrum for the contemporary American detective has formed, the centers of which I term comedic, invested, and violent. As what is now contemporary becomes contextualized by time and a growing oeuvre, these identities may be renamed or redefined. However, in the tenuous academic study of contemporary popular culture, I argue that they provide a relatively stable set of terms and a useful lens through which to explore relevant authors and their increasingly ironic, sympathetic, or violent protagonists.[1]

To briefly expand on the more detailed image and broadly define terms I have coined, the comedic detective takes the redemption that Chandler posits may be of "raucous laughter" and takes it past absurdity or irony into the realm of sit-com sleuths and laughably good "Bad Boys," while the invested detective leans into the Chandlerian detective's homosocial yearning, expanding this desire and centering relationships as their motivating factor. Finally, the violent detective undertakes the grimmest transition of the three, stripping the Chandlerian detective of his moral code and resilient hope that he might be able to do some good in an evil world. Instead, the violent detective leans fully into the existentialism that Marlowe fought against, not bound by social loyalty, moral codes, or a belief in his role as a singular hero. The bitter perspective of the Chandlerian detective is a pair of rose-colored glasses compared to the existential nightmare of the contemporary violent detective's worldview. James Ellroy's novels present a perfect example of the violent detective—the heir to Chandler's macabre legacy—and shape a side of the contemporary conceptualization of the detective. None of his works display the dread of men without honor pursuing truth for their own purpose more than *L.A. Confidential*.[2]

The third novel in Ellroy's L.A. Quartet is almost five hundred pages of dirty cops and dirtier precincts. The increasingly desperate and sordid lives of Bud White, Ed Exley, and Jack Vincennes intertwine and undercut each other for eight years, beginning with the (real) "Bloody Christmas" scandal and ending only with "A glory that costs everything and means nothing." An undercurrent of existentialism thrives in the novel alongside a callousness toward others' deaths and the systemic violence that Bud, Ed, and Jack rely on for self-preservation. As quintessential examples of the violent detective, this trio of LAPD officers shoot, steal, murder, and beat their way deeper and deeper into the corrupt structures of the city. Published in 1990, this novel is admittedly outside of the twenty-first-century parameters of the spectrum I just established. However, the foundational nature of Ellroy's work in the field, the continued relevance of his work, and the spot-on depictions of violent detectives in the novel lead me to forgive the fact that it was a few years too early. Moving through the violent detective's relationship with violence and self, I will demonstrate how James Ellroy's *L.A. Confidential* provides an emblematic example of the violent detective through its characters' utilization of and dependence on systems of harm to enact their reactionary and deliberate acts of violence.

THE VIOLENT DETECTIVE AND VIOLENCE

It goes (almost!) without saying that violence is a prerequisite for successful detective and crime fiction. There is no work for the detective without violence; this is one of the genre's unwritten rules. Even Nancy Drew's tamest cases involve violence against social norms or local laws, and most contain at least one good sap to the head or a kidnapping. Violence is inevitable in the detective's journey. However, the various questions about detective types and subgenres tend to boil down to the detective figure's relationship to this violence. For example, softer-boiled detectives have a hands-off relationship with violence, while their pulp and noir peers have a more heuristic approach. Whether and how a detective views, enacts, or solves individual acts of violence is intertwined with their relationship with themselves and society. The Chandlerian detective's view and utilization of violence directly impact his view of himself and society, and, more importantly, whether he moves in this society as a "man of honor, by instinct and inevitability."[3]

Chandler and other authors of American hard-boiled detective fiction understood honor as an all-important mark of a man qualified to know how to counterbalance their addition to the general violence of the world. However, this idea of honor was not bound to acts of courtesy or social mores of gentility; whether he seduces or imparts "dispassionate revenge" on someone does not sully his honor so long as he does not do so dishonestly. The social constraints of polite language have no bearing, nor does the fact that he is "common."[4] A man's honor was self-fulfilled and self-realized; even a man whom the courts denounced a criminal could have a measure of honor if he stayed true to a personal code of honor, the detective more so because of his ability to see the corroding world around him and construct this code outside the blindness of a society caught up in the irrelevant. This man is honorable "by instinct and inevitability," which seems a tricky characteristic to claim in the nebulous morality of the world he writes.[5] However, this tightrope trick is achieved through an actual contract instead of the unwritten social contract. The required "fifteen dollars a day plus expenses" for services rendered means that any necessary violence committed while upholding it is virtuous because it falls under the protection of that contract. Violence is necessary on LA's seedy streets, but if these acts can be redeemed, it is only because *not* to do so would be to take a client's money dishonestly.[6] Chandler saw the detective-client contract as a tangible or legalized foundation that served as the detective's justification for relationships with a society he wishes he could trust but cannot. This is particularly noticeable in how these men repeatedly attempt (and fail) to form homosocial bonds, an aspect of the hard-boiled detective that scholars such as Leonard Cassuto and Sean McCann have enumerated. The contemporary violent detective, however, pushes past the Chandlerian boundaries of written-out and financially compensated relationships toward a mindset centered on self-preservation instead.

We can see this change in the detective's relationship to violence even in the trope of the calloused cop standing over yet another horrifically mangled body; an attitude of apathy—it is not his first ugly scene, and it won't be his last!—is almost expected at this point in the genre, a throwaway line meant to demonstrate the character's relationship to violence from the outset. To put it differently, *the violent detective is no longer thrown off by the violence he confronts nor guilty for the violence he enacts.* The irony or horror of overwhelming death and violence is left for the reader to confront, be shocked by, or recoil from. As one of the earliest examples of contemporary detective fiction in the violent detective subgenre, *L.A. Confidential* provides these elements while exemplifying the shift away from Chandlerian ideals of just(ifiable) violence. Violence is not a means to an end or a necessity of fulfilling his job requirements; it is the detective figure's primary means of self-preservation, even if more upstanding options are available. Bud, Ed, and Jack refuse to hurt their chances at social and physical survival, even if that would be the "right" thing to do. Consider just one of many scenes where this plays out, Jack's remarks outside of the courtroom after testifying: "'I'm snitching three old-timers who'll be fishing in Oregon next week. Next to you, I'm clean. And smart.'"[7] Snitching is not about right or wrong or justice, only better or worse chances of survival. Instead, what might have been framed as a socially or personally moral decision is a question of self-preservation. Nothing is owed to God, society, or personal qualms and beliefs. The better decision is whatever gives you the best chance of survival. Virtuous violence is replaced by violent survival; there is no honor in Ellroy's LA.

Chandler was direct in his depiction of the world he saw, the corruption on each side of the tracks, and, most importantly, the detective's singular ability to enact limited justice as someone outside of these systems. He knows that "it is not a fragrant world" but that it is the world the reader and detective live in.[8] It was "not enough" for this man to know that relationships and sentiment are bound to fail; the detective must continue to look through his grimy glasses of reality to be the only "hero" to hope for.[9] Chandler wrote of himself as a "realist in murder," but Ellroy can also be described this way as well; however, their departure begins where the violent detective's hope in redemption and justice ends.[10] Ellroy's novels do not challenge the Chandlerian dedication to a code of conduct outright. Instead, they seem to ask if a contract is still enough or if it is only barely possible to save yourself by any means necessary; their characters utilize violent systems as the only means of self-preservation. This is distinctly different from the approach of invested detective fiction which centers on the victims of these violent systems and provides an alternate view of the genre's violence.

Violence is enacted suddenly throughout the novel; Ellroy's LA is violent. Bud, Ed, and Jack are violent men, but violence comes to violent and innocent alike. This element of the novel is easy to identify, and it hardly seems relevant to attempt to comprehensively list the mentally, physically, emotionally, and socially violent moments in the book; the citation would read something along the lines of (Ellroy 1990, 497). What I would draw attention to, instead, are the specific instances of *unjust violence enacted by those who are meant to represent the system of justice*. The depraved or corrupt actions of the novel's central detectives emphasize Ellroy's maturation and deterioration of Chandler's un-fragrant world into one that is difficult to separate from the world of true crime or the nightly news. This element of realism that Woody Haut explores in his discussion of neon noir fiction in the late twentieth century continues in much of crime fiction today. Regardless of Ellroy's (lack of) intent to comment on the outside world, which I explore in a later section, the detective's relationship to violence in their fictional world is critical to examine. Acts of unjust violence by those who represent a system of justice demonstrate systems of harm and the detective's *modus operandis* when pursuing hidden truth for their own preservation instead of others. Hidden truth and these men's adventures in search of it are at the heart of Ellroy's *L.A. Confidential.* Some search for the truth to play out revenge, while others look to bury it further to protect themselves, but the search is imperative for each. For the violent detective, truth is not the infallible tool of justice; rather, it is a kidnapped character that is ransomed, bought, and stolen. At the novel's end, it is disposed of like all the other inconvenient witnesses.

"THE JUSTICE IN HIS RAGE . . . "[11]

Perhaps the clearest example of this deterioration from a vocationally required search for truth and justice to violent self-preservation is Ed Exley's character development throughout the novel. Following the Bloody Christmas massacre at the novel's start, Ed questions law enforcement officers' role in revealing the truth and enforcing justice when filing the police report. The pressure of deciding what to write and whom to blame weighs on him, as does his father's legacy and example. Preston Exley's intimidating shadow shapes Ed's determination for professional achievement and his guilt, an increasingly strained relationship captured in the scrapbook he compiles for his sons. The burning recollection Ed has of the clippings impresses upon the reader a measure of parental instruction in absolutes: "Preston Exley keeps copies of the death photos; he shows them to his policemen sons—so that they will know the brutality of crimes that require absolute justice."[12] As Ed conceives of his father's belief, absolute justice is *required* for brutal crimes and must be brutally meted out. The seemingly black-and-white nature of this job requirement is muddled when he confronts the task of writing the Bloody Christmas report. Ed considers the "truth" of what happened, the "truth" that these crimes required justice, and the truth that he must now decide where "justice" would land; the truth "twisted a few turns" before he decides which one would survive as codified history.[13] Fraternal allegiance wins out; Ed commits to the third edited version of the truth: "no whimpers, no *madre mia,* the cop beaters inciting other inmates. He wondered how his father would rate the crimes: brother officers assaulted, the assaulters ravaged. Which required absolute justice?"[14] Echoing his father, Ed reveals the first facets of his relationship with violence—when justice and violence intertwine, he has the responsibility and authority to sort them out as he believes necessary for the department, his fellow officers, and himself.

Ed continues to wrestle with whether hiding truths or making them known results in absolute justice, but somewhere along the way, the justice of protecting and avenging his fraternity morphs into the self-preservation of the violent detective. The (mis)step of the Bloody Christmas report is soon followed by the questioning of Sugar Ray Coates, Leroy Fontaine, and Tyrone Jones. Ed skims the arrest report and is tasked with obtaining confessions from the Black boys, the arresting officers liked for the Nite Owl murders. Although they confess to the kidnap and rape of Inez Soto, the young men continue to deny that they were behind the massacre. Ed is confronted with another decision, feeling "himself buzzing, electric chair, a sign on top: THEY DIDN'T DO IT."[15] The truth of their crimes is violent but would his acknowledging their innocence of a different violence result in the necessary violence against them that justice requires? In the end, Ed twists along with the truth and takes on the seemingly department-wide "any means necessary" view of retributive and violent justice. This, like the writing of the Bloody Christmas police report, is another step in his journey toward craven self-preservation. Although he later attempts to mitigate the fallout, his goal is still self-preservation instead of justice—preserving his position in the department as his father's son and protecting his ability to live with himself. What seems to be some measure of moral motivation to make things right is only a subconscious drive to avoid his depravity and save his own perception of himself as a real man, if not a good one. As Ellroy remarks, "real men do not wallow in self-pity" or "revel in [their] own grotesque."[16] Ed's delusion of acting in pursuit of absolute justice keeps him from realizing that he is following in his colleagues' footsteps.

Slowly, even the language Ed uses to explain his actions starts to mirror the callous justifications of Bud and Jack. When talking to Inez, he brushes off her anger, saying, "You wanted them in the gas chamber, they're going there. You didn't want to testify, now I doubt if you'll have to. [. . .] This is a case that demands absolute justice."[17] Inez sees through Ed's moral delusion, laughing, "absolute justice fits you like this robe fits me, *pendejo*."[18] The pursuit of porn and women drives the other men to acts of self-interested violence and their justifications for them, but Ed's violence is more obviously centered on his own fears and hidden behind a public image and the tinny repetition of his father's favorite phrase. Eventually, even Ed acknowledges that adding the slogan to the end of his arguments and excuses does not elevate them to the moral stratosphere he once imagined them at. His violence is only "a weak man's rage" taken out on Black bodies and given meaning by labeling them the Nite Owl Killers.[19] Under this banner, his violence becomes "absolute justice boldly taken," his murders become vouchers for public accolades and fatherly pride, and his manipulation becomes a badge to prove he does not have to be afraid of knowing who he truly is.[20]

The gold plating of this assurance is cheap, though; Inez rubs the shine off and forces Ed to look at it. She mocks his honorable words and acknowledges her manipulations of the capital-T truth, saying, "I lied because I didn't want you to feel bad that you'd killed four men for me. And you want to know what the big lie is? You and your precious absolute justice."[21] In this crucial moment, Ed faces a critical decision: he can attempt to break a system of harm at significant personal risk or lean into it, purposely utilizing systems of harm and brutalizing the truth to avoid what he fears. *This decision encapsulates his relationship to violence and demonstrates why Ed is a clear example of the violent detective*. Twisting the truth to keep the accolades a reality, Ed answers the knocking opportunity clear-eyed and decided, weaponizing the conscious self-adulation and preservation of the violent detective.

By the novel's end, the safety is irrevocably off of this weapon of violence, even when confronted with the tatters of his conscience. His hate-filled goodbye to his father, "Goddamn you for the bad things you made me," is an ironic moment between the two men.[22] Preston is "unbudging, unyielding, unflinching" in his lack of remorse, even as Ed argues against the same justification of an unjust murder he has been using throughout the novel.[23] Ed's hatred toward his father is a proxy, a way to hate who he is and what he has done without violating his own need to self-preserve. Like father, like son. The same devil Preston sold his soul to has made a generational deal with Ed, and Ed knows it. The final report on Preston mentions none of his violence or corruption, only how he "personified the grand and good dreams that have built this city."[24] The end of Preston's story is the best-case scenario for Ed, who can only hope to subvert justice forever or die humiliated. As a violent detective, there is only one option: he is left on the final page with "Gold stars[,] alone with his dead."[25]

"RUTHLESS MEN IN LOVE . . ."[26]

The relationship between Bud White and Ed Exley is as turbulent as the latter's journey to remorseless killing but hardly resembles the former's relationship with violence. Bud White is straightforward, singular, and unbothered in his determination to get what he wants. Ed describes Bud as a man "too stupid" to grasp his revenge and manipulated by his emotions: "a simple cuckold accompanied by a woman's few words had him treading lies at the top, thrashing for a way to make his stale glory real."[27] His violence is one of the characteristics he is known for in the department and characterizes much of his interactions throughout the novel, including his romantic and sexual adventures. Much like Ed, Bud is afraid of not being the man he thinks he is, but this image of himself has nothing to do with justice or good police work. Instead, Bud needs affirmation that he is the sort of man a strong woman is right to love. This is demonstrated throughout the book, from his "wife-beater spiel" and "pervert patrol" to his conflicted desire for and guilt toward Inez and Lynn.[28] This juxtaposition of violence and women is only meant to protect his existential doubt in the same way that Ed's pursuit of "absolute justice" is a cover for his self-interests. Luce describes this inclination of Ellroy's characters as a critical element of his writing; Ellroy writes of "bad men in love with strong women—damaged cops seeking redemption from the opposite sex."[29] When those women fail Bud, they are subject to the same violence he employed to protect them; they prove their strength by understanding his rage and facing his violence. A brutal example of these ties is Bud's assault on Lynn after she sleeps with Ed; he hits her until he sees that he cannot break her, but this is justified in his eyes because she understands where this stems from, and she chooses him in the end.[30] She has proven herself a strong woman, and he is proven worthy of redemption by her love. As a violent detective, saving and screwing women are emotional reactions—a grasp at the redemption and glory he associates with their love.

Bud's thrashing and violence are nothing more than desperate attempts to remedy his doubts about himself. Vulnerable after sex, Bud talks and talks to Lynn but is still frustrated because

> he wasn't that smart, he wasn't really a Homicide detective—he was the guy they brought in to scare other guys shitless. After a while, the talk petered out—Bud felt restless, pissed at himself for spilling too much too fast.[31]

Not the weak man's rage that drives Ed's violence, Bud's violence is born from an acknowledgment that he is damaged and his belief that he can change that. Because of this, he risks his life and "doesn't weigh the consequences" of his actions.[32] Instead, he is driven by his emotions in each moment; rage, revenge, lust, despair, and even impatience motivate his uncensored violence. A different man might doubt Bud's brutal hands-on methods, but the vicious punishment meted out by his "own two wounded hands" is the natural choice for him in the face of his emotional response.[33] These unfettered personal motivations are emblematic of the violent detective, and Bud White demonstrates this characteristic in a wholly untainted way. While Ed hides behind his "precious absolute justice" and Jack cowers behind the false apology of his own self-loathing, Bud knows who he is and who the people around him are.[34] He faces the parts of him that make him a violent detective figure as violently head-on as he does any other fact.

Some characters see this as a pragmatic trait that makes him the ideal person to intimidate witnesses into involuntary confessions.[35] For others, like Inez, it is only honesty born of stupidity.[36] For Ed, it is why he ultimately respects Bud; he has done what Ed could never hope to achieve. He sees Bud for the first time: "The notes were a limited man reaching for the stars. Pulling most of them down. Limits exceeded through a brilliantly persistent rage. Absolute justice—anonymous, no rank and glory."[37] Ed sees Bud as his redemption, but if that redemption ends with Ed's purposeful violence in pursuit and protection of his interests, then Bud plays out a purer form of this violent detective figure. Somewhat fittingly, as the detective most unflinching in his violence, he is served this violence back in an equally straightforward manner.

For Bud White, the novel ends differently than it does for the others. While Ed must live with his weakness and Jack dies for his, Bud takes his blows on the chin, quite literally, and seems to gain the object of his pursuit. When the dust settles, Bud has gotten the girl and the glory he pursued, left the department with more respect than he entered it, and handed the responsibility of his revenge off to Ed. However, the unknown ellipsis at the end of the novel leaves a lingering question: Can a strong woman ever truly redeem the damaged man? Has he broken out of the cycle of the violent detective, or will he inevitably turn to violence in more desperate attempts at self-preservation?

"PERFECT MATCHES TO MURDER MUTILATIONS"

Of the three violent detective figures, Jack Vincennes relies the most on corrupt systems of harm while desiring his violence more distantly, more grotesquely. He has no desire for justice or redemption from women; Jack's violence is driven by his need to see systems of harm in their ultimate and inevitable form—death. The deaths he orchestrates and seeks out are not general, however. The bodies that he subjects to unjust execution and eroticized death are vulnerable bodies, disposable because of their place within the systems he operates in. Even the most benign of his corruptions, "counting lies," is motivated by the desire to bring about the death of someone vulnerable.[38] He risks his involvement in an investigation to ensure that the falsely accused Black men die:

> He didn't tell him his reports were all bullshit. He didn't tell him he didn't care if the smut gig and the Nite Owl were doubled up from here to Mars. He didn't tell him he wouldn't rest easy until he had Sid Hudgens' file in his hand and the n***ers sucked gas—guilty or not.[39]

No literary analysis is necessary to draw out his motivation for and relationship with violence; Jack *does not care* about the violent results of his silence or his desire for dead Black bodies. Even though Black and Brown bodies are brutalized and victimized throughout the novel, Jack most clearly correlates this disregard for justice, personal motivation for violence, and racist attitudes and epithets at this moment. Capitalizing on the vulnerable and exploiting systems of harm for his benefit and protection grounds the actions of the violent detective, and Jack epitomizes this habit of violent utilization in ways more straightforward than Ed or Bud do.

The violence that Jack inflicts and wants to inflict is not limited to the Nite Owl innocents, however. His extensive desire for violence and death is also channeled toward the "obscene perfection" of violent smut, a rather on-the-nose example of an officer of justice's reliance on systems of harm and a grotesque extension of the genre's strained relationship with women. Where Chandler built a world with rough, bitter sex and the inevitable fallibility of *femme fatales*, Ellroy constructs absurdity—meaningless fulfillment in the wake of prioritizing self. Even the most violent tropes of the genre are pushed to the limits of publication; sex is not just a threat but every variety of bloody, severed, violated death that "artful little swirls" can produce.[40] If they are allowed to live, women are not just betraying men—they are doing it by fucking their sons on roller skates. The apex of this absurdity is that Jack enjoys the accentuated violence, is addicted to it, and is fundamentally changed because he cannot live without it:

> What drove him was the smut. [. . .] Nothing he did changed things—Karen just learned who he was. [. . .] He got bored with Karen, ran to the smut, went crazy with it. [. . .] no way to have the real thing—he decided to fake it. He bought hookers, shook down call girls. He fixed them up to look like the girls in his books. He had them three and four at a pop, chains of bodies on quilts. He costumed them, choreographed them. He aped the pictures, took his own pictures, recaptured; sometimes he thought of the blood pix and got scared: perfect matches to murder mutilations. Real women never thrilled him like the pictures did.[41]

The detective is not battling against existentialism or nihilism anymore, nor has he lost the battle. As a violent detective figure, Jack instead melds his violence and apathy together, wielding the destructive combination as he pleases until he is killed. The violent deaths he was aroused by and intent on executing were twisted reflections of his fear of dying wrongly and his public image being sullied after death. As the only one of the three central detectives to be killed, Jack embodies the inevitable end of the violent detective who cannot save himself through the prioritization of self or the utilization of systems of harm any longer.

Though Bud and Ed may not die within the pages of the novel, the fear underneath their violence will also be realized. The conscious and unconscious shenanigans to mask their corruption and violence become cyclical; if they cannot look beyond their fear the first time, their self-preservation will not let them reverse and face the mounting crimes. The violent detective will inevitably fail, die, or become "doped up, boozed up, [and] going psycho."[42] The violent detective's relationship with violence is ultimately rooted in fear and self-preservation. Ed fears becoming the man he eventually does, Bud fears that the love and glory he finds are fake, and Jack fears dying. This motivates why they smother justice and lose themselves in revenge, why they fuck and kill before they can be fucked or killed. At the novel's end, they are either destroyed by or stuck in the violent cycles of this fear. As the last section header of the novel asks, what happens "After You're Gone" and after your last attempt to save yourself fails? The violent detective perpetually lives with the fear he so doggedly corrupts himself to avoid and inevitably dies by it. It is not that any of the men are more emblematic of the violent detective and his future than any of the others, but rather that they display the various means and consequences of the violence he acts out and the different ways he relies on systems of harm. Because the violent detective's relationship with violence is centered around self-preservation, it is crucial to ask what happens to the communities and individuals victimized by the systems that allow the detective his violence. Who pays the tab?

THE VIOLENT DETECTIVE'S DEPENDENCE ON SYSTEMS OF HARM

It is crucial to look at how this violence is rooted in and reliant on systems of harm and consider the sociopolitical critique that has always accompanied the genre. In his history of hard-boiled crime fiction and New Deal liberalism, McCann notes the undercurrent of social critique that defines the genre's interaction with its milieu, defining the "ethical drama" of the detective tale as "a drama of the commitment to civil society," portraying both the "hopes and failures of its authors' cultural ambitions."[43] Chandler struggled against the inevitability of failure with the mindset that while a minimal commitment to society is the most you can aim for, this is also what you *should* aim for. In the same way he acknowledges that the genre's bridging of culture and intellectual expertise must fail and yet endeavors toward it anyway, his novels continually return to demonstrations of sentiment's inability to defeat or suppress systems of corruption and harm. McCann describes Chandler's "grandiose aim" and his awareness that it must fail as a bridge between high and low culture:

> building on the vernacular language of the pulps so as to create a public taste capable of overcoming the constraints of literary tradition, [in the same way that] the detective works to expand mundane affiliations and common emotions in order to create a popular coalition that might surpass the limits of corrupt institutions.[44]

More simply, the genre asks questions not only of crime but of the society that produces and condemns it; the corrupt should be cleansed, justice enacted, and (the detective's particular definition of) social order reinstated. American detective fiction is fundamentally entrenched in social critique and commentary, historically interested in the reinscription of the status quo as a demonstration of this struggle in bridging that personal/social gap.

However, Ellroy wastes no time demonstrating the looming failure of sentiment and relationships; he presents the violent detective figure through characters who have internalized this ideology of inevitable failure and are showcasing that belief in every physical or emotional act of violence committed. He keeps his characters in a world where they understand what social contracts they are *expected* to be acting out of but replaces the traditional moral struggle with a core disbelief in the merit of meeting those expectations. To put it bluntly, because Ed, Jack, and Bud believe, in some conscious or unconscious part of their core, that sentiment and social mores are fundamentally incapable of keeping or making the world and society survivable, they have decided to do whatever is necessary to make *their* world survivable, including utilizing the same systems of harm that support the corrupt and broken machinations of society around them.

I look at the elements of sociopolitical critique last because it is in looking at the systems which support the violence of the plot and the characters that we are able to more fully see how violent detective fiction has separated from the other subgenres of contemporary detective fiction, namely the invested detective. However, the root of this separation can be traced to what they share—authorially crafted worlds that unblinkingly reflect a real one. The indistinguishability of fictional worlds and reality is a shared trait of the violent and invested detective; it is the detective's reaction to the crime and the author's intent in crafting the world as such that differentiates the two. Authors of invested detective fiction, such as Alicia Gaspar de Alba and Kalisha Buckhanon, are vocal in their intent to present a fictional reality that mirrors the one they live in as marginalized voices and look to the genre as an opportunity to show what systems of harm can do in hopes that it will be seen and understood by those less marginalized than themselves and changed. However, James Ellroy is equally vocal that he has not buried any deeper political meaning in his novels. Consistently refusing to answer questions on current political leaders or extrapolations of hidden meanings in his novels, Ellroy maintains his stance that "what happens today is of no interest"[45] to him and that even his much-noted, self-termed introduction as the "white knight of the far right" is only a "schtick."[46]

Ellroy has remarked on multiple occasions that his works are not political and are "as deep as a tortilla," which is an ironic choice of words for an author whose novels continually subject Mexican and Mexican-American bodies, as well as Black bodies, to violence, disgrace, and discrimination.[47] This claim of disassociation holds for most of the other prominent authors in this subgenre; any sociopolitical critique that might be drawn out is done so expressly at the scholar's hand. On the other side of the coin, however, invested detective fiction is expressly meant to draw the reader into a reading experience that causes them to confront systems of harm drawn from all-too-real social realities. This intent is seen intra-textually, through the character's dialogues and the problems they face as a result of violent marginalization, as well as extra-textually, in their authors' statements of intent and forewords or epilogues written to the reader.

How does this separation of the subgenres become productive? I argue that it is through the examination of the mirrored worlds that they present; the violence of the one becomes the crime to be solved in the other. In the world of the violent detective, characters *must* subjugate marginalized bodies to preserve their own; in the world of the invested detective, these subjugated side characters are the central figures. Invested detective fiction crafts a world that mirrors the same reality as violent detective fiction does but is written to bring attention to the glossed-over, "not political," brutalization of men and women of color who are harmed by the systems that the violent detective depends on. Both of these subgenres utilize American sociopolitical systems, which is a crucial element of the conversation surrounding the violence of the violent detective. Even if our critique is limited to the novels and not the world they clearly reflect, the counterpoint of invested detective fiction necessitates a conversation about the use of marginalized bodies in contemporary violent detective fiction.

Social structures built on and reiterating racism and sexism are the foundation of the stage where the drama of the detective novel is played out. Detective fiction's excess of violence demands an excess of recipients of that violence. Bluntly, Black and Brown bodies are dispensable, unimportant, obvious targets to channel the violent detective's uncontrolled urge for violence. These men and women bear the consequences of the detective's self-prioritization, left paying the bill after the violent detective's departure from a social contract. Ellroy comments that the central theme of *L.A. Confidential* is "three men working out their destiny," but the price of those men's journeys is ultimately paid by helpless others.[48] The detective characters' fears drive the novel's plot, but it is the murder of Inez Soto, Raymond Coates, Tyrone Jones, Leroy Fontaine, and several others that enables both. While Inez plays a more prominent role in the Nite Owl case and the resulting tumult of the novel, each of these characters plays a vital role in establishing the violent detectives' character. Not only this, but they are brutally aware of their innocence and helplessness in their situations. Regardless of whether those who perpetuate systems of harm are aware that they do, those who cannot escape their machinations cannot choose not to see them at work against them.

Admittedly, Raymond, Tyrone, and Leroy are guilty of Inez's kidnapping and rape, and she is guilty of the lie that results in their deaths. This does not mitigate how they are subjected to systems of harm; rather, it explicates it. Because of these systems, the boys are arrested and executed for the Nite Owl murders rather than tried for their assault. It is because of systems of racism and sexism that Inez is assaulted. It is because she *knows* that she is a victim of these systems that she knows "six white people are more important than a Mexican girl from Boyle Heights."[49] It is because she cannot escape these systems that she resolves to twist the truth. Systems of biased violence inform the fact that although both Lynn and Inez move from detective's bed to detective's bed, it is Inez who is found dead. Notedly, it is not just in these specific, more blatant instances that we see these larger systems of harm; they are woven into the fabric of the world and the plot in multiple insidious ways. There is violence in the slurs, in the pornography, in the correlation of virginity and criminality, and in the explicit details of assaults and deaths. The pages are drenched with violence and blood, held together by systems of interlaced prejudices and harm.

Yes, violence is necessary for a crime fiction novel. However, *L.A. Confidential* and violent detective fiction create this violence by assuming and utilizing systems of harm. The violent detective is so consumed with shoring up the cracks in his defense against what he fears that he uses these social structures to benefit and protect himself at any (one else's) cost. Ed, Bud, and Jack all embody this critical characteristic of the contemporary violent detective as they work out their destiny at the expense of marginalized communities. The city they rage and thrash about in is as emblematic of the genre as the novel that houses it—there is no honor in (Ellroy's) *L.A. (Confidential)*.

NOTES

1. All italicized quotes are pulled from Chandler's "The Simple Art of Murder" and point toward the moments in his exploration of his own hero that, when played on and extrapolated out, become relevant markers for the contemporary character.
2. All the books in the original LA Quartet (*The Black Dahlia, The Big Nowhere, LA Confidential, White Jazz)* feature equally corrupt characters and revoltingly murky police operations; why choose *L.A. Confidential* to explicate the violent detective and his dependence on systems of harm? First, with the beginning of his second LA Quartet (*Perfidia, This Storm*) and the backstory they provide, it is clear that Ellroy's commitment to mirroring the complicated crossings of police, deceit, politics, and crime in LA leads him to circle back to the characters of *L.A. Confidential*. Second, these characters (as I will soon expand on) live out the tenets of exemplarily violent detectives in clear and remarkable ways—a boon to academic inquiry and conversation. Third, I simply enjoy *L.A. Confidential* the most.
3. Chandler 1988, originally 1950, 18.
4. Ibid.
5. Ibid.
6. Ibid.
7. Ellroy 1990, 67.
8. Chandler 1988, 18.
9. Ibid.
10. Ibid.
11. Ibid., 286.
12. Ibid., 48.

13. Ibid., 32.
14. Ibid., 32.
15. Ibid., 132.
16. Luce 2019.
17. Ellroy 1990, 240.
18. Ibid.
19. Ibid., 302.
20. Ibid.
21. Ibid., 289.
22. Ibid., 484.
23. Ibid.
24. Ibid., 491.
25. Ibid., 496.
26. Ibid., 254.
27. Ibid., 302.
28. Ibid., 12, 202.
29. Luce 2019.
30. Ibid., 401.
31. Ibid., 238.
32. Ibid., 241.
33. Ibid., 470.
34. Ibid., 289.
35. Ibid., 124.
36. Ibid., 241
37. Ibid., 477.
38. Ibid., 196.
39. Ibid., 215, censorship mine.
40. Ibid., 111.
41. Ibid., 299.
42. Ibid., 379.
43. McCann 2000, 15, 37.
44. Ibid. 149, 160.
45. Luce 2019.
46. Anthony 2019.
47. Brown 2019.
48. Lyttelton 2012.
49. Ellroy 1990, 152.

BIBLIOGRAPHY

Anthony, Andrew. "James Ellroy: 'I've Been Canonised. And That's a Gas.'" *The Guardian*, May 18, 2019, sec. Books. https://www.theguardian.com/books/2019/may/18/james-ellroy-this-storm-ive-been-canonised-interview.

Brown, Mark, and Mark Brown Arts correspondent. "James Ellroy Says Film Adaptation of LA Confidential Was 'as Deep as a Tortilla.'" *The Guardian*, June 2, 2019, sec. Books. https://www.theguardian.com/books/2019/jun/02/james-ellroy-says-film-adaptation-of-la-confidential-was-as-deep-as-a-tortilla.

Cassuto, Leonard. *Hard-Boiled Sentimentality: The Secret History of American Crime Stories*. Columbia University Press, 2008.

Chandler, Raymond. "The Simple Art of Murder." In *The Simple Art of Murder*, 1–18. Boston: Houghton, 1950.

Ellroy, James. *L.A. Confidential*. L.A. Quartet 3. Grand Central Publishing, 1990.

Luce, Edward. "James Ellroy on Time Warps, His New Novel and Trump." Australian Financial Review, June 5, 2019. https://www.afr.com/life-and-luxury/arts-and-culture/james-ellroy-on-time-warps-his-new-novel-and-trump-20190604-p51u8a.

Lyttelton, Oliver. "5 Things You Might Not Know About 'L.A. Confidential.'" *IndieWire* (blog), September 19, 2012. https://www.indiewire.com/2012/09/5-things-you-might-not-know-about-l-a-confidential-105871/.

McCann, Sean. *Gumshoe America: Hard-Boiled Crime Fiction and the Rise and Fall of New Deal Liberalism*. New Americanists. Durham, NC: Duke University Press, 2000.

Chapter 6

Policing, Corruption, and Criminality

The Politics of the Legitimate Use of Force and the Rule of Law in James Ellroy's LA Quartet

Jeffrey Becker

James Ellroy's LA Quartet novels (*The Black Dahlia*, *The Big Nowhere*, *L.A. Confidential*, and *White Jazz*) portray an unsettling dynamic about Los Angeles that reflects (and shapes) how Americans understand policing, the rule of law, and the use of force. Ellroy's Los Angeles of the 1940s and 1950s is a city that blurs the lines between cops and criminals in ways that show contemporary Americans' expectations of good heroes and bad villains to be simplistic and infantile. Ellroy creates a world of uncertainty where one's status, power, and success are always fluctuating and fleeting. In this light the line between obeying the law and breaking the law is bound up with a fight between competing groups for identity, power, and standing in the evolving civic order of postwar Los Angeles. The LA Quartet reveals a Los Angeles that is a microcosm of American life: a city that, by its nature, generates an anxiety often expressed through violence and the desire to dominate and control the civic environment. And it is this undercurrent of continual jockeying for power and status that generates the kind of anxiety that actress Ana de Armas described in 2022: "the feeling of something that you don't have, something missing."[1] Ellroy's LA Quartet captures the contradictory social demands that drive contemporary debates about the place of policing in the United States. To make sense of policing in the United States is to understand the complex ways racial and social status are bound up with definitions of who and who does not count as a criminal. For Ellroy, that line is rarely as clear or bright as his audiences may expect.

Ellroy's novels pull the curtain back on the cinematic fantasy of the morally pure police keeping a degenerate citizenry from threateningthe civic order. In doing so, Ellroy's novels parallel recent social movements questioning the purpose and effects of policing in a society that believes—at least publicly—in rule of the people through law. Just as the proliferation of cell phone video surveillance rapidly expanded public scrutiny of the police use of force disproportionately applied to Black Americans, Ellroy's LA Quartet also questions the purpose (and effect) of state-sanctioned use of force by police officers. Though Ellroy does not engage in an overt critique of policing under a democratic republic, his novels question the human costs imposed by the state-sanctioned use of force that often serves private and corrupt ends. Ellroy reveals the paradoxes of a city that proclaims (at least publicly) that the power of the state (through the police) exists to serve the people, yet entrusts that power to tyrants, who, under the guise of "serving public good" betray those ideals to enrich themselves and satisfy base desires.

Ellroy's LA Quartet is set during the founding of William (Bill) Parkers' efforts to reform and professionalize the LAPD in the 1950s. Parker's implementation of the motto "to protect and to serve" institutes a "Hollywood ideal" of policing: noble servants of the public good. For many the LAPD motto"to protect and to serve" adopted in 1955 under Bill Parker has stood as an ideal against which Ellroy's novels implicitly pose the questions: who is being protected and what interests are being served.[2] Ellroy's LA Quartet implicitly challenges the comfortable assumptions that the police always represent and defend the noble ideals of American democratic life: to protect and serve the public good. Yet, Ellroy's novels also hold open the possibility that the decency necessary for democratic life can be found in the quiet actions of his police protagonists, who, in their own ways, fight to sustain a measure of human empathy needed to build common purposes through civic relationships.

Ellroy shows how the police, charged with the responsibility to maintain order, not only protect and enforce a regime of power but also, in their own way, *create* a regime of political power. To do so requires that the police use force and violence that values and rewards *some* people, *some* values, and *some* practices as more worthy than others. Ellroy shows that what the *police* value may not align with what the public expects and values, which, in turn, reveals the contradictory and at times hypocritical demands on policing of the American public.

The numerous shootings, arrests, and incidents appearing on social media since 2013 have highlighted the contradictory role the public expects the police to play as defenders of American ideals *and* upholders of regimes of power often seen as at odds with those ideals. For critics, the police do not "protect and serve" all the people, rather they only protect and serve those who hold power. In response to shootings, the "Black Lives Matter" movement called for reforms such as community policing, better training of officers, body cameras, and tighter guidelines for the police use of deadly force. These reforms reflect a call for American police to live up to ideals that Ellroy portrays as a Hollywood mirage. Though reformers outraged by recent events seek a less brutalizing relationship between the police and citizens, many pay little attention to the complex way policing practices evolve in response to the contradictory demands of people who publicly claim to live by one set of civic values, while privately pursuing more licentious desires for self-gratification or domination and control over other people. Though Americans profess one set of values, they/we often live by another. Yet, amidst protests and proposed reforms, broader questions about who should enforce the law, what divides criminals from cops, and what the rule of law preserves in democratic states remain assumed and unexamined. It is far easier—and more comfortable—to hold onto illusory ideals about good and noble cops protecting a virtuous (yet helpless) citizenry from marauding criminals and predators, then to blur the lines between cops and criminals, or between citizens and predators. Though Ellroy's novels do not presume easy answers, Ellroy's protagonists, at their core, attempt to be "reluctantly decent" or "retain a tenacious dignity."[3] Despite Ellroy's vivid descriptions of civic corruption, his characters seek to redeem their actions. And it is this effort at redemption, at recovering human decency amidst an environment that fosters social isolation and rewards vice that offers moments of hope for the human condition.

Ellroy's LA Quartet shows characters caught up in the contest for power where defending civic ideals is often secondary, or instrumental, to personal ambitions. Characters driven by venal motives of power and greed appear contradictory to the presumed public trust between the police and the communities they are empowered to protect and serve. Americans want to believe the ideals and fantasies Hollywood produces but cannot fathom the truth that American ideals and American identity also hinge on making ideals and fantasies true through the inequitable use of force where some people get policed, and some do not. The aggressive policing of the disproportionately nonwhite communities, of finding black suspects as scapegoats for the Nite Owl murders in *L.A. Confidential* reveals how the promise of glamour offered by 1950s LA depends upon limiting access to realizing that promise. To change policing of a community, it is necessary to understand this duality: the way a community simultaneously educates and *undermines* the values that attach people to obeying the law. Fairness and justice for *some* may come at the cost of dominating others. While public institutions may consciously teach certain values of liberty and equality, there are the unconscious private values of greed and lust for power taught by the emerging geographic place and circumstances that is Los Angeles. Ellroy shows how the place and circumstances of Los Angeles teach unconscious civic values that dignity is to be won through the adoration of strangers.

James Ellroy's LA Quartet depicts an emerging civic culture in 1940s and 1950s Los Angeles where crime and depravity belie the grand public pronouncements of elected officials and public servants. Ellroy's characters search for something to stand for, some order or moral code to defend in the face of the perversion and violence they confront from criminals, prominent citizens, fellow officers, and public officials. His protagonists are police officers who the public expects to sort through, and make sense of, the vicious crimes they encounter. And in telling their stories, the LA Quartet reflects American illusions about crime and policing. Despite public condemnation of crime, democratic cultures make exceptions for the vices of some, while sanctioning the use of brutal force to punish those same vices in others. The LA Quartet shows how policing preserves hierarchies of social power in an evolving multicultural Los Angeles; yet Ellroy frames his stories through the personal futility of police empowered to maintain those hierarchies. Criminality and policing in Ellroy's Los Angeles are contradictory yet interdependent.

By exposing the dichotomies of virtuous cops and bad citizens, or corrupt cops and virtuous citizens as mythic, Ellroy's LA Quartet shows a Los Angeles where civic values become lost amidst a nihilism that threatens an already fragile social order. When everything people trust about the bonds holding civic institutions together becomes suspect, people lose the ability to publicly defend moral codes that distinguish right from wrong conduct. Ellroy's novels implicitly ask whether a civic order premised on the rule of law can survive when citizens disparage shared ideals, and corrupt police enforce the rule of law to suit their own ambitions and prurient interests. The crime and police corruption in Ellroy's Los Angeles provide audiences with little hope for preserving what Martha Nussbaum calls the "security of cherished values in times of stress."[4] Ellroy explores what happens to characters when virtuous behavior goes unrewarded, and corrupt behavior emerges as the norm. Characters face the prospect that there may be no civic ideals worth defending, no enduring values worthy of sacrifice. Yet, the protagonist cops of the LA Quartet struggle to preserve a modicum of law and order in a climate hostile to both. And in this respect, the struggle of Ellroy's characters is also the struggle of democratic citizenship: Can a people find the promise of self-government worthy of personal sacrifice, even when all human incentives suggest they are not?

Because the ideals of a regime are not self-executing, or self-enacting, citizens have to exercise their power to stake out, and express, the civic ideals that express a collective identity. Exercising power allows a people to participate in constructing a world of shared norms and behaviors. Yet, this forging of shared norms does not take place on equal terms. And policing codifies, as well as mitigates, such inequality using force and often violence. At its core policing is how a society manages violence. When speech and words fail to adjudicate conflict, policing becomes the mechanism of coercion for generating compliance and conformity. The question of who gets policed and why, for Ellroy, is not just a reductively forceful application of racial animus, class privilege, or gendered power; policing is not solely a reaction to existing cultural and social identities. Policing in the LA Quartet reflects how overlapping civic identities come to be formed in response to the competition for resources, status, and power in Los Angeles. Cross-group collaboration (or intersectional coalitional politics) takes place all the time—and often in the service of criminal activity, corruption, and pecuniary gain. Alliances and conflicts that intersect multiple cultures and civic groups are the norm, though the goals of such alliances are rarely in the service of noble public goods.

THE DUALITY OF THE RULE OF LAW AND THE DESIRE FOR ORDER IN DEMOCRATIC STATES

Ellroy's novels capture the dual quality that the rule of law and desire for order play in democratic societies as both protectors and threats to civic peace. Democratic states establish government by the rule of law to protect the public welfare from arbitrary power. Laws are intended to protect shared processes of self-government from the capricious and unaccountable rule of tyrants and mobs. Yet, citizens who value their liberty of self-government do not uniformly agree about what arbitrary power is injurious to the public welfare. Laws do not enjoy universal assent. And political communities are rarely unanimous in choosing which values the community accepts, and which values are so unacceptable as to merit sanction and punishment. Self-determination fractures agreement about what counts as lawful conduct. Lacking clear consensus on what constitutes the "public good," or what actions best promote the public interest, democracies continually, imperfectly, sort and divide lawful behavior from criminal/unlawful behavior. Though citizens are responsible for executing the law, laws are not self-executing; laws do not enforce themselves. Citizens empower police forces to create socially recognized order out of perceived chaos. When laws break down, or fail to corral violence, political communities rely on the police to enforce laws on those who do not (or will not) enforce it on themselves. Policing, at base, involves using force or the threat of force to compel some people to comply with social rules that other people regard as legitimate and just. To establish a police force is to recognize that *not all* democratic citizens abide by the laws they impose on themselves.

Nonetheless the state needs to balance the need for citizens to obey the law against the chaos created when police exercise power in ways citizens see as arbitrary. Following the rudimentary terms of a Hobbesian social contract, people surrender their right to seek private revenge for harm by entrusting the police to protect *us* from *one another*. The police are entrusted to defend what the public considers right; policing is the public exercise of power done in the public's interest. From the perspective of the police, maintaining order against the threat of chaos *is* the primary concern. Citizens who trust the police to enforce their will do not see a need to protect the public *from* a police force empowered to act in the public's interest. Citizens do not *expect* the police to become the threat themselves. Yet critics of policing rightly point out the folly of blindly trusting government and its agents, arguing that citizens often need protection from government—specifically protections from the use of force by the police. Ellroy's LA Quartet shows a police force that routinely uses violence against the people in the service of its own motives—motives often at odds with stated public interest. Rather than seeing the police as protecting citizens from themselves, citizens come to see the police as the instruments of chaos and tyranny.

Ellroy's LA Quartet expresses this duality: the police are empowered to contain brutality and violence, yet they also instigate their own brutality and violence. In Ellroy's fiction, the police subdue criminal vice and violence to maintain "law and order" while also engaging in vice advantageous to arrangements of power and control. For Ellroy, "'Brutality and cold calculation rule. It's a more truthful account of American history . . . than the official version and the Marxist revisionist version,' both of which . . . 'should be judged as equally fallacious.'"[5] Crime for Ellroy is not a simple case of deviant people breaking rules, nor is policing a simple case of chasing down bad people. Ellroy's LA Quartet embodies America's contradictory relationship with crime: Americans say they/we want law and order but their/our motives suggest that they/we remain enraptured by venal desires and perversions. The motives of criminals and cops are indistinct for Ellroy's characters, which makes the relationship between crime and policing in his novels more nuanced and interdependent than much of the surrounding mythology that characterizes crime as a contest between good/order and evil/chaos. In the LA Quartet, characters empowered to protect the public good often use that power in the service of baser motives; and characters' use of *power* tends to corrupt themselves and those around them. Power is used to dominate others, rather than resolve personal demons or elevate civic principles. As Ellroy describes, the struggle to preserve order and control is as much personal as social.

> Sloth and disorder could be sensual and seductive . . . You had to control. You had to assert. It got crazy and forced you to capitulate and surrender. Cheap pleasure was a damnable temptation. Booze and dope and random sex gave you back a cheap version of the power you're out to relinquish. They destroyed

> your will to live a decent life. They sparked crime. They destroyed social contracts. . . . Pundits blamed crime on poverty and racism. They were right. I saw crime as a concurrent moral plague with entirely empathetic origins. Crime was male energy displaced. Crime was a mass yearning for ecstatic surrender. Crime was romantic yearning gone bad. Crime was the sloth and disorder of individual default on an epidemic scale.[6]

Ellroy's characters pursue their own self-destruction while simultaneously longing for public and personal redemption. The use of violence and brutality in Ellroy's work is always searching for a justifying purpose. As ex-LAPD inspector and developer Preston Exley is fond of toasting in *L.A. Confidential*, "To the solving of crimes that require absolute justice."[7] In this respect, Ellroy's novels ask whether the public life of the implied social contract taking shape in Los Angeles during the 1940s and 1950s is worthy of preservation, survival, and the loyalty of its residents. Ellroy, in effect, asks whether the forgotten crimes and sins of previous generations can be redeemed by the emerging metropolis of Los Angeles. As Ed Exley learns In *L.A. Confidential*, the careers of current police and government officials are based upon corrupt deals from the past (some involving his father) built and secured out of the brutal acts of police violence (often disproportionately applied against black and brown Angelenos). Ellroy's novels question whether the virtue of "absolute justice" promised by a new Los Angeles can be freed from the vices of greed for wealth and fame, and the violence that accompanies that greed.

LOS ANGELES: A CITY OF FUTURE PROMISES AND PRESENT BRUTALITY

Behind Ellroy's fiction is a vision of civic life where the corrupt enforcing of virtues by the police is often indistinguishable from the debasing vices of criminals. Heroes do bad things, and villains are capable of heroic moments. Ellroy consciously deflates the hero worship of LA's celebrity culture that sells the illusion that people (and the police) are the best of what people *imagine* them to be (in the same way the history of Los Angeles is a civic history where developers manufacture and market ideals to build a city on the mythic appeal of sensual comfort and admiration). Los Angeles in the 1940s and 1950s is a city built on dreams of a beautiful and luxurious future. And to achieve this nirvana the current city needs to conceal the brutal and violent acts that could dispel the illusion. Ellroy sees something false and elusive about the American love of this popular fantasy. In talking about Bette Davis, but also reflecting on a broader American sentiment, Ellroy remarked, "She was always performing, she had the diva's phoney baloney affection for the hoi polloi. She had that effusive warmth that you see in actors that isn't real but is surely convincing,

American actors at least"[8] For Ellroy, the social order of Los Angeles is based on the ephemeral promise of the happiness that comes from adoration, of trying to feed the hunger to be loved and admired, a hunger that frustrates because it can never be satiated. And for Ellroy, *The Black Dahlia*, in a way, embodies this longing, a yearning for a love that, because it forever escapes people's grasp, generates frustrations that find release in perverse brutality.

THE BLACK DAHLIA AND VOYEURISTIC CULTURE

Ellroy's *The Black Dahlia* captures the trappings of a Los Angeles that promises wealth, status, and euphoria but delivers little. And this is part of the legacy of Southern California (and California more broadly), a region where promises of future paradise entice people to seek their fortunes by abandoning their homes, their familiar surroundings, and moving west. Early settlers in the mid-1840s migrated to California seeking this better life. The journalist Carey McWilliams once described these early residents of California's dream culture: "a large body of restless, adventuresome, single men . . . suddenly catapulted into a new and foreign land, with the excitement of gold in the air, and with no settled government to curb their predilection for violence and direct action."[9] In a similar fashion, Jim Mancall describes Ellroy's Los Angeles as "populated by orphans and failed families."[10] Faced with seemingly boundless possibilities to conquer a new land by starting anew, people migrating to California came to experience a frustration when promised future wealth did not come to fruition. By leaving their familiar worlds and traditions behind, these newcomers inadvertently cut themselves off from cultural restraints and institutions that tempered venal impulses. It is this movement of people away from the familiar, to chase visions of fame and success that Ellroy exposes as having a darker, more depraved, and potentially murderous quality. Once people cut themselves off from others, from those who know them, by geographically moving west, the resulting conditions of anonymity and isolation produce a longing to reach out to others, to connect, to *matter* to someone else.

Yet Ellroy's Los Angeles distorts this hunger for connection in *The Black Dahlia*. Ellroy's Los Angeles is a civic culture premised on voyeurism. Voyeurism implies a control without risking vulnerability. Those who derive pleasure from watching others do so without touching, without ever risking personal connection. The voyeur makes others (like the Black Dahlia/Elizabeth Short) the object of personal fantasy. Like all fantasies, the voyeur's dreams are based wholly on illusions. And when the fantasy of love and connection prove to be continually elusive and ephemeral, frustration quickly turns to a rage against the unattainable ideals of beauty and love.

In Ellroy's Los Angeles, the voyeuristic quality generates a civically destabilizing hunger for connection: a hunger for an imagined connection with the images other people represent. Ellroy's characters yearn for a meaningful human connection, yet seek solace with others through the emotionally distancing act of idealization. Such attempts at connection remain unsatisfying, leaving people less able to *see* one another as human beings with whom a common purpose can be found outside of bodily desires. Voyeurs covet (and create) visual images of others they long to connect with, yet they risk nothing of their own vulnerability in the process. Because the promise of human connection without human vulnerability cannot serve as a foundation for civic life, the needs of affection and friendship necessary for citizenship never get met. As a result, the civic life atrophies: Los Angeles in the 1940s and 1950s develops into a growing metropolis that does not bring people together, but rather reinforces their separateness. What civic cohesion exists in Ellroy's novels is brought together through force and the ever-present threat of violence.

The Black Dahlia centers around a partnership between two cops and one woman (Lee Blanchard, Dwight Bleichert, and Kay Lake) who try to maintain relative codes of honor and moral conduct in a city that appears to only value the hollow prestige of glory and appearance.

Bleichert recognizes that the foundations that bind him to Lee and Kay, for example, are tenuous and threatened by the deceptions of their past. "I thought of all the things I'd have to explain to Kay, evidence to keep a new foundation of lies from destroying the two—or three—of us."[11] Maintaining a sense of right and wrong allows people to condemn, stand up to, and challenge corruption as wrong. Amidst perversions, there *must be* a code or an ethic to guide personal actions.

Ellroy shows how police officers, who do not embody *pure* ethical codes, defend values that serve as touchstones amidst a climate of depravity. Even though Bleichert gets a reputation as a "sob sister" who is cited in a fitness report for his "reluctance to employ sufficient force with recalcitrant misdemeanants"[12] he maintains an ethical line he will not cross, separating him from the "truly corrupt" cop Fritzie Vogel (who knowingly tortures innocent people to extract a confession). As Bleichert reflects, "my horror pushed me where I'd been too scared and stupid to go for a long, long time."[13] Despite the deceptions and double-crosses, Ellroy's protagonist Bleichert maintains a struggle to uphold a moral code by continuing to investigate the murder of The Black Dhalia Elizabeth Short. Without collective civic principles that serve as a moral compass the lines between enemies and friends are not as reliable or clear as Elloy's characters might hope. And without a code or standard by which one can judge conduct as right or wrong, the rule of force can end up creating its own standards. As Ellroy shows, the police then become the instruments of force empowered to impose those standards of right and wrong.

WILLIAM PARKER'S "THE THIN BLUE LINE" AND THE MYTHOLOGY OF POLICING

Ellroy's LA Quartet stands at the inflection point of the police force as a law unto themselves and efforts by William Parker to transform the LAPD into a more professionalized police department. Prior to the reforms of former Los Angeles police chief William H. Parker, the LAPD was viewed as a kind of mercenary army at the service of mob faction who could afford to buy or bribe the police. As John Buntin describes this early period in the history of the LAPD,

> Officers on the front lines of the effort to police the underworld often faced a stark choice: break the law and accept bribes from the saloonkeepers, madams, and gambling house operators who were bankrolling the politicians or refuse bribes, enforce the law, and risk being fired or assigned to direct traffic on the graveyard shift down at the port of San Pedro.[14]

But modern policing in America embodies Chief William H. Parker's metaphor that the police function as a "thin blue line" that protects civilians from criminals. Parker, Chief of the LAPD from 1950–1966 thought the LAPD should emulate the United States Marines in structure and operations. For Parker, the LAPD should become the "thin blue line" protecting vulnerable citizens from predatory criminal forces of evil. Parker's effort to transform the LAPD from a community-policing model, where the police officers were beholden to elected officials and ward politicians to a more professional, yet militaristic, force was both a response to circumstances and generated new dynamics of social unrest. Parker developed a media relations strategy and professionalized police force that was answerable to administrative oversight rather than politicians. His more professional civil servant model of the police was modeled on a military peacekeeping strategy of heavily armed mobile response units. As George Kelling describes, Parker's moralistic transformation of the LAPD took hold in the popular imagination during the 1950s. And it is this image of the police as the morally pure defenders of good that Ellroy's LA Quartet challenges.

> In Parker's day, police reformers' most important goal was to transform the nation's police forces from sloppy, patronage-ridden, often corrupt municipal agencies with a distracting array of duties into highly disciplined, professional anticrime forces. To do this, they tried to make police forces more like military

> units. Parker's image of a "thin blue line" arrayed against the "forces of evil" captured the imagination of police and public alike and helped build that military ethos. Decades after Parker coined it, the image still wields considerable power, showing up not only in self-congratulatory speeches at union meetings, but in police textbooks as well.[15]

For Ellroy these metaphors of policing and crime shield citizens from the perversions and violence that define the world depicted in the LA Quartet: a world shaped more by depravity than the illusory and virtuous "order" promoted and promised by Parker's LAPD. Though Ellroy exposes Parker's vision as an illusion, it is an illusion capable of creating its own truth. By moving away from foot patrols to officer patrolling in cars (Parker believed isolating officers from the streets would reduce opportunities for corruption), the LAPD exacerbated tensions between different cultures in Los Angeles, heightening animosity toward (and between) African Americans and Latinos.[16]

This ideal of policing sees the police as protectors of community, dedicated civil servants, sworn to protect and serve. Yet, at base, Parker's model of policing represents the failure of a community to inculcate its values into the population. If there are police, then there are criminals, people who disobey the law; people who are not doing what they are told, or what they should be doing. Yet, the public good is not defined by reflexively obeying the law; nor is disobeying the law neither automatically a threat to the common good. In a culture where the attractions and rewards of obeying the law, "playing by the rules" do not offer rewards that compete with the desire to be famous or admired, Parker wanted the police empowered to protect the public good. But obeying the laws of the regime must prove to be its own reward, and not just stand as an elusive ideal. Civic ideals must hold value in the larger culture, and Ellroy shows that the civic ideals of postwar Los Angeles are betrayed by violent contests for power and status. There is no coherent collective goal driving the LAPD in Ellroy's Los Angeles. The alluring desire for power, fame, and glamour draws people away from publicly defending the collective values that sustain democratic life.

Ellroy's LA Quartet does not dress up vice as virtue, or pretend that heroes are purifying forces for the causes of democratic goodness. In this respect, there is a democratic humanist quality to Ellroy: the protagonists are not heroes who transcend the human condition of having to wrestle with the pull of virtues and vices. In this respect, Ellroy's LA Quartet embodies part of the condition of democratic life where citizens must choose between good and evil courses of action without having complete information or knowing whether their choice is the morally good choice or not. Ellroy strips democratic life of the illusions and myths that allow citizens to rest comfortably in the confidence that the ends of *their* political community are unassailable and virtuous.

When a police officer once asked Ellroy, "why all the cops (in his novel *White Jazz*) were extortionists and perverts" Ellroy responded that "good cops made for bad fiction."[17] Ellroy's response captures the pervasive acceptance of Parker's metaphor for how the public expects the police *should* relate to citizens. As Kelling describes,

> this vivid image has many implications. It splits the world into friend and foe. On one side are citizens; on the other, forces of evil; between them, the thin blue line of heroes. The metaphor urges a passive citizenry: Police keep the beast at bay, while citizens are noncombatants, ceding streets to barbarians and police.[18]

This invitation to passivity reduces citizens to obedient subjects. In safe and orderly neighborhoods, citizens, not police, are the prime keepers of the peace. In unsafe and chaotic neighborhoods, the police are at war with criminals who threaten the civic peace. Countering this image of the police as keepers of the peace, Jane Jacobs writes,

> the first thing to understand is that the public peace—the sidewalk and street peace—of cities is not kept primarily by the police, necessary as police are. It is kept primarily by an intricate, almost unconscious, network of voluntary control and standards among the people themselves, and enforced by the people themselves.[19]

Despite Jacobs' faith in a "network of voluntary control and standards", the lack of order and control does not automatically generate the goods of democratic life. Americans find "bad cops" entertaining because bad cops are largely the dramatic exception, rather than the rule. And though Americans will acknowledge a criminal justice system as corrupt, they/we will not accept a criminal justice system that is irredeemably corrupt. When the public regards the whole system of dispensing justice as corrupt, then citizens lose confidence in civic institutions designed to secure public justice. As Killing remarks, "[d]isorder, left untended, increases citizen fear and leads to more severe disorder, resulting, as a good deal of research has shown, in serious crime."[20] And in the face of such disorder, violence becomes a more common response. Corruption erodes the place of civic values to guide conduct, leaving the rule of force and violence to take its place. As Buntin describes, "Cops sometimes acted violently because they believed the system was corrupt."[21]

To remedy corruption, and restore public trust in law enforcement, community policing is offered as a possible reform for rebuilding connections between the police and the communities they serve. Yet, as Ellroy's LA Quartet shows, community policing slips easily into corruption when the police become *too* responsive and beholden to politicians and community patronage. The unspoken partnerships between organized crime and the LAPD fostered by Dudley Smith in *L.A. Confidential*, where "a certain organized crime element should be allowed to exist and perpetuate acceptable vices that hurt no one" reflect a degenerate application of the cooperative partnership imagined by ideals of community policing.[22] Community policing, despite its noble intentions, may mean making peace with the kind of corruption that comes with bending to local standards, where people plead (and pay) officers to "look the other way" to let *their* transgression of the law pass. Policing can also suffer from the corruption of becoming too professional, too much like the military, where civilians are to be corralled and managed, rather than being treated as citizens, who share responsibility for self-governance and enforcing the law.

THE ILLUSION OF "ABSOLUTE JUSTICE"

Ellroy's epigraph to *L.A. Confidential* captures the conceit animating real-life William H. Parker's quest to reform the LAPD during the 1950s. Confronted with a police force regarded as notoriously corrupt for partnering with partisan political groups and organized crime to operate vice and street corruption, Parker sought to become a police chief not beholden to elected politicians or mob bosses. *L.A. Confidential* challenges the assumption that order will inevitably vanquish chaos; that the police will reliably preserve the good; and that civic order will elevate virtue while suppressing vice. This idealism is encapsulated by Preston Exley's favorite toast: "[t]o the solving of crimes that require absolute justice."[23] The pursuit of "absolute justice" becomes an ideal around which to anchor the diverse cultures and communities that continually shift and change in postwar Los Angeles. Ellroy's LA of the 1940s and 1950s is an expansive, sprawling metropolis where people come to reinvent themselves in the quest for fame and a new start. Lacking the established attachments of tradition and inherited geographic customs, newly arrived residents to LA form civic attachments to narrower communities of race, neighborhood, and ethnicity. And the human diversity of an evolving Los Angeles does not coalesce around the ideals of absolute justice—at least the absolute justice represented by the police characters in Ellroy's novels.

Ellroy's characters show the way contradictions between professed ideals, personal ambitions, and lived experiences are never fully resolved: sometimes what is best in people wins, sometimes what is worst wins, and sometimes all that characters (and readers) are left with are inconclusive stalemates. Despite the nihilistic implications of the novels, Ellroy's characters continue the struggle to preserve what they/we believe to be right, while also seeking an elusive redemption for their sins and transgressions. Ellroy's protagonists in the LA Quartet still recognize that doing wrong *does* defile one's character. And Ellroy's characters still build, and depend upon, bonds of friendship that support one another. In the end, even though Ellory blurs the lines between heroes and villains, the larger civic order is still preserved and protected by characters who actively defend principles capable of promoting civic life.

CONCLUSION: THE NIHILISM DEMOCRATIC CITIZENS HAVE TO FEAR

Ellroy's LA Quartet depicts a world of civic corruption and venal motives that democratic communities still have to defend against. In this respect, the novels offer insights into the dualism of a utopian temperament in LA that relies on force and violence to maintain order. Writing in the magazine PM in 1945, Max Lerner remarked that

> Our living standards are higher than in any other country in the world, but there is also a greater gap between lowest and highest than anywhere else. Ours is the land of success, but for every successful man there are hundreds unsuccessful. We have deep psychic hungers, all of us—hungers for money or power or dazzling beauty or acclaim.[24]

Ellroy's LA exacerbates that hunger, and amplifies it. Amidst the competition for status and fame, Ellroy shows a side of America that indirectly wills a kind of nihilism, people caught up in seeking the glamour and power that comes from appearing desirable. Such people do not seek the recognition that comes from enduring friendships and embracing responsibility for maintaining civic values. This is the paradox of Ellroy's police officers: though they are servants of the public trust who work to "protect and serve" they also cannot escape the allure of Hollywood glamour, as well as its inevitable moral trappings and compromises.

Yet, when the institutions people trust fail to meet public demands for justice, and reprehensible private conduct (though publicly condemned) is largely given a pass, then the deep psychic hungers Max Lerner describes generate an aimless mob anger. Such mob anger expresses its rage indiscriminately and often violently. Mob justice and tyranny continue to threaten democratic life since both silence citizens into forms of voicelessness. Amidst the isolation and anonymity of the mob (online and in public) no one person's voice matters, only the most extreme and strident voices get heard. Widespread support that makes policing and the criminal justice system legitimate depends upon the public's claims for justice being heard and then made part of the institutions of government. When the public does not support the police or regard the criminal justice procedures as only benefiting some at the expense of others, public confidence in the principles that animate the regime fades. And if people question the justice of the rule of law, then the legitimacy of the democratic state is at risk—with the alternatives being ruled by the tyranny of force or the capricious whims of mob justice.

Southern Californians, journalist Carey McWilliams once wrote, are "haunted by a vague and nameless fear of future disaster."[25] For Ellroy, growing up in 1950s Los Angeles, that fear was, in part, the threat of a nuclear World War III. For contemporary Americans, the "nameless fear of future disaster" now has many names: government corruption; pollution; climate change; war; global pandemics; economic or financial collapse (to name only a few).[26] This haunting feeling can dispel hope, and turn people toward hedonistic nihilism. Ellroy's novels capture a perverse self-indulgence fueled by Los Angeles, a place where defending civic values of compromise and sacrifice cannot deliver the glitz or glamour promised by Hollywood. A place where people are encouraged to indulge their private debauchery rather than build the public confidence necessary for imagining a better collective future. Writing in 1946, Carey McWilliams observed,

> Incessant migration has made Los Angeles a vast drama of maladjustment: social, familial, civic, and personal. . . . When so many people have nothing meaningful to do with their time, nothing real with which to occupy their minds, they indulge in fantasy, in silly daydreams, in perversions, and occasionally, in monstrous crimes. Social neuroticism is a distinct phenomenon in Los Angeles. . . . Los Angeles is the kind of place where perversion is perverted and prostitution prostituted. . . . There can be no doubt that Los Angeles has paid a high price for its repaid growth. The price is indicated in the pathology rates in many categories: suicides, divorces, crime, juvenile delinquency, bankruptcies, narcotic addition, and so forth. In a community made up largely of newcomers, as Charles N. Reynolds has pointed out "social control agencies such as the opinion of neighbors, friends, or relatives are weakened or absent and the law itself fails to function as it should." The boom-cycle largely accounts for the curious lack of social continuity in Southern California.[27]

This lack of social continuity puts the question of reforming policing in a fragile light. Without a criminal justice system that citizens regard as fair or just, citizens will continue to regard policing as the imposition of arbitrary rules by the strong over the weak, by the well-connected over the disenfranchised, and by the wealthy over the destitute. There is no civic hope for such a community, no belief or faith in a common better future. Such emptiness may lie in the heart of Ellroy's LA Quartet, novels that portray Los Angeles as a paradigm, and a warning, for an American form of nihilism: the false promise that fame and glamour can satisfy Americans' "psychic hungers for money or power or dazzling beauty or acclaim."

NOTES

1. https://www.elle.com/culture/celebrities/a40679818/ana-de-armas-boyfriend-paul-boukadakis-tinder-exec/
2. https://www.lapdonline.org/lapd-motto/ (Accessed November 23, 2022).
3. James Ellroy, *The Black Dahlia* (New York: Grand Central Publishing, 2006), 369.
4. Martha Nussbaum, *Political Emotions* (Cambridge, MA: Belknap/Harvard University Press, 2015), 2.
5. Chris Harvey interview with James Ellroy, September 10, 2014. http://www.telegraph.co.uk/culture/books/booknews/11048653/James-Ellroy-interview-for-Perfidia-I-have-a-penchant-for-the-extreme.html
6. Ellroy, *My Dark Places*, 354.
7. James Ellroy, *L.A. Confidential* (New York: Grand Central Publishing, 1997), 19.
8. Chris Harvey interview with James Ellroy, September 10, 2014. http://www.telegraph.co.uk/culture/books/booknews/11048653/James-Ellroy-interview-for-Perfidia-I-have-a-penchant-for-the-extreme.html
9. McWilliams, *Southern California*, 58.
10. Jim Mancall, *James Ellroy: A Companion to the Mystery Fiction* (Jefferson, NC: McFarland and Company, 2014), 36.
11. Ellroy, *The Black Dahlia*, 357.
12. Ellroy, *The Black Dahlia*, 215.
13. Ellroy, *The Black Dahlia*, 213.
14. John Buntin, *L.A. Noir: The Struggle for the Soul of America's Most Seductive City* (New York, NY: Broadway Books, 2009), 34.
15. George L. Kelling, "Crime and Metaphor: Toward a New Concept of Policing," *City Journal*, Autumn 1991 (https://www.city-journal.org/html/crime-and-metaphor-toward-new-concept-policing-12733.html). Accessed January 6, 2023.
16. Kelling, "Crime and Metaphor: Toward a New Concept of Policing."
17. James Ellroy, *My Dark Places* (New York: Vintage Books, 1996), 254.
18. Kelling, "Crime and Metaphor: Toward a New Concept of Policing."
19. Kelling, "Crime and Metaphor: Toward a New Concept of Policing."
20. Kelling, "Crime and Metaphor: Toward a New Concept of Policing."
21. Buntin, *L.A. Noir*, 36
22. Ellroy, *L.A. Confidential*, 70.
23. Ellroy, *L.A. Confidential*, 19.
24. Max Lerner, quoted in McWilliams, *Southern California*, 310.
25. McWilliams, *Southern California*, 199.
26. https://blogs.chapman.edu/wilkinson/2022/10/14/the-top-10-fears-in-america-2022/ (Accessed March 15, 2023).
27. McWilliams, *Southern California*, 239.

BIBLIOGRAPHY

Buntin, John. *L.A. Noir: The Struggle for the Soul of America's Most Seductive City*. New York: Broadway Books, 2009.

Ellroy, James. *The Black Dahlia*. New York: Grand Central Publishing, 2006.

The Big Nowhere. New York: Grand Central Publishing, 1998.

L.A. Confidential. New York: Grand Central Publishing, 1997.

White Jazz. New York: Vintage Books, 1992.

My Dark Places: An L.A. Crime Memoir. New York: Vintage Books, 1997.

Mancall, Jim. *James Ellroy: A Companion to the Mystery Fiction*. Jefferson, NC: McFarland and Company, 2014.

McWilliams, Carey. *Southern California: An Island on the Land*. Layton, UT: Gibbs Smith, 1973.

Chapter 7

The Guy Who Gets Away with It

Law, Justice, and Violence in the Film LA Confidential

Paul Babbitt

INTRODUCTION

LA Confidential is a highly regarded film, nominated for nine Oscars including Best Picture and winning two. Almost all reviews available on the website Rotten Tomatoes are positive. However, Ellroy himself seems to be unhappy with the film, saying "it is about as deep as a tortilla." Nevertheless, Ellroy does think *LA Confidential* is the best film adaptation of his work.[1] As the film proceeds, it takes some time before the viewer (especially a viewer unfamiliar with the novel) can begin to understand how the various episodes and characters relate to one another. While there has been considerable scholarly attention to detective fiction in general, and James Ellroy's work in particular, including *LA Confidential*, scholars have not looked much at the film adaptation of the novel. Police corruption is an important theme as well, but the film does not present "dirty cops" as an exception to be ferreted out but rather as norm of police conduct. Police are not enforcers of a law, but are rather entitled to use their monopoly on violence and all police are to a greater or lesser degree complicit. The film, like the writings discussed throughout this book, explores the "dark places" of Los Angeles and the United States: There is no real line between the law-abiding and the lawbreakers, there are merely those agents of violence who are recognized as legitimate—the police—and those who are not—the criminals.

Noir is a genre found in both films and literature. A clear and concise definition of noir is elusive, but for our purposes, the film *LA Confidential* includes violence, a suspicion of sex and sexuality especially female sexuality verging on the puritanical, a general posture of amorality, and of course a setting in the Los Angeles of the 1950s. In many respects, noir films are more well regarded as classic of cinema than the novels on which they were based, many now forgotten. Ellroy's novels, however, have resisted successful adaptation, with *LA Confidential* being an exception. Though there are common elements in both in terms of plotting and character, film, as visual medium, has specific stylistic cues of its own. Both the novel and the film depict a great deal of violence, but the visual depiction of the violence results in it becoming a central subject in the narrative. *LA Confidential* was one of several violent "neo-noir" films of the 1990s that presented an amoral fantasy world that reflected the widespread anxieties about crime, but also one where there were concerns with the abuse of police power. These films were not realistic, nor were they intended to be. Finally, though much is made of Ellroy's biography when approaching his writing, the film, as an adaptation, is somewhat removed from Ellroy's life.

The film deserves attention on its own merit, not simply as a derivative work of the novel. There are some critical differences, especially in the ending. Furthermore, the film by necessity streamlines the plot, with the result that the complex racial and economic geography of Los Angeles, and the construction of its now emblematic and problematic highways and theme parks receiving substantially less attention. Another critical difference is time. The events depicted in the novel take place over seven years. The film is not specific in the duration of the events, but it is a substantially compressed timeline. One other point of contrast is the muting of Ellroy's distinctive style from the film. Many critics note Ellroy's staccato voice that runs in the novel, with clauses and other fragments in place of sentences. However, the clipped descriptive sentences are mostly missing from the dialog. Instead, the film's dialog is natural. While the novel is clearly the work of an author with an immediately recognizable voice, the film depends on extensive use of close-ups and adherence to a historically consistent look. The music tends toward the popular music of the era, with a handful of jazz pieces that are often associated with Ellroy's writing. Perhaps the most striking difference, though, was how the audience would perceive the event in the film. It was released in 1997, as police violence was receiving more attention, particularly, though not exclusively in Los Angeles. Whether or not the filmmakers intended to make such commentary, the film could not help but remind the audience of cases of police brutality such as that against Abner Louima and Rodney King. However, the 1990s were also a period of heightened concern about crime. Many places, including California, passed draconian sentencing laws such as the "three strikes you're out" which provided for lengthy sentences after three felony convictions even if the third conviction was for a minor offense. The California law was passed by voter initiative in 1994.

Police violence is a major element of the film, and while it is set in the past, the reality of police violence was highly salient to the contemporary viewers of the film as it is today. The film presents police violence (and most of the violence in the film is in fact committed by the police) as systematic and routine. On the other hand, much like harsh criminal laws passed during the 1990s, the police and the political leadership believe that the "law-abiding" people demand these extreme tactics. Thus, it provides its viewer an explanation as to why police violence occurs. To be sure, the motivations of the characters differ—for some it is a means to further the corruption, while for others it is vengeance. None, however question whether violence is appropriate. It is not an aberrant behavior on the part of a few bad cops. Instead, it serves several purposes, among those are it maintains racial and other hierarchies. Furthermore, it provides a foundation for all social and political authority. At the same time, the police are increasingly concerned about their image, which serves to establish that the police are the "good guys" even as they routinely violate the civil rights and civil liberties of their victims. Though the use of violence may be justified as necessary to stop violent criminals, it turns out that routine police violence provides important tools to help the police cover up their own criminal activities. The routine acceptance of violence in law enforcement means violence can be used in the commission of crime as well without receiving unwanted attention.

The film has a second theme, intertwined with, and ultimately merged with the first: The political use of illusion in maintaining authority. Many characters in the film construct and maintain a fantasy of life in postwar Los Angeles—Hollywood entertainment of course, but city officials and of course law enforcement. Law and justice are the fantasy, violence is the reality. But more than that, power is essential to maintain the fantasy. As the film progresses, it illustrates the way that authority itself is an illusion. Illusion and authority serve to reinforce one another. Neither by themselves are sufficient to establish authority, much less legitimate it. There needs to be a narrative. Violence and illusion are both part of the narrative necessary for the maintenance of authority.

The film makes clear that it intends to offer some social and political commentary in its opening sequence, a brief introduction about the fantasy of a Los Angeles good life that does not exist. This introduction uses film clips that appear to be from historical archives, and they are shots that could be from civic promotional material as well as clips of celebrities from the 1950s such as Frank Sinatra and Marilyn Monroe, though the narration, provided by Danny Devito who plays reporter Sid Hudgens is sardonic. These opening scenes also explain how the television show "Badge of Honor" (based on Dragnet) provide "copaganda," essentially an hour every week extolling the virtues of the Los Angeles Police Department. This introduction then moves to black-and-white clips of people with what appear to be heroin and large amounts of cash, interspersed with new footage specifically from the film shot in the 1990s. It also turns out that Hudgens who writes for the tabloid *Hush Hush* will be an important figure as the film unfolds. These clips conclude with a discussion of the arrest of an organized crime boss Mickey Cohen. Eventually, we learn that the arrest of Cohen serves as the catalyst of the action of the film.

These clips establish a historical context of the film's setting. Though the use of what appears to be historical footage might suggest otherwise, the purpose is not to evoke nostalgia. Rather, the gradual transition, moving back and forth from historical to contemporary footage, and clips of the good life to clips of criminal activity serve to establish continuity from the world the film depicts, the 1950s, to the world in which the film was released, the 1990s. *LA Confidential* shows the social and political problems regarding crime and race, and especially the problem of police using violence without consequence has a long and dark history. Its historical setting reflects our contemporary issues back onto us. The film remains a potent if ambivalent comment on the relationship between the law and violence, and ways in which state authority ultimately depends on its willingness to use violence beyond the proscription of the law. That is, the law is not statutes and constitutions, but how the state authority uses violence to enforce racial and other hierarchies. Especially the first half of the film is an exploration of how violence is the foundation of power and authority.

This first part of the film presents a series of seemingly unconnected episodes of police enforcing and reinforcing these hierarchies. Before the viewer can really grasp the plot, these scenes establish the manner in which the police use violence to maintain the hierarchies. The police are not vigilantes; their use of violence is officially sanctioned and encouraged by those in power. This violence is acceptable because of the illusion that the police are good, they "walk on water" to use the phrase from the beginning of the film. Courts and judges, even prisons, barely exist. In order to be able to enforce and thus establish the law the police not only solve crimes and apprehend suspects, but also deliver punishment. Many suspects in fact are summarily executed, not charged and tried, and this is considered justice. The political leadership of the police and the city itself believe, likely correctly, that the public (at least the white public) demands this violent, direct approach to law enforcement. Law and justice are distinct ways in which power and violence manifest themselves. Thus, the movie provides an illustration of a Hobbesian sovereign, one where power is the source of not just authority, but law and justice.

THE FILM

LA Confidential was one of several notable neo-noir films of the 1990s. It shares with these films a Los Angeles setting, which allows a contrast between Southern California's natural beauty and favorable weather and the corruption and sordidness of the people who live there. It is notable that some of the climatic scenes are set during heavy rain, thus pushing the contrast even further. Costuming, sets, props, and dialog serve to locate the film in a specific time and place, Los Angeles of the 1950s. Locating the film in this time period establishes its "neo-noir" atmosphere (though the film eschews many conventions of film noir) and by setting the viewer at a distance, the film is more able to allow its characters to express the racist, sexist, and homophobic prejudices of its day.[2] Ironically, though, it turns out that the real Los Angeles of the 1950s was closer to the fantasy laid out in the beginning than the violent and corrupt city where the film is set. Good jobs were available, and land was cheap. Thus, crime itself was part of an illusion used to justify police violence which served the interests of police corruption.

Like the novel, the film centers around three detectives, Bud White, Jack Vincennes, and Ed Exley. They are wrapped up in a set of sensational and horrific but seemingly unconnected crimes—a series of murders of organized crime figures, a pornography and prostitution ring, and a brutal multiple homicide in the Nite Owl coffee shop. Each is connected with one of the three detectives who exhibit contrasting and incompatible types of police officers. Bud White (played by Russell Crowe) is a detective who engages in vigilante prosecution of men who commit domestic violence. He is a cruel and violent man, lacking the ability to control his anger. Jack Vincennes (Kevin Spacey) works as a technical consultant to the show "Badge of Honor" but also provides the tabloid *Hush Hush* with exclusive coverage of arrests of minor Hollywood figures. Edmund Exley (Guy Pearce) is young, very politically savvy, and ambitious but also idealistic. He is presented as uptight, following the letter of the law and college-educated. All are, in their own way, complicit in the corruption of the police department and serve to support the power that runs the city. Though all have a sense of personal morality, all also easily compromise that morality with little regret or hesitation. The three crimes and the detectives engaged with them turn out to be intertwined in a conspiracy that reaches the highest levels. The detectives come together when three suspects, accused of attacking police officers, are arrested and subject to a beating by the police who had been drinking during a Christmas party. White refuses to testify against the other police. Exley by contrast works out a way to salvage the department's reputation which involves White temporarily losing his position and pressuring Vincennes to testify. Thus, the three main characters are now enemies. Exley also earns the hostility of most other police officers.

Though the novel has a considerable number of secondary characters, the film has four critical supporting roles—Ellis Loew, the district attorney, and Dudley Smith, a police captain who are working together to take over organized crime in Los Angeles. Sid Hudgens, a tabloid reporter for *Hush Hush* who works with Vincennes and finds personal profit in exposing the illusions of Hollywood while creating his own. Finally, Lynn Bracken is a prostitute made up to look like Veronica Lake, one of several prostitutes working for Pierce Patchett who often has them undergo plastic surgery to look like movie stars.

POLICE VIOLENCE

Racially charged police violence could not be presented in the film as part of a shameful past. Between the publication of the novel in 1990 and the release of the film in 1997, the police beating of Rodney King highlighted the continuing problem of police violence in Los Angeles and the United States more generally. Viewers of the film would see police violence in a different context than readers of the book. Specifically, filmgoers would not see the kind of violence portrayed in the film as something from a distant past, but as an ongoing problem that if anything was more severe in the 1990s. A reader of the novel might be able to consider that the events depicted occurred before major Supreme Court decisions such as *Miranda v. Arizona*, *Mapp v. Ohio*, and *Gideon v. Wainright* and guaranteed civil liberties for those accused of crimes. The Rodney King case, combined with revelations from the O. J. Simpson trial exposed the routine violation of these rights. By the 1990s, the Los Angeles Police Department was increasingly perceived as a paramilitary organization under the leadership of its chief Darrell Gates. Its role was less law enforcement than occupying force. This is clearly depicted in the film in the scenes taking place in African-American neighborhoods. The film therefore forces the viewer to confront ways in which police violence is far from an anomaly, the result of a few "bad cops" who abuse their authority but instead use violence as a way to institute an authoritarian ideology under which the designation of "criminal" has to do with one's relation to power rather than one's activity. The criminal is labeled as such regardless of whether such a person has broken any laws, while a police officer is above the law. Setting the film in the 1950s, in the context of increasing attention to police violence in the 1990s, serves as a commentary on how despite civil rights and court precedents protecting the rights of the accused, little has changed.

Compared to the novel, the film may seem to downplay the racism of its characters and the system in which they work. Race and white supremacy are but part of the historical context of the film. The main characters themselves do not directly express racist sentiments, though they have no problem accepting and exploiting the racial hierarchies that place them at the top. At least some critics of Ellroy's work claim that much of the racism and sexism expressed by those characters are not central characteristics but instead used for effect.[3] The film therefore may be seen as consistent with the novel. Regardless of their personal bigotry and racial animosity or lack thereof, the characters work to preserve the racial hierarchies. Merely changing laws and procedures are inadequate; their racism is not merely structural but involves the character's "soul blindness" where Black lives do not matter.[4] The film itself need not make this claim explicit, as the fact that racially motivated police violence remains a serious problem in the late 1990s or beyond. Thus, racism is presented as a product of socially embedded hierarchies. Racially motivated police violence is not the problem of individual bigoted police officers (though many are bigots) but of a racist system.

As far as gender, even more so than the novel, women are essentially invisible, victims but little else. Even Lynn Bracken, played by Kim Basinger who is credited with a starring role, has little agency. Unlike the racial hierarchies the film presents, gender hierarchies are left unexamined and accepted as natural. To be sure, White, himself a victim of domestic violence as a boy that resulted in his murder, takes it upon himself to try to protect women who are victims of violence, but there is little analysis or exploration of this motif beyond seeing it as a consequence of White's trauma. Not only does White not see how gender hierarchies are at the root of this problem, but he himself beats Bracken when he discovers she has had sex with Exley, thus demonstrating that he fails to question gender hierarchies.

Finally, the film continues to comment on these hierarchies in its treatment of sexuality, particularly homosexuality. Like most noir, sexual attraction of any kind commonly results in the character's downfall—it is something dark and dangerous, something that cannot be controlled. *LA Confidential* like much noir, presents men's desire as a weakness to be exploited. Though the *femme fatale* is not as prominent in *LA Confidential* as it is in other neo-noir films, it is present. Furthermore, several characters, including District Attorney Loew, are vulnerable to blackmail due to their homosexuality. *Hush Hush* commonly accuses Hollywood celebrities of homosexual behavior.

Since *LA Confidential* is a work of fiction and not a work of political philosophy, its commitments regarding politics, justice, and violence are ambiguous. However, it provides an illustration of the relationship between violence, power, and authority. It shows how those forces work to maintain social hierarchies, especially along racial and economic dimensions. The hierarchy matters more than law or justice. The police are not enforcing the law so much as creating a law, and thus are able to provide the delivery of illegal vices including heroin, prostitution, and pornography, but in such a way that the presence of these services does not disrupt the lives of ordinary, law-abiding citizens referenced in the beginning of the film. It presents a world where not only do the police have a monopoly on the legitimate use of violence in order to enforce the law, but they also have a monopoly on the "legitimate" use of violence in committing illegal activities. Thus, in short, the government, backed by police violence, is really nothing more than a protection racket. However, it may be the case that like Hobbes, the film is arguing that justice is nothing more nor less than the use of legitimate violence.

The police are a criminal organization that functions with immunity. They are not trying to prevent crime so much as they are trying to control it. There is in fact a conspiracy within the department, headed by Smith, that is trying to establish a monopoly on criminal activities in Los Angeles. Their job is to maintain order within this underworld and make sure underworld activities are contained to neighborhoods populated by lower-income communities and communities of color. There are several characteristics presented in the film that demonstrate this. When two suspects are severely beaten by police officers who had been drinking at a Christmas party, White refuses to testify against his partner or any other police officer. Exley, commenting on this, says the other police officers "believe silence and integrity are the same thing." Exley does not yet understand that since the foundation of police authority is not their integrity, but their capacity to inflict violence, that in fact silence is the same thing as integrity given how the police function. That is, if the police are subject to the law, then they cannot perform their function. Thus, silence is necessary to avoid prosecution by laws. White, who participated in the violence, avoids significant punishment because Smith sees him as a "valuable police officer" specifically because he is willing to do those things Exley would not. Nevertheless, because he is willing to cooperate with the investigation into the police violence, he receives a promotion to detective lieutenant.

This scene is followed by a significant scene where Smith gives White his badge back, and sets up a contrast between "direct" men like Smith and politicians like Exley, though both are necessary. The film also makes clear that there is now a central conflict between White and Exley. In the world of *LA Confidential*, there is no effective independent standard of justice or law. There is only power and force; the willingness to use violence. This is not to say the world is an anarchical state of nature. Rule of law prevails. However, it is not the rule of law of the Enlightenment, one that functions to preserve the social order necessary for liberty. Rather, owing to the distinction developed by Judith Shklar, it is an Aristotelian rule of law. This version of the rule of law only applies to men, with women and slaves outside of public justice, ruled by a "domestic economy."[5] These people are not fully human and thus may be subject to whatever brutality deemed is necessary to keep them subservient. The police are the instrument assigned the role of maintaining that hierarchy while those at the top of the hierarchy are subject to different standards of law. Therefore, the film makes the argument that a pre-modern account of law and justice is still influential in American law enforcement.

Another important lens to consider in viewing the film is the purpose of violence. A common definition of the state is that it has a monopoly on the legitimate use of force. The police in *LA Confidential* use violence as a matter of routine. Since as police officers, they are representative of the state, the violence they use is state-sanctioned. Thus, we are forced to confront the idea that the violence suits the purpose of the state. The film then makes clear that what government means is the ability of the strong to inflict violence on the weak. As with Hobbes, the individual officers and the police department believe state violence is justified in the preservation of order. The sovereignty of the police entails that the police cannot violate the law; they make the law. The question is whether the film supports this view. Violence is central to establishing the authority of the police department and by extension the power brokers of the city itself. That is, police violence does not undermine the authority of the city's establishment by making the police an institution outside the control of the city's political and economic elite. Rather, the violence serves to establish and maintain that elite. Even beyond that, violence is constitutive of law and authority, creating its legitimacy.

Violence is a critical concept in politics and political science, but its political and social function can be difficult to analyze, and there seems to be little consensus about its functional and normative role in political society. Film generally, and *LA Confidential* specifically can expose the difficulty of attempting to make general claims about the politics of violence. Raymond Geuss argues that violence is best understood as a description of behavior, one that need not have any political content. It can serve a specific purpose, or no purpose at all. Coercion, by contrast, may entail the use of violence.[6] In *LA Confidential*, we see violence used for several reasons, including following Geuss for coercive purposes as well as blind rage.

The use of violence goes beyond an attempt to establish "law and order" though. More to the point, a violent and unaccountable police force serves the authoritarian government. The film might be making a point along the lines of Judith Shklar's liberalism of fear:

> Given the inevitability of that inequality of military, police, and persuasive power which is called government, there is evidently always much to be afraid of. And one may, thus, be less inclined to celebrate the blessings of liberty than to consider the dangers of tyranny and war that threaten it. For this liberalism the basic units of political life are not discursive and reflecting persons, nor friends, and enemies, nor patriotic soldier-citizens, nor energetic litigants, but the weak and the powerful. And the freedom it seeks to secure is freedom from the abuse of power and intimidation of the defenseless that this difference invites.[7]

Since much of the violence is racist, it perpetuates an ideology of white supremacy. That is, it is organized and rational despite appearances: "Violence in interracial struggle is always murderous, but it is not 'irrational,' it is the logical and rational consequence of racism, by which I do not mean some rather vague prejudices on either side, but an explicit ideological system."[8] The film portrays what this ideological system looks like in practice. Though the film is set in the 1950s, there is no mention of anything like a civil rights movement. However, it is clear that police violence is part of an ideological struggle, in addition to serving the interests of corruption.

There is an important contrast as the film progresses between the routine police violence committed against those who lack power, and the way in which similar violent tactics are used against those with power. Smith has Vincennes and Hudgens killed, and he tries to set up White to kill Exley. White uses the same violent tactics he used in the beginning of the film against those without power against District Attorney Loew who White knows is implicated in Smith's criminal activities. That is, the victims of violence evolve from those without power increasingly to those with power. Influential men are killed as they struggle over who will control organized crime in Los Angeles. The problem is that this plays into the film as a kind of revenge fantasy, since in reality, elites are rarely subject to extra-legal police violence. Efforts of reform are never considered, all that matters is power, and the illusion of justice. Even Exley, who may try to make the system more just, really has no idea how to achieve this other than working within the system itself.

The idea that Exley believes in, and represents, a modern approach to law enforcement is signaled by his glasses. Smith insists that no one in the detective bureau wears them. No explanation for this is offered. From that point on, Exley is shown in some scenes with the glasses, but when he is trying to make an impression on other police officers, he does not wear them, even if his inability to see well puts others at risk. The glasses represent reason and civilization. They serve as a contrast between Exley's intelligence and the "directness" of the other police officers.

JUSTICE

Justice, as both a term and a concept, is mentioned multiple times throughout the film. The film presents a debate about the meaning of justice, with different characters, notably Exley and White, presenting competing and incompatible ideas. Exley believes justice lies in consistency with the law, while White understands justice as vengeance. In political philosophy, justice is a central subject of debate. Even if a theory of justice were to achieve consensus, implementing that idea would require compromise and trade-offs. In addition, modern politics makes a distinction between law, which is imperfect but known and practical, in contrast with justice, which is often conceived as an aspirational ideal. All this is at play in the film, which resists taking a clear stand on which conception of justice it favors. One might even come away from the film believing that justice itself fails as a political good since it seems its pursuit often leads to further injustices.

Here the second theme of illusion comes into play as well. Though the characters in the film talk a great deal about justice, there is no evidence of justice itself in the film. Throughout the film, it is emphasized that what really matters to the police and their leadership is not justice but the *appearance* of justice. For example, the three men charged with the murders at the Nite Owl are shot and killed having escaped from jail. It does not matter that they did not commit the murder, all that matters is whether people think they did. It also does not matter that the actual murderers will not be held accountable for their crimes. The illusion of justice interferes with achieving actual justice. Furthermore, the illusion of justice, the illusion that the police are in fact solving crimes and punishing wrongdoers serves the interest of the police more than actual justice would. This raises questions about the noir genre more generally. At its heart, the genre is one of cynicism. If the protagonists live by a code, it is an individual one, and as such cannot be lawful.

As presented in the film, the idea that justice requires following the law appears to be unworkable. Jack Vincennes is corrupt, staging arrests and receiving payouts from the tabloid *Hush Hush*. Once however he attempts to make amends, he is killed and becomes a martyr for justice. This is noted by his final words, "Rollo Tomasi" a reference to the man who killed Exley's father. Rollo Tomasi was a name Exley used to attach to the man who killed his father and was never caught. It too is an illusion, and thus Exley's pursuit of justice is revealed to be a pursuit of an illusion.

Exley's initial conception of justice means he rejects the "dirty hands" idea that one must from time to time sacrifice common moral principles in service of a greater good. Instead, Exley seems to have in mind an idea that law and justice reach their ultimate expression when they exist without distinction. Despite this view, Exley is also politically savvy and suggests ways that the police department can avoid damaging its reputation while making sure some police are held accountable for the "Bloody Christmas" scandal where police severely beat two suspects accused of injuring police officers during an attempted arrest. Exley's view of justice however evolves as the plot unfolds. Before the Bloody Christmas events, Smith asked Exley whether he would be willing to violate the law in order to ensure the guilty are punished—planting evidence, beating a confession out of a suspect, and even shooting a suspect to ensure he is not acquitted on a technicality. In the beginning, Exley firmly rejects this idea but by the end of the film Exley has abandoned these principles. When Smith and he have a final confrontation, Smith tempts Exley with career advancement and more if he is willing to work with Smith: "Good lad. Always the politician. Let me do the talkin'. After I've done, they'll make you chief of detectives." After a pause, the two characters go outside, and Smith instructs Exley: "Hold up your badge so they'll know you're a policeman." At that point, Exley betrays the idea of law he had articulated in the beginning of the film by shooting Smith in the back. Yet, it is clear he believes doing so was the only way to stop Smith's continuing injustices. Exley's idea of justice has changed to resemble that of the other police officers, where justice serves as an excuse to violate not just the law, but basic precepts of morality.

Several characters in the film go beyond or outside the law to pursue their own idea of justice. By doing this, the film shows how the personal conception of justice is incompatible with law. The film uses this to explore the idea of vigilante justice. The questions though go deeper. At first, we might dismiss the questions posed as simply whether Exley is willing to violate what might be called "technicalities" in order to ensure the guilty are punished. But we realize that the question of guilt or innocence is irrelevant here. One is suspect because of who one is, not what one does. Thus, in the end, the corrupt police officer gets away with it, while the three suspects do not. The film adds a layer of complexity to this. The "innocent" people subject to police violence in the film may be innocent of the specific crimes for which they are subject to extra-legal punishment, but they are presented as guilty of *something*. This thus can be interpreted as making the film implicit in the ideology it seeks to criticize, or one might even see the film as justifying the system it portrays. In several scenes where criminals who would fill the vacuum left by the arrest of Mickey Cohen are beaten and threatened if they do not leave Southern California, Smith justifies his corruption by arguing that vices like drug use, prostitution, and pornography are inevitable. Thus, it is better if the provider of those vices is a local and a member of law enforcement rather than an outsider because such a system will be better able to preserve order.

By contrast, though White cares little about the formalities of law and law enforcement, he cares a great deal about seeing the guilty, especially those who victimize women, punished. Though he is the most violent of the police officers in the film, he is also the least concerned with expediency and the most concerned with justice. In the Nite Owl Killings, White realizes the police shot the wrong suspects. Though he does not care about their innocence (since they had raped and beat a woman, as far as White is concerned, they deserved to be killed) he does care about identifying the person who killed his partner. White's probing of what had been thought a closed case unravels a conspiracy, one in which White himself turns out to be implicated. Exley and Vincennes join forces with White, and they begin to uncover connections between the Nite Owl murders and other murders as well as heroin dealing and pornography. Everyone else in the department is satisfied with the case being closed. Exley at first too seems willing to put his career ahead of the pursuit of justice. He then remembers that he became a police officer "to catch the guys who thought they could get away with it." That is his definition of justice, and it turns out that White and Exley despite their hatred of each other find common ground. It is significant that this common ground is found by Exley compromising his idea of justice toward that of White. Exley is made to realize that he cannot pursue justice in a lawful way in a corrupt system and must embrace something more like White's ideas of justice.

Violence is also central to the idea of justice for many of the characters. In assaulting criminal suspects, the police are, in their view, doing justice. In some regards, the film is even sympathetic with this view. White frequently assaults men involved in domestic violence. He believes that the criminal justice system does not do enough to protect the victims of violence. Thus, violence is an essential part of justice. In the end, Exley accepts this. He is not so much corrupted by the lawlessness and violence but learns to use it to serve his own ends. He understands its inevitability. Whatever doubts Exley may have had toward the use of violence in the beginning of the film, by the end he recognizes the necessity of violence in supporting the ideology to which he has committed himself.

Violence is also a critical element in the relationship between law and justice. The police believe that justice cannot depend on law and thus they must rely on violence to establish their authority. Like the novel, the characters in the movie have moved beyond the political idea of "dirty hands" where ends can be argued to justify the means. Walter Benjamin describes the relationship thus: "If justice is the criterion of ends, legality is that of means."[9] *LA Confidential* undermines this idea, because legality interferes with the ends. Violence is the means, not the law. In the novel, the characters are not without values, but in defending those values betray them.[10] Thomas Hobbes famously argued

> To this ware of every man, this also is consequent; that nothing can be Unjust. The notions of Right and Wrong, Justice and Injustice have there no place. Where there is no common Power, there is no Law: where no law, no Injustice. Force, and Fraud are in warre the Cardinall virtues.[11]

LA Confidential raises the question of whether justice does in fact rely on law, or whether violence alone suffices as a foundation for justice. It is the Hobbesian concept of law and justice in operation, in the sense that for

Hobbes, the law was the will of the sovereign. The police are not under the law, nor obligated by it since they are shown as sovereign.

Law in the "law and order" sense is presented in the opening scenes as both an illusion and a goal. The novel depicts those charged with enforcing the law as themselves involved in criminal activity. Critically, these characters have different motivations for smearing the distinction between lawful and unlawful. For some, it is greed; for others, personal ambition; and for others an attempt to squeeze some justice out of a thoroughly corrupt system. To work within the law is impossible because the law as such does not exist.[12] The film is no different. The law-abiding people supposedly working in good jobs and living on cheap land as depicted in the film's introduction never intrude upon the action of the film.

Based on this, the film is presenting an example of the ways Walter Benjamin argued police violence is connected to the state, law, and justice:

> The assertion that the ends of police violence are always identical or even connected to those of general law is entirely untrue. Rather, the "law" of the police really marks the point at which the state, whether from impotence or because of the immanent connections within any legal system, can no longer guarantee through the legal system the empirical ends it desires at any price to attain.[13]

Organized crime is one threat to the legal system that the state is impotent against. Violent crime in general, portrayed as the murder at the Nite Owl café and the murder of Vincennes, among other crimes, also illustrate the state's impotence.

"HUSH HUSH"

Hush Hush is a fictional tabloid that reports on celebrities indulging their vices, especisally those involving illegal drugs and homosexuality. On one hand, the tabloid exposes the reality Hollywood celebrities try to hide. On the other hand, we see ways in which the exposure is itself as much a construction as any other Hollywood reality. This is made apparent when Vincennes and Hudgens collaborate on arresting a minor celebrity for marijuana. Before the arrest, they make sure the cameras are in place, the lighting is flattering to the detective, and a large movie marquee appears in the background. Though central to the plot, Sam Hudgens' character and his journalistic efforts appear as a satire of the tabloid, providing perhaps the only moments in the film that are even close to comic relief. Hudgens concludes his stories with his trademark phrase "Off the record, on the QT, and very hush hush" providing his readers with the illusion that they are privy to exclusive, inside information.

In some sense, for the first half of the film, *Hush Hush* provides a narrative center. Los Angeles and Hollywood, and its crime and corruption, are the central characters. Hollywood figures lead a double life—a cultivated fantasy of all-American values, and a private life of drug use, sexual perversion, and support for communism. At this point, the film lacks a single protagonist, featuring three detectives in three distinct plotlines that only come together later in the film. As the film proceeds, secrets are exposed and the ugly reality that lies underneath the fantasy emerges. *Hush Hush* takes as its project the exposure of the reality, but it does so in a way that preserves the interests of those in power.

Once in possession of information that could expose the reality of powerful people, Hudgens is killed by Smith. His death is in fact a baroque illustration of narrative fantasy in service to the preservation of power in reality. Hudgens agrees with Smith to serve as bait and is tortured in order to provoke White to kill Exley by "confessing" that he has pictures of Exley having sex with Bracken (who, as a prostitute, was paid to seduce Exley and make sure there were photographs.) Rather than risk Hudgens exposing this plot, Smith kills him once White leaves, presumably to kill Exley. Though unpacking the layers of deception of these may be a little confusing, suffice it to say that power requires maintaining an illusion, and will do what it must to preserve the illusion. Though the scene where Hudgens is killed is not the final scene of the movie, it brings us back to the fantasy described in the film's opening scene. *Hush Hush* is tolerated as long as its exposures do not undermine the edifice of Los Angeles power.

CONCLUSION

"Are you going to shoot me, or arrest me?" are the final words spoken by Smith to Exley. Despite the appearance of a stark choice, works of art resist simple interpretations. Rather, they derive their power and interest by highlighting the ambivalent and ambiguous moral problems of real life. Adapting the novel to film inevitably results in loss of much of that nuance. For all its complexity, the film is ultimately about a fight for control of prostitution and heroin distribution in Los Angeles. Though it seems to resist a Hollywood resolution, it ultimately offers if not a moralistic ending with the good guys prevailing and the bad guys duly punished, it is an ending where those left alive seem satisfied with how things turn out. A film that begins with commentary about the image of Los Angeles as paradise, and police officers committing brutal and racially motivated beatings, ends with a shootout between bad cops and only somewhat morally compromised cops. In the concluding scenes, the police chief presents Exley with his second "Medal of Valor" where he says Exley is the model of the "new" police officer, where "Los Angeles will finally have the police force it deserves." This simple phrase though presents layer upon layer of ambiguity. One wonders if the film is saying that Los Angeles exactly does deserve the kind of lawless rogue and corrupt police officers the film portrays. In 1997, and today, this kind of question turns the controversy surrounding police violence on its head. It may very well be we are getting the kind of police we deserve because these are the kind of police we want and reward.

There are a series of critical moral compromises at the end of the film and the final scenes offer a potential return of the film's moral ambiguity. Exley is tempted to let Smith get away with for political advancement, but ultimately, shoots Smith in the back. This is a direct reference to the scene where Smith had asked Exley if he was willing to shoot a hardened criminal in the back in case a lawyer was able to get him off on a technicality. It turns out Exley was in fact quite willing to kill in order to prevent a guilty person from "getting away with it." It appears that Exley is willing to throw his career away in order to tell the truth. Ultimately, though, a complete fabrication becomes the official story. And, far from throwing his career away, Exley will get the promotion and prestige he appeared to reject when he shot Smith. Moreover, at the film's conclusion, there is no way to know how Exley will handle his power and his new position. Did he make these compromises in order to achieve a greater good? Or is he merely ambitious, using whatever means available to advance his career, or even engage and profit from the same corruption Smith attempted?[14]

Importantly, only White gets redemption at the end of the movie. Vincennes is killed, and it is clear that what matters to Exley is his own career. Even if he refuses to going along with Smith's corruption, he has come to believe that one must be willing to go outside the law in the pursuit of justice, having lost the naiveté that characterized him in the opening scenes. He may not be corrupt, but he is more than willing to fabricate a story about Smith and his role in the spectacular crimes the film recounts in order to salvage the reputation of the Los Angeles Police Department and his own career. White, by contrast, drives off with Bracken, back to Bisbee, Arizona.

Ultimately, from the perspective of its politics, we have two different and contrasting films. This leads to several competing and conflicting interpretations. Perhaps the most troubling conclusion the viewer can have is the film not only portrays and explains police violence, but excuses and perhaps even celebrates it. It is important to note that even if at points the *LA Confidential* presents police violence as disproportionate, its victims are presented as deserving punishment. The unspoken point is that ordinary law-abiding citizens will not be victims of police brutality. This is made clear in shortly after the opening of the film when Bud White notices a scene of domestic violence and beats and threatens to charge the perpetrator with charges of pedophilia before handcuffing him to the railing and calling other police officers to arrest him on a parole violation. This interpretation presents law and justice as distinct—police officers must deploy violence in order to see justice done. Bud White, the most violent of the three central police officers, is also presented as the one who has motivations beyond personal ambition. Though all the film's characters are deeply flawed, White is ultimately the most sympathetic of the three main detectives of the story. Though his pursuit of justice goes well beyond anything that is or should be legal, he is doing these acts for their own sake. White really has no other agenda than his personal account of justice.

One might take the opposite view though—that there can be no justice without law, and the illegal violence portrayed in the movie also violates justice. The film cannot simply be dismissed as an ordinary police revenge fantasy. In a just world, Smith would not be presented posthumously as a hero. One might suggest that the story of Ed Exley is one of becoming corrupt, rather than one of the triumph of good. To be sure, in the final scenes, Exley seems ambivalent about what he has done. Yet, he does, more than any other character in the film, "get away with it." That is, the more Exley does what is necessary and what is expedient instead of what is lawful, he flourishes. It seems as if Exley never needs compromise. Unlike the tragic White or the corrupt Vincennes, he comes out on top through a cynical presentation of self. The illusion is that Exley is the man with the glasses, upright and law-abiding. But the reality is he is blindingly ambitious and the more he gives up his stated principles, the more his career advances. The film explores the interplay of violence and power. Importantly, the police commit most of the acts of violence presented in the film, and thus the film shows how the authority of government depends on physical force and coercion.

No one watching the film would come away with the idea that the police are to be admired. The film is unflinching in its presentation of their violence and lawlessness. Unlike many films that present police violence as an occasionally necessary tactic, that limits on police activities are put in place by politicians and bureaucrats who do not understand the realities of law enforcement, that is, films such as *Dirty Harry* that present the police vigilante as a hero, police violence in *LA Confidential* serves the interest of police engaged in criminal activities. The idea of police as vigilante is a common trope in American crime fiction and cinema.[15] As a law enforcement tactic, the violence is counterproductive—the shortcuts police take often result in the wrong person being accused of a crime while the guilty go free. It even puts police officers themselves at risk—when Exley shoots the three Nite Owl killing suspects, another officer is fatally shot as well. Nevertheless, Exley receives his first Medal of Valor and earns the respect of his fellow officers.

No one would consider *LA Confidential* "copaganda," rather, the film is critical of presentations of the police as noble heroes of law enforcement. Thus, the film can be seen as an argument against common police practices, particularly those that involve police spending more effort and energy maintaining its public image than solving crimes.

There is a further difficulty here. The characters in the film are racist, sexist, and homophobic, attitudes that are frequently exhibited not just in their language but also in their violence. Ellroy himself is not progressive on these issues. The novel does not really suggest that there is anything wrong with the attitudes of the police detectives. The film shares the viewpoint of the novel, even as its presentation of the language and the violence is less explicit. In its (necessary) simplifications, the film removes much of the novel's ambivalence and complications even as it tones down the racist language and violence. However, only the white male characters have any agency themselves. The othersThey do not act; they are acted upon. We know nothing about them as human beings. Given this portrayal, it is difficult to maintain the idea that these characters are treated unjustly, even as they are treated with violence and cruelty.

Instead of ambiguity though, perhaps the real problem with the film is reading any kind of positive moral or political message into one. It is Hobbesian not just in terms of the strategies used to impose order but as an inevitable consequence of how human beings are. Exley may have begun the film as an idealist (though one with almost supernatural political instincts) but the film concludes that even if Exley maintains his commitment to a better, fairer, more just Los Angeles, he can only contribute to that project by going outside and beyond the law. One might make this claim about noir more generally. That is, the genre is cynical, and while characters might have a personal code that structures their attitudes and actions, these codes are not really moral codes in that there is no attempt to universalize them. More than that, there is no politics that could emerge from these codes.

NOTES

1. Mark Brown, "James Ellroy says film adaptation of *LA Confidential* is "as deep as a tortilla" *The Guardian* June 2, 2019. url: https://www.theguardian.com/books/2019/jun/02/james-ellroy-says-film-adaptation-of-la-confidential-was-as-deep-as-a-tortilla retrieved February 15, 2023.
2. William Marlin, *The American Roman Noir: Hammett, Cain, and Chandler* (Athens, GA: University of Georgia Press, 1995), 242.
3. Nathan Ashman, *James Ellroy and Voyeur Fiction* (Lexington: Lanham, MD, 2018), xxi.

4. Jonathan Havercroft and David Owen, "Soul-Blindness, Police Orders and Black Lives Matter: Wittgenstein, Cavell, and Ranciere," *Political Theory* 44, no. 6 (2016), 751.

5. Judith Shklar, "Political Theory and Rule of Law" in *Political Thought and Political Thinkers,* ed. Stanley Hoffman (Chicago: University of Chicago Press, 1998), 24.

6. Raymond Geuss, *History and Illusion in Politics* (Cambridge: Cambridge University press, 2001), 21–22.

7. Judith Shklar, "The Liberalism of Fear" in *Political Thought and Political Thinkers*, ed. Stanley Hoffmann (Chicago: University of Chicago Press, 1998), 9.

8. Hannah Arendt, *On Violence* (New York: Harcourt, Brace, and World, 1970), 76.

9. Walter Benjamin, "Critique of Violence" in *Selected Writings* v. 1 edited by Marcus Bullock and Michael W. Jennings (Cambridge, MA: Harvard U Press, 1996), 237.

10. Lee Spinks, "Except for Law: Raymond Chandler, James Ellroy, and the Politics of Exception." *South Atlantic Quarterly* 107, no. 1 (2008), 136.

11. Thomas Hobbes, *Leviathan*, ed. Richard Tuck. (Cambridge University Press: Cambridge, 1991), 90.

12. Spinks, 137.

13. Benjamin, 243.

14. Though in the *Black Dahlia*, the fourth novel in Ellroy's LA Quartet, Exley in fact remains committed to rooting out corruption in the LA Police Department as Smith is not killed in the novel. However, by this point the plots of the film and the novel have diverged substantially and thus there is no reason to think the film Exley will have the same outcome as the novel Exley.

15. Sim, 16.

BIBLIOGRAPHY

Arendt, Hannah. 1970. *On Violence*. New York: Harcourt, Brace, and World.

Ashman, Nathan. 2018. *James Ellroy and Voyear Fiction.* Lanham, MD: Lexington.

Benjamin, Walter. 1996. *Critique of Violence.* Vol. 1, in *Selected Writings*, by Walter Benjamin, edited by Michael W. Jennings Marcus Bullock, 236–252. Cambridge, MA: Harvard University Press.

Brown, Mark. 2019. "James Ellroy Says Film Adapation of LA Confidential Was 'As Deep as a Tortilla.'" *The Guardian.* Manchester, June 2. Accessed February 15, 2023. https://www.theguardian.com/books/2019/jun/02/james-ellroy-says-film-adaptation-of-la-confidential-was-as-deep-as-a-tortilla.

Geuss, Raymond. 2001. *History and Illusion in Politics.* Cambridge: Cambridge University Press.

1997. *LA Confidential.* Directed by Curtis Hanson.

Havercroft, Jonathan, and David Owen. 2016. "Soul-Blindness, Police Order and Black Lives Matter: Wittgenstein, Cavell, and Ranciere." *Political Theory* 44 (6): 739–763.

Marling, William. 1995. *The American Roman Noir: Hammett, Cain, and Chandler.* Athens, GA: The University of Georgia Press.

Shklar, Judith. 1998. "Political Theory and Rule of Law." In *Political Thought and Political Thinkers*, by Judith Shklar, edited by Stanley Hoffman, 21–37. Chicago: University of Chicago Press.

Shklar, Judith. 1998. "The Liberalism of Fear." In *Political Thought and Political Thinkers*, by Judith Shklar, edited by Stanley Hoffmann, 3–20. Chicago: University of Chicago Press.

Sim, Stuart. 2015. *Justice and Revenge in Contemporary American Crime Fiction.* New York: Palgrave Macmillan.

Spinks, Lee. 2008. "Except for Law: Raymond Chandler, James Ellroy, and the Politics of Exception." *South Atlantic Quarterly* 107 (1): 121–143.

Chapter 8

Ellroy's Wetworkers

Soldiers and Spooks, Paramilitaries and Assassins, Cops, G-Men, Wise Guys, Latinos, and Gringos in the Underworld USA Trilogy

W. John Green

In James Ellroy's world, one thing is clear: elites are not nice people. They are all generally corrupt, potentially violent, and many are obvious psychopaths; in fact, criminal elites *are* the elite. Power and violence go together naturally in the Underworld USA Trilogy, and these elites need people to do their bidding. This essay, therefore, will focus on the muscle and their world.

In Ellroy, noir becomes explicitly political with an intense focus on right-wing worldviews, diving into the politics of conspiracy theory, murder, and assassination. (Ellroy, after all, cites Don Delillo's *Libra* about the JFK assassination as an inspiration for *American Tabloid*). Yet making his vision in the Underworld USA Trilogy strikingly original, Ellroy melds familiar noir conventions about the politics of assassination in the United States during the 1960s with Latin American political violence and murder, death squads, and dirty war. Professional killers, known matter-of-factly as "wetworkers" among intelligence professionals, are at the center of his stories. And the relationships among these professionals point to the United States' role as part of a hemispheric political culture of murder as a paid-up member, with connections that are ideological, political, military, and economic. Ellroy overtly acknowledges the somewhat taboo and ignored fact that powerful people in the United States are known to employ armed retainers, just as elites in Latin America often do. There is no "American Exceptionalism" here, no "shinning city on a hill." (And it's probably worse than you think.)

Not surprisingly, Ellroy's work parallels a flourishing subspecies of the genre, politically inflected Latin American noir novels. As Misha Kokotovic has noted, many works written in the aftermath of the civil and dirty wars that racked Central America from the 1970s to the 1990s "do not fit neatly within the generic boundaries of the detective or mystery novel," though "most of them do allude to and play with the conventions of the genre." What is more, "all of them share a noir sensibility characterized by a pervasive sense of corruption, decay, and disillusionment, in which the social order itself, and particularly of the state, is the ultimate source of criminality, rather than justice."[1]

These three novels capture a murky and twisted world of power, north and south of the U.S.-Mexico border, built upon the interlocking foundations of intimidation, violence, and murder. Rodney Taveira notes that in these works Ellroy is focused on "the unblinking representation of bad men doing bad things."[2] But more to the point, Ellroy's "bad men" work for powerful people with grim and shadowy agendas, and in so doing (he insists in the prologue of *American Tabloid*), they are the true agents of history. Ellroy writes that our "continuing narrative line is blurred past truth and hindsight," and only "a reckless verisimilitude can set that line straight." The actions of his "rogue cops and shakedown artists," his "wiretappers and soldiers of fortune and faggot lounge entertainers" blaze the path and had

> one second of their lives deviated off course, American History would not exist as we know it. It's time to demythologize an era and build a new myth from the gutter to the stars. It's time to embrace bad men and the price they paid to secretly define their time.

On the surface Ellroy is writing classic hard-boiled noir, but he is also clearly attempting (and succeeding) to write well-researched historical fiction that ties together dark networks of power across the Western Hemisphere through the actions of his wetwork protagonists.

A HEMISPHERIC POLITICAL CULTURE OF MURDER

In his Underworld USA Trilogy, Ellroy exposes the fully integrated and interconnected world of wetwork throughout the Americas. Following clear noir convention (and much left-leaning scholarship), the Gringos were not, and never were, the white hats. To return to Ellroy's prologue of *American Tabloid*, he insists that

> America was never innocent. We popped our cherry on the boat over and looked back with no regrets. You can't ascribe our fall from grace to any single event or set of circumstances. You can't lose what you lacked at conception.

And just in case one were inclined to dismiss Ellroy's vision of this world of wetwork as too extreme to be believed, here is some context. The U.S. military gave useful insight into its mindset by openly discussing the use of the "Salvador Option" in Iraq (that is, running death squads there), providing strong evidence that many people in power in the United States believe in the utility of political murder. U.S. special operations units such as the "Intelligence Support Activity" of the U.S. Army, SEAL Team Six (that took out Osama Bin Ladin), and CIA paramilitary squads all ply the trade. There are also "contractors" and U.S. versions of the Latin American paramilitary entities, best represented by Xe Services, LLC, formerly known as BlackwaterUSA and Blackwater Worldwide, a "private military" company founded in 1997. Such companies, many observers believe, regularly act very much like their Latin American counterparts, often reportedly outside the confines of international law.[3]

Clearly, this mindset lives on among U.S. elites of a murderous bent, as the popular FOX television thriller "24" demonstrated. The brainchild of conservative writer Joel Surnow, it followed the adventures of Agent "Jack Bauer" (played by Kiefer Sutherland), who wrestled manfully with terrorist threats to the "American way of life." Bauer killed a lot of bad guys and tortured "terrorists" (in myriad gruesome ways). He even disemboweled one evil doer to recover a cell phone SIM card, all for the most patriotic reasons. His victims were always dangerous scumbags, and their information was always useful (and time-sensitive). It was a reactionary fantasy, but it had loud echoes in the broader political culture of the United States. Supreme Court justice Antonin Scalia, for example, cited the show's "ticking time bomb scenarios" as justification for repressive tactics.[4] (He was in good neo-fascist company. Hitler-apologist Vicente Massot made similar arguments justifying the Argentine Dirty War.) Television evangelist Pat Robertson did Scalia one better, and openly called for the assassination of then Venezuelan president Hugo Chávez, to prevent Venezuela from becoming "a launching pad for communist infiltration and Muslim extremism all over the continent."[5] Yet beyond television Realpolitik, right-wing politicians continue to embrace murderous policies in the United States. Sharron Angle, Republican candidate for the Senate from Nevada, made her position clear enough in a January 2010 interview: "You know if this Congress keeps going the way it is, people are really looking toward those Second Amendment remedies." That is, they will use guns to counter the kind of change represented by the Obama administration. Later that year, Georgia State representative John Yates stressed that troops stationed on the border with Mexico "ought to be armed" and that Mexicans should understand that "we will shoot to kill if anybody crosses." And most famously, in January 2011 Michel Bachmann, Republican congresswoman for Minnesota, leader of the House "Tea Party" Caucus, and candidate for the Republican presidential nomination, wanted people to be "armed and dangerous" to resist liberal legislation on the climate.[6] Given this background, the events at the U.S. Capitol ten years later were all too predictable. It also underscores that Ellroy is hardly exaggerating.

Much scholarship credits the corrupting power of the "American Empire" with driving political murders in Latin America. Ellroy, however, recognizes that this is a partnership. The Gringos are not "teaching" the Latin Americans this stuff; rather, they're collaborating. They're the essential enablers of an existing tradition of violence in support of elite power, and the influences run both ways. Political murder has served the interests of Latin America's most powerful and privileged citizens rather well. Certainly, political murder was widely employed in the twentieth century and is still quite common in the twenty-first century. Such murder generally seeks to eliminate the bearers of ill tidings for hegemonic structures. One can safely argue that this, the most widely exercised form of political murder in the region, has been carried out by states, elites, or their proxies, against a variety of closely related enemies. These have included the unnervingly popular leaders of mass political movements, politically minded former revolutionaries and demobilized guerrillas, pesky agitators, intellectuals, artists, journalists, academics, subversive activists and ambitious labor organizers, troublesome lawyers, prosecutors and judges, and even crusading priests and nuns. In other words, power elites in Latin America aimed to purge their societies of all "bad influences" and the individuals whom they considered the cause of any social or political unrest fall into that category.[7]

Many studies, nonetheless, begin with the assumption, implicitly or explicitly, that U.S. government and North American corporate interests are the driving force behind the practice of political murder in the region.[8] It is a seductive argument because with one handy variable, the Gringo/Yankee connection, one can explain the widespread use of political murder across time and in very different countries. Unquestionably, U.S. imperial activity on the periphery has done a great deal to drive the phenomenon of political murder. There are plenty of cases where the United States organized and bankrolled the killing, and generally called the shots (as with the Contras), and many more in which its involvement was secondary but significant. Yet there are a variety of problems with this mechanistic and simplistic interpretation, beginning with the fact that it leaves out a great deal of political murder that had no connection to U.S. influence. Another complicating factor is that the United States has not followed a consistent policy in the region, emphasizing first the fight against subversion and later that against drugs, advocating human rights, democracy, and the rule of law, or U.S. economic interests, in alternating fashion, or all at once. Also, the tendency to privilege U.S. contributions creates an ever more awkward dilemma in that it shifts the focus away from the Latin American murderous elites, downplays their roles and degrees of responsibility, and generates a strangely condescending outlook which ignores Latin America's long history of repressive government and elite domination.

But even if the United States is not the root of all political evil in Latin America, it hardly follows that the United States can be absolved of its share of guilt. The record of the United States is a deeply troubling one for a country that sees itself as a paragon of democratic virtue and an example to the rest of the world. The United States has often, as during the early 1980s, acted as the perfect codependent in Latin America's political murder habit, bringing out and allowing to flourish some of the region's worst tendencies. So while the United States did not create the use of political murder, it did readily facilitate it. Far from being exonerated, parts of the U.S. government and many U.S. corporations have been and continue to be active participants in political murder endeavors, highlighting the fact that many Gringos partake of the elite political culture of murder, and hold the same assumptions. It is a shared collaboration, a partnership, in which the United States is one of many players. The United States is an enabler and more—it is one who sits down and joins in, part of a united hemispheric murderous elite acting to protect a broader status quo.[9]

Ellroy captures this history. In these three interconnected novels, he lays bare the seamless world of power and muscle that exists both north and south of the U.S. border. In *American Tabloid*, his "bad men" attempt to entrap JFK with a call girl, but the plot fizzles. Post Cuban Revolution they moonlight for the CIA, working with the Mob and Cuban exiles to overthrow Fidel Castro. With the failure of the Bay of Pigs invasion, which the players blame on JFK's refusal to provide air cover, plots are set in motion that lead to the president's assassination. *The Cold Six Thousand* jumps into the coverup of JFK's murder. New characters join the crew in a complex set of intrigues that involve rogue members of the CIA, the KKK, organized crime, the Cuban exile community, the Dallas Police Department, and FBI operatives directly connected to J. Edgar Hoover that lead to the assassination of RFK and MLK. In *Blood's A Rover* they strive to carry out Hoover's racist agenda while helping parts of the Mafia attempt to recreate the lost Cuban Mecca of sin in the Dominican Republic with spillover into Haiti. There is the plenty of mayhem and murder carried out by "La Banda," the death squad working for Joaquín Balaguer in the DR, as well as Papa Doc Duvalier in Haita and his murderous Tontons Macoutes. And of course, the CIA is on hand to help the DR avoid becoming another revolutionary stronghold like Cuba. Laid next to the actual history, it seems indistinguishable.

OVERLAPPING JURISDICTIONS

The intertwining of this world is not just geopolitical. In Ellroy's take, there are no real hard and fast boundaries for individuals: the CIA, the FBI, the Mob, criminals of various stripes, intelligence operatives, the military, law enforcement, Latin American *pistoleros*, right-wingers, thugs, paramilitaries, *narcos*, wise-guys, and G-men, are all first cousins, or even siblings; overlap is the norm. They are professionals and coworkers and most of them move widely within these interconnected realms. In Ellroy, we find clear patterns in his characters' bios.

Pete Bondurant is perhaps the key representative. Born in Quebec, "Pete joined the U.S. Marines to bag a green card." He is a hulking and clever ex-LA. Deputy Sheriff who beat a wino in the drunk tank to death "bare-fisted." Howard Hughes "sensed strongarm potential" and "got the beef quashed." Ellroy called him "Renaissance Man Pete: pimp, dope procurer, licensed PI goon."[10] At various times he works for Hughes, for the CIA running an anti-Castro paramilitary group, organizes a heroin distribution ring to finance it, and serves as an enforcer for the mob. And of course, he helps assassinate President Kennedy and later brother Bobby.

Kemper Boyd is a Yale Law School grad, an FBI agent who had been "a long-time FBI-sanctioned car booster" who "rigged auto-job evidence and skimmed money off of it for years."[11] Hoover recognizes his special talents and tasks him with sabotaging RFK's anti-Mob McClellan Committee. He helps the CIA organize Pete's paramilitary group in Miami of anti-Castro right-wing Cubans and works for the Mob. In *American Tabloid* Kemper Boyd's "plethora of affiliations" was described by CIA agent John Stanton: "an FBI agent on Tuesday, a prospective pimp for Jack Kennedy on Wednesday, and a McClellan Committee investigator on Thursday."[12]

Ward Littell is an FBI agent with leftwing sympathies who early in the novels idolizes RFK and admires his anti-mob crusade. Littell eventually leaves the Bureau, but after being slighted by RFK, works for Hoover to undermine his former hero. He becomes a mob lawyer and fixer while also working for Hughes. Seeking revenge on Bobby, he helps kill his brother and later helps bring down MLK.

Wayne Tedrow Jr. is the son of Wayne Sr., a violent, right-wing, rich, and powerful Mormon mover and shaker in Nevada. Junior is an Army vet, Brigham Young grad with a chem degree, summa cum laude; a onetime Sargent with the Vegas P.D., a reluctant mob hitman, and eventual heroin runner. He kills his father with the help of his stepmom, who is his lover. He also helps turn the DR into a new Mob-friendly enclave like the old Havana.

Dwight Holly, "The Enforcer," is a former FBI, later of the Nevada Federal Bureau of Narcotics. He plays an elemental role in the MLK assassination and helps his friend Wayne whack his dad. As Rodney Taveira also has observed, "The protagonists of the Underworld USA Trilogy are double and triple agents working for the FBI, CIA, local police forces, Cuban loyalist groups, leftist revolutionaries, and the Mafia."[13] And one should add, Latin American death squads.

DEATH SQUADS: AN OVERVIEW

The mechanisms of murder, disappearance, assassination, and mass killing in Latin America are diverse.[14] The repressive apparatus that a state or part of a state or elite might employ, therefore, can vary widely, as can the actual methods of butchery. Jeffrey Sluka pointed out that the victims of political murder have been "gunned down in groups and shot individually, blown up with bombs and artillery, stabbed, strangled, hacked to death, or poisoned." They are often "tortured to death" or "sexually abused before being killed."[15] There is, consequently, no single "Latin American style" of killing. Latin Americans are inventive, and in this context, their creativity unfortunately translates into processes that are messy and convoluted by design. No one is ever supposed to sort it all out. Each country or period has its own favored routes to the common destination of killing troublemakers. There is, however, an important caveat: variations tend to get repeated. Certain techniques, tried and true, find widespread employment. So while there is no single organizational method or means of slaughter, there seems to be a shared playbook, evident in the recurring patterns found across Latin America.

The basic building block, of course, has been the "death squad." Bruce Campbell defined death squads as "clandestine and usually irregular organizations, often paramilitary in nature, which carry out extrajudicial executions and other violent acts . . . against clearly defined individuals or groups of people. Murder is their primary or even sole activity." He argues that death squad members tend not to wear uniforms, and strive to give governments "deniability;" regimes routinely disavow any connection to them. At the same time, however, he stresses that death squads generally "operate with the overt support, complicity, or acquiescence of government, or at least some parts of it."[16]

Yet there has been plenty of variation on the death squad theme. In fact, one can identify a continuum that begins with regular military operations, in which the various services act like death squads (or form smaller covert units for that purpose, peopled by active duty soldiers and sailors) and encompasses police detachments hunting subversives or weeding out undesirables, political parties fielding their own partisan civilians or henchmen, mixed-membership hit squads with multiple connections, paramilitary organizations in the pay of national or local government or regional elites (both "legitimate" and "criminal") as well as paramilitary proxy armies funded from abroad, and finally, stretches to freelancers and rogue players, professional paid assassins, often working in pairs from the backs of speeding motorcycles (a practice known in Colombia as the parrillero), with loyalties that are frequently unclear.

Considering this spectrum, two things are apparent. First, while the general categories are clear enough, some groups and individuals can fall into more than one. Untidy historical reality laughingly defies crisp typologies. Overlap is particularly apparent regarding membership in death squads which, like the categories themselves, can be quite fluid. The practitioners are skilled specialists in high demand (including the ones with criminal backgrounds), and move from group to group, while many military, police, and paramilitary organizations, along with various death squads in between, have often operated in closely coordinated fashion, and even in combined squads. In Argentina, El Salvador, and Guatemala, for instance, an assortment of units from the army, navy, various police agencies, and even the customs and treasury services had their own groups and were known to treat each other as rivals. But in practice, they often hunted together.

The second thing we can say about death squads is that their relationships to the state are far from consistent or completely predictable. Admittedly, some students stress the connections. Sluka noted that death squads are "usually linked directly or indirectly with the regular security forces," though sometimes "they are part of paramilitary 'defense' forces, civilian right-wing paramilitary groups who kill people the state wants, or doesn't mind being, killed." But he insisted that "there is always overlap in membership and other forms of direct or indirect collusion between death squads and the army and police, and the death squads are usually directly or indirectly under official or unofficial state control." He contended that though they are "outside the law," death squads enjoy impunity and "are generally and secretly fully integrated into the state's regular security network."[17] This, however, is something of an exaggeration in that it over-emphasizes the role of the state at the expense of non-state elites. While Kees Koonings and Dirk Kruijt have reasonably argued that all death squads have a common tendency "to defend or restore established interests by applying violence to 'undesired' social categories and political opponents," it does not follow that death squads only do this work for "the state." Indeed, Campbell recognized a "mix of state and private interests" behind death squads.[18] What is more, states themselves are not monolithic entities. Regional governments and security forces within central governments may have varying degrees of involvement, and can also be decidedly independent. The relationships death squads have to the state are therefore usually close but also complex. They experience ruptures and discontinuities, and once again, exhibit a spectrum ranging from direct, government-sponsored and organized varieties to indirect "private" enterprises serving other power players that may at times operate against the wishes of a particular national government.

Ellroy brings this supposedly "Latin American" phenomenon into the U.S. sphere of influence. While in Vietnam, protecting their dope ring, Ellroy's "bad men" know how to pull off death squad ops. (The ring raised money for "The Cause"—defeating the Cuban Revolution—which motivated everything: "Cuba drove them. Cuba drove Pete. Cuba drove the dope plan. Cuba drove Viet ops. Something said Cuba drove Dallas.") After an attack, they know what a true death squad would do. "Pete said no burials. Chuck said no evidence. Mesplede said guts lured wild pigs. Bob disemboweled the Marvs. Pete disemboweled Chaffee. Bob disemboweled the VC. Wayne flipped a coin. Marv Three called heads. Wayne got tails-tough luck. He disemboweled Fido. He thought of Maynard Moore. He smelled the rest stop near Dallas. They walked away. Chuck left hate tracks. Bob left an ace of spades."[19]

Undoubtedly in the Latin American mind, Gringos seem perfectly attuned to death squad wet work. An excellent representation of this belief can be found in the Argentine cartoon character, Boogie "El Aceitoso" (the Oily One), created by Roberto Fontanarrosa. In this comic, which ran from 1974 to 1995, Boogie is a "Yankee" formed in his profession of hit man, bodyguard, and mercenary during his tours fighting in Vietnam. (He was Rambo before Rambo.)[20] Boogie is a coldblooded psychopath, for sure, but he is also supremely competent, controlled, and "principled." Though a fiercely independent freelance, he will work as a violence contractor for anyone who will pay him. He is chummy with police (he believes in law and order, after all) and occasionally works for the CIA, in Africa, and later in Central America, where he provides his services to the Contras in Honduras and Nicaragua. He even serves in the First Gulf War.

Indeed, Ellroy (and Fontanarrosa) offer fiction that is well grounded in the real world; they get this right, to a large degree. The careers of Pete Bondurant, Wayne Tedrow, (and Boogie) parallel those of many of their real-life countrymen. Of course, not all military veterans were converted into murderous sociopaths, but many embody the mercenary stereotype. A case in point was Billy Waugh, World War II vet, "special forces legend, seasoned CIA paramilitary, renowned assassin, covert operator, and the world's longest operating 'Green-Badger' or CIA contractor," (in addition to his days as a direct "company" employee, or "Blue-Badger"). His general counsel was "kill them . . . Flatten the place. You have to not mind killing innocents. Even the women and children."[21]

DARK, REACTIONARY, YET COOL

Ellroy's world of wetwork is not only political, it swings decidedly alt-right. Yet this violent world is chic, ominous, and plugged in, savvy, cynical, and jacked up on speed. It's reminiscent of the way Nazis or Fascists always seem to have the best and most stylish uniforms in old movies. The air is heavy with threatening possibility. Even the Mormons are menacing, a throwback to their rough and tumble nineteenth-century forbearers: from Howard Hughes' Mormon "goons" to Wayne Tedrow Senior, "a big Mormon fat cat." "He ran a kitchen-help union. He rigged low pay. He had coin. He had pull." He "was jungled up all over the nut Right. He did Klan ops for Mr. Hoover and Dwight Holly. He pushed high-line hate tracks. He rode the far-Right zeitgeist and stayed in the know. He knew about the JFK hit."[22]

Rubén Peinado Abarrio observes that Ellroy's work "seems to beg" for a look at "the restrictive, negative workings of institutionalized power." It is true that far from being a portrait of a "unified apparatus" of class domination in the Althusserian sense, Ellroy's depiction of the CIA, FBI, and various police departments involved in repressive operations point to plenty of "collisions and turbulence." But just like their heterogeneous Latin American death squad counterparts, they all seem to pull in the same reactionary direction, working closely with the Ku Klux Klan and organized crime in battling the 1960s progressive agenda. Ellroy's wetworkers, in large part, reflect and accept the ideological notion that "socialism is unfair, communism is anti-American," "black people are lazy and lascivious," and "civil rights laws threaten U.S. free enterprise."[23] Ellroy is definitely onto something authentic, and other writers have also noted it. Returning to the parallel case of Boogie, he is a firm believer in the American "free enterprise system." He hates communists, blacks, Asians, Latinos, Arabs, and he routinely slaps women around (when they need it).[24]

Ellroy's fiction captures a real-world rightwing dynamic and mindset, portraying various kinds of elites that are unified on key elements of a repressive regime. J. Edgar Hoover, one of the primary forces moving in the shadows, owed his rise, of course, to the "post-World War I Red Scare." This was his milieu: "Civil liberties suspended, abrogated, quashed, interdicted, suppressed. First Amendment rights shat upon. Political round-ups, false imprisoning, deportation at whim. A concurrent resurgence of nativist groups and the Klan."[25] Hoover understands that among his natural allies are "the nice Italian folks" who helped keep Las Vegas "clean."[26] As Rubén Peinado Abarrio points out, "the trilogy's Mob leaders share Hoover's hate for communists."[27] So it is no surprise that Hoover wants to shut down RFK's attempt "to expose labor unions collusively linked to organized crime."[28] Beyond Hoover, the CIA and members of the Mafia are very much on the same page about the need to quash the Cuban Revolution, but for slightly different reasons. The former are Cold Warriors and the latter want to protect (or recreate) a lucrative status quo of prostitution and gambling in Havana.

Their wetworker minions concur. Most of these guys want nothing to do with the forces of social, economic, and political change, and throw in a serious helping of racism. Ellroy notes that the Outfit, as the FBI called the Mob, hated MLK. A wiretap in a St. Louis "dump" frequented by "Outfit guys and sub-lease hoods" catches them "talking up a fifty-grand bounty" on him.[29] Dallas cop Maynard Moore is "Joe Redneck—tall and fat. He wore a Stetson. He wore big boots. He wore a mother-of-pearl .45." He tells Wayne Jr. that "DPD runs to the right side of the street. We got some Klan and we got some John Birch."[30] Moore is also given to spectacular feats of repressive racist violence against black people. In Ellroy's world (and in the "real" world), the muscle, or at least a lot of its members, are true believers, and they also feel double-crossed, sold-out, and betrayed by their superiors when they seem to waver in their devotion to "the Cause." Indeed, "hit-man" Pete Bondurant and "mercenary" Jean Phillipe Mesplede carry out their "professional underground war" because they are clearly "fueled by anti-communist feelings."[31] And even when they have leftist leanings politically and socially (see Littell and Wayne Jr.) they get pulled into the right-wing agenda.

Ellroy's reactionary hipster thugs would seem at home in a Quentin Tarantino movie, except that they are more believable.

THE VIEW FROM THE STREET

At his most basic, Ellroy gives us a picture of how this world functions from the "worker" perspective of cops, FBI agents, hit men, enforcers, killers, grunts, and journeymen assassins. They're players and hustlers, always looking for the angle, having much in common with traditional noir gumshoes, but possessing additional murderous flair. This is professional, but it can get personal fast. They have their own agendas even as they serve their intimidating paymasters. It usually does not turn out well for them.

Ellroy called novelist/true crime writer Joseph Wambaugh "Big. The major influence." As Jim Mancall noted, he credited him "with 'single handedly' obliterating 'the jive, whiny, poetic, utterly disingenuous, first-person private eye' novel and creating 'a new iconic figure, the traumatized police officer.'" Ellroy said "the great themes" of his work (from Wambaugh), especially in the LA Quartet novels followed "the lives of police officers and bad men in love with strong women."[32] Ellroy's focus subsequently made a logical progression from the LA Quartet to the Underworld USA Trilogy, and it was not surprising, since it is a short trip from his bent cops to professional killers.

And the jive and poetic aspects survived and thrived in Ellroy; his wetworkers are decidedly traumatized by war, violence, and so on. In fact, it seems to be a necessary precondition.

Ellroy's wetworkers have complicated lives and backstories. They are multidimensional, nuanced, flawed, and in no way black and white. They become "bad guys" because of their life trajectories, and they all seem to be drawn to their dooms. Ellroy exposes their beliefs, fears, and motivations; he unpacks their heavy baggage, and there is plenty of it. They are driven, compelled by machismo and self-doubt of their masculinity, fearing to show cowardice.[33] They feel regret, guilt, remorse, betrayal, and desire for revenge. They cannot escape their own macho worldview. They evolve and dissolve, and many of his key characters eventually break under the pressure. Kemper Boyd idolized and envied Jack Kennedy, who met Boyd's admiration with shorn and contempt, driving Boyd into the conspiracy to assassinate him. Pete Bondurant, easily the most compelling and charismatic of Ellroy's killers, ends up a broken man, physically and mentally. He sees his anti-communist efforts betrayed, barely fights off his old comrades tasked with killing him, and has to take part in the RFK assassination before he and his wife are allowed to leave "the Life." Finally, the disillusioned and guilt-ridden Ward Littell betrayed much of what he believed in, tried and failed to save Bobby Kennedy, and killed himself, after binging on news coverage of the assassination.

In these novels, Ellroy becomes the bard and chronicler of wetworkers with PTSD.

CONCLUSION

Ellroy's take on these guys rings true. He demonstrates the defendable cliché about how fiction can reflect the "truth" of history. In these novels, actual representatives of the U.S. murderous elites, such as J. Edgar Hoover, Howard Hughes, the Mafia, and the KKK, mesh with their Latin American counterparts, the anti-Castro Cubans, Joaquín Balaguer in the DR, and Papa Doc Duvalier in Haiti. The muscle, Ellroy's "bad men" and rogue cops, seem to step right out of the pages of classic hard-boiled noir, complete with fixations on sultry dames in low-cut dresses who need their help, though one can argue that his novels should actually be read as historical fiction. Yet however one approaches these works, in the Underworld USA Trilogy, Ellroy's wetworkers move through an utterly politicized landscape, both north and south of the U.S. border. And they kill a lot of people, largely in the service of elite interests, while driving history forward.

NOTES

1. Misha Kokotovic, "NeoLiberal Noir: Contemporary Central American Crime Fiction as Social Criticism," *Clues*, vol. 24, Issue 3 (Spring 2006), 15. Kokotovic also notes that "Central American noir generally expresses a deep disillusionment with the outcome of revolutionary struggles," 16.

2. Rodney Taveira, "The Divine Violence of the Underworld USA Trilogy," in *The Big Somewhere: Essays on James Ellroy's Noir World*, ed. Steven Powell (Bloomsbury Academic, 2018), 126.

3. See Michael Smith, *Killer Elite: The Inside Story of America's Most Secret Special Operations Team* (New York: St. Martin's Press, 2007); Jeremy Scahill, *Blackwater: The Rise of the World's Most Powerful Mercenary Army* (New York: Nation Book, 2007); and Robert Young Pelton, *Licensed to Kill: Hired Guns in the War on Terror* (New York: Crown Publishers, 2006).

4. Dahlia Lithwick, "The Fiction Behind Torture Policy," *Newsweek*, July 26, 2008.

5. From the August 22, 2005, broadcast of *The 700 Club.*

6. Cited by Greg Sargent's "The Plum Line" in the *Washington Post Online*, June 15, 2010; Broadcast report on Fox 5 Atlanta, October 14, 2010; noted by *Washington Post* columnist Dana Milbank, January 26, 2011.

7. See W. John Green, *A History of Political Murder in Latin America: Killing the Messengers of Change* (New York: SUNY, 2015), Introduction.

8. See Cecilia Menjívar and Nestor Rodríguez, eds. *When States Kill: Latin America, the U.S., and Technologies of Terror* (Austin: University of Texas Press, 2005); Lesley Gill, *The School of the Americas: Military Training and Political Violence in the Americas* (Durham: Duke University Press, 2004); Greg Grandin, *Empire's Workshop: Latin America, the United States, and the Rise of the New Imperialism* (New York: Owl Books, 2006); J. Patrice McSherry, *Predatory States: Operation Condor and Covert War in Latin America* (New York: Rowman and Littlefield, 2005); and most recently, Marcia Esparza, "Introduction: Globalizing Latin American Studies of State Violence and Genocide," in *State Violence and Genocide in Latin America: The Cold War Years,* eds. Marcia Esparza, et al. (New York: Routledge, 2010), 9.

9. See Green, *A History of Political Murder in Latin America*, chapter 5.

10. *American Tabloid*, 8.

11. *American Tabloid*, 20.

12. Rubén Peinado Abarrio, "Between Althusser and Foucault: Power Relations in James Ellroy's Underworld USA Trilogy," in *The Big Somewhere: Essays on James Ellroy's Noir World,* ed. Steven Powell (Bloomsbury Academic, 2018), 99.

13. Taveira, "The Divine Violence of the Underworld USA Trilogy," 127.

14. For an expanded discussion of dirty war mechanics, see Green, *A History of Political Murder in Latin America*, chapter 2.

15. Jeffrey A. Sluka, "Introduction: State Terror and Anthropology," in *Death Squad: The Anthropology of State Terror*, ed. Jeffrey A. Sluka (Philadelphia: University of Pennsylvania Press, 2000), 3.

16. Bruce B. Campbell, "Death Squads: Definition, Problems, and Historical Context," in *Death Squads in Global Perspective: Murder with Deniability*, eds. Bruce B. Campell and Arthur D. Brenner (New York: Palgrave Macmillan, 2000), 1–2, 5.

17. Sluka, "Introduction: State Terror," 4–5.

18. Dirk Kruijt and Kees Koonings, "The Military and Their Shadowy Brothers-In-Arms," in *Armed Actors: Organised Violence and State Failure in Latin America*, eds. Kees Koonings and Dirk Kruijt (New York: Zed Books, 2004), 27; Campbell, "Death Squads: Definition," 1.

19. *The Cold Six Thousand*, 322–323.

20. See Roberto Fontananrrosa, *Todo Boogie El Aceitoso* (Buenos Aires: Ediciones de la Flor, Quinta edición, 2009).

21. Pelton, *Licensed to Kill*, 17–41. For memoirs, see Stuart Herrington, *Stalking the Vietcong: Inside Operation Phoenix: A Personal Account (*New York: Presidio Press, 2004); Michael J. Walsh and Greg Walker, *Seal!: From Vietnam's Phoenix Program to Central America's Drug Wars* (New York: Pocket Books, 1995), and G. LaVerne Cromwell, *ICEX Intelligence: Vietnam's Phoenix Program* (Baltimore: PublishAmerica, 2006).

22. *The Cold Six Thousand*, 4. *Blood's A Rover*, 16.

23. Peinado Abarrio, "Between Althusser and Foucault," 94–95.

24. See Fontananrrosa, *Todo Boogie*.

25. *Blood's a Rover*, 582.

26. *The Cold Six Thousand*, 5.

27. Peinado Abarrio, "Between Althusser and Foucault," 95.

28. *American Tabloid*, 22–23.

29. *The Cold Six Thousand*, 559.

30. *The Cold Six Thousand*, 4 and 22.

31. Peinado Abarrio, "Between Althusser and Foucault," 95.

32. Jim Mancall, "'No-Man's Land': Broken Men and Traumatized Police Officers in *The Onion Field* and *The Black Dahlia*," in *The Big Somewhere: Essays on James Ellroy's Noir World,* ed. Steven Powell (Bloomsbury Academic, 2018), 32.

33. See the "special memorandum" by Inspector John Powers, who was known as "the Patton of the Los Angeles force." He was, "as Wambaugh puts it, a 'cop's cop' who 'talked like a real man.'" This was a macho Prime Directive: "the manner of a man's living and dying was of paramount importance." Mancall, "'No-Man's Land': Broken Men and Traumatized Police Officers," 37.

BIBLIOGRAPHY

Campbell, Bruce B. "Death Squads: Definition, Problems, and Historical Context," in *Death Squads in Global Perspective: Murder with Deniability*, eds. Bruce B. Campell and Arthur D. Brenner. New York: Palgrave Macmillan, 2000. 1–26.

Cromwell, G. LaVerne. *ICEX Intelligence: Vietnam's Phoenix Program.* Baltimore: PublishAmerica, 2006.

Esparza, Marcia. "Introduction: Globalizing Latin American Studies of State Violence and Genocide," in *State Violence and Genocide in Latin America: The Cold War Years,* eds. Marcia Esparza, et al. New York: Routledge, 2010. 1–19.

Fontananrrosa, Roberto. *Todo Boogie El Aceitoso*. Buenos Aires: Ediciones de la Flor, Quinta edición, 2009.

Fox 5 Atlanta, Broadcast Report October 14, 2010.

Gill, Lesley. *The School of the Americas: Military Training and Political Violence in the Americas*. Durham: Duke University Press, 2004.

Grandin, Greg. *Empire's Workshop: Latin America, the United States, and the Rise of the New Imperialism*. New York: Owl Books, 2006.

Green, W. John. *A History of Political Murder in Latin America: Killing the Messengers of Change*. New York: SUNY, 2015.

Herrington, Stuart. *Stalking the Vietcong: Inside Operation Phoenix: A Personal Account.* New York: Presidio Press, 2004.

Kokotovic, Misha. "NeoLiberal Noir: Contemporary Central American Crime Fiction as Social Criticism," *Clues* vol. 24, Issue 3, Spring 2006. 15–29.

Kruijt, Dirk and Kees Koonings, "The Military and Their Shadowy Brothers-In-Arms," in *Armed Actors: Organised Violence and State Failure in Latin America*, eds. Kees Koonings and Dirk Kruijt. New York: Zed Books, 2004. 16–32.

Lithwick, Dahlia. "The Fiction Behind Torture Policy," *Newsweek*, July 26, 2008.

Mancall, Jim. "'No-Man's Land': Broken Men and Traumatized Police Officers in *The Onion Field* and *The Black Dahlia*," in *The Big Somewhere: Essays on James Ellroy's Noir World,* ed. Steven Powell. Bloomsbury Academic, 2018. 31–49.

McSherry, J. Patrice. *Predatory States: Operation Condor and Covert War in Latin America*. New York: Rowman and Littlefield, 2005.

Menjívar, Cecilia and Nestor Rodríguez, eds. *When States Kill: Latin America, the U.S., and Technologies of Terror.* Austin: University of Texas Press, 2005.

Milbank, Dana. *Washington Post* columnist, January 26, 2011.

Peinado Abarrio, Rubén. "Between Althusser and Foucault: Power Relations in James Ellroy's Underworld USA Trilogy," in *The Big Somewhere: Essays on James Ellroy's Noir World,* ed. Steven Powell. Bloomsbury Academic, 2018. 91–106.

Pelton, Robert Young. *Licensed to Kill: Hired Guns in the War on Terror*. New York: Crown Publishers, 2006.

Sargent, Greg. "The Plum Line" in the *WashingtonpostOnline*, June 15, 2010.

Scahill, Jeremy. *Blackwater: The Rise of the World's Most Powerful Mercenary Army*. New York: Nation Book, 2007.

Sluka, Jeffrey A. "Introduction: State Terror and Anthropology," in *Death Squad: The Anthropology of State Terror*, ed. Jeffrey A. Sluka. Philadelphia: University of Pennsylvania Press, 2000. 1–45.

Smith, Michael. *Killer Elite: The Inside Story of America's Most Secret Special Operations Team*. New York: St. Martin's Press, 2007.

Taveira, Rodney. "The Divine Violence of the Underworld USA Trilogy," in *The Big Somewhere: Essays on James Ellroy's Noir World,* ed. Steven Powell. Bloomsbury Academic, 2018. 126–145.

The 700 Club August 22, 2005, broadcast.

Walsh, Michael J. and Greg Walker, *Seal!: From Vietnam's Phoenix Program to Central America's Drug Wars*. New York: Pocket Books, 1995.

Chapter 9

Knowledge Is Danger

The Kennedy Assassination in Ellroy and Don DeLillo

Joseph Romance

The assassination of John F. Kennedy continues to have an extraordinary hold over the minds of Americans. Did people in the 1950s obsess over the details of the McKinley assassination? No. Did people in the 1930s wonder about what might have been if Garfield had lived? No. Do people still concern themselves with Lincoln's death? Well, actually, on this last question, the answer is yes. But that just opens us up to more questions about Kennedy. Lincoln's assassination, coming at the end of the Civil War, a war that dealt with slavery, gives his death an almost Christlike dimension with the president dying for the political sins of the nation—sins he worked to remove. Kennedy's death did not mark the end of an administration that accomplished great things, though his successor would use the martyrdom to advance transformative policy changes, particularly with regard to race.

So what does his death mean? Why should we be so fascinated with it? Commentators and scholars of politics often look at the concrete. They like to consider what can be counted, proven with numbers. And there is nothing wrong with that. But politics is also about myth and concerns events that have extraordinary emotional resonance that we can hear even to the present day. How are we to respond to such distant but powerful moments? What are we to make of America's "mystic chords of memory" when it comes to JFK? What makes the Kennedy assassination so powerful and so troubling?

In a poll conducted in October 2017, over 60 percent of Americans believed that more than one person was involved in the Kennedy assassination.[1] Although, there was some variation among various demographic groups, almost all groups believed that Oswald did not act alone. In an era when Americans are divided along so many fault lines, it seems they are united on one thing—the Kennedy assassination requires a better explanation than the one offered by the Warren Commission. Indeed, there are a number of persistent theories, far different than the official account, to explain the event.[2] And, most of these involve disturbing conspiracies—the CIA is responsible, Castro is at fault, or the Russians or the Mob.[3] This was not the case with the earlier assassinations of Garfield or McKinley. Lincoln's was the result of a very real conspiracy but not one that was particularly mysterious. Indeed, the details may fascinate, but the cause of Booth and his fellow conspirators is painfully obvious.

All of these alternative explanations to the Kennedy assassination point to sinister and secret forces at work in the world. In some ways, this is not surprising. It is not unexpected in part because of the level of hopes surrounding Kennedy. John F. Kennedy, the man, continues to maintain a very special place in the hearts of Americans. In a recent Ipsos/University of Virginia poll, asking people to rank all the presidents from Eisenhower on (including Trump), Kennedy took the top spot. One of the reasons he ranked number one was that he was popular with Democrats, Republicans, and Independents.[4] Such bipartisan approval is rare in today's politics. Yet, the Kennedy administration accomplished relatively little in terms of concrete policy actions. During the less than three years in office, he was stymied by a difficult Congress, despite Democratic party majorities.[5] Home and abroad there were looming crises, civil rights, and Vietnam, for instance, that were difficult to solve. Yet, Kennedy the man was the locus of enormous expectations and hopes. He spoke during his life, and in more in his death, to the aspirations of so many. And, as Thomas Mallon argues, despite historical revisionism that "nearly shattered the idealized image of Kennedy . . . public opinion remained largely indifferent to what scholars and pundits had to say."[6] Many people simply project onto Kennedy as the man of their greatest political aspirations and dreams. Given the incompleteness of his administration, people can look back and imagine what might have been. They tell themselves if only Kennedy had lived X or Y would have happened—or not have happened. For instance, one common belief is that the United States would have pulled out of Vietnam sparing the nation that horrible trauma. Or, conversely, he would have committed troops even more readily and maybe won the war. Kennedy's own words can be used to support either position on Vietnam and it is probably that his mind was not settled on what to do in that part of the world.

His rhetoric about "getting the country moving again," but not really fully articulating where that movement would take us, allows people to see what they want to. Kennedy often called for sacrifice ("Ask not what your country could do for you—but what you could do for your country" is his most famous poetic example of this) for some greater purpose. At times it seemed that almost any purpose would do.[7] As "court" historian Arthur Schlesinger wrote about Kennedy's moment, "The capital city, somnolent in the Eisenhower years, had suddenly come alive . . . with the release of energy which occurs when men with ideas have a chance to put them into practice."[8] It is almost as if energy and movement are the very raison d'etre of the Kennedy moment.

Although, toward the end of his life he tantalizingly appeared to be embracing the moral demands of the civil rights movement. As he said, just months before the horror in Dallas:

> We are confronted primarily with a moral issue. It is as old as the Scriptures and is as clear as the American Constitution. The heart of the question is whether all Americans are to be afforded equal rights and equal opportunities, whether we are going to treat our fellow Americans as we want to be treated.[9]

Moreover, after his death, Kennedy seems to have transcended partisan divides—although he was a Democrat and seen as a liberal (though a pragmatic and even technocratic one) in his day, some contemporary conservatives seek to claim him as one of their own.[10] As the historian Alan Brinkley observes, "He remains a powerful symbol of a lost moment, of a soaring idealism and hopefulness that subsequent generations still try to recover. His allure—romantic, almost mythic, associations his name evokes—not only survive but flourish."[11] And, Brinkley adds, "More than anything, perhaps, Kennedy reminds us of a time when the national's capacities looked limitless, when its future seemed unbounded, when Americans believed that they could solve hard problems and accomplish bold deeds."[12] More recent administrations seem to either end in failure or, at best, show an ability to manage affairs reasonably well. But boldness is not an adjective that springs to mind with any major politician in recent decades. (Ronald Reagan would be the only president for whom a plausible case for boldness could be made.) Instead of greatness we are left with failure or managerial competence.[13]

What troubles many people, and I believe nurtures conspiracy thinking, is that given the great events that came to pass it is too horrible to think that one man, a non-entity like Lee Harvey Oswald, had such extraordinary influence. Kennedy's life plays very well with the idea of the great man in history that so many people want to believe. Despite the fact that many historians rank Kennedy as, at best, a good president but certainly not a great one, many average citizens see him as one of the greatest.[14] Kennedy's death, thus, forces us to consider the very uncomfortable idea of the small, pathetic man in history who absurdly wields a sickly power. There is something too horrible to contemplate about a hero being brought down by a bumbling non-entity such as Oswald. History should *not* be changed by a sickly and deadly "pratfall."[15] Of course, DeLillo suggests another possible result of the Kennedy assassination:

> After Oswald, men in American are no longer required to lead lives of quiet desperation. You apply for a credit card, buy a handgun, travel through cities, suburbs and shopping malls, anonymous, looking for a chance to take a shot at the first puffy empty famous face, just to let people know there is someone out there who reads the papers.[16]

The anonymous, sad, defeated among us can take down the famous just because they can—for no other reason than a desperate man act but only to make a mark on history. The mark, and nothing else, being the sole point.

Thus, it is not surprising, then, that such a turn of events has compelled some of our most gifted and challenging novelists to consider and write. Don DeLillo and James Ellroy are two who have looked at the Kennedy assassination and imagined what could explain it. In DeLillo's *Libra* and Ellroy's *Underworld USA Trilogy* (made up of the novels *American Tabloid, The Cold Six Thousand*, and *Blood's a Rover*) we enter a world where the Kennedy story is neatly explained and the truth comes forward. The story, as presented by DeLillo and Ellory is a complex one but one that makes a kind of sense. In neither case is this truth comforting but at least it points us away from the disturbing idea that one, lone, sad little man brought the country low and twisted that country away from a bright future.

Furthermore, I believe as upsetting as it might be that the CIA or the Mob did this awful thing there is something oddly encouraging about conspiracy theories. They tell us that there are forces in control of events. Life is not one of randomness and unpredictable chaos. Psychologist and expert on conspiracy theories, Jan-Willem van Prooijen defines such theories as "the belief that a group of people—often powerful people collude in secret in order to make plans that are widely seen as malevolent or evil."[17] Thus, in the case of most conspiracy theories wicked or misguided forces control events but that means simply that bad people and corrupted institutions are in charge. As Brian Resnick observes, "The theories [conspiracy theories] are a tool by which people can feel more in control, and find explanations in a scary and turbulent world."[18] And, if the malevolent men can be exposed, and the truth comes out, then presumably good people and rightly ordered institutions can be restored to power. Every conspiracy theory is, in essence, a plea for a kind of restoration. On one level conspiracy theories are alarming but at another level they are unexpectedly reassuring. Of course, DeLillo and Ellroy sketch no picture of a restored world where the conspiracy is exposed and the good triumphs. There is a deep pessimism that pervades their works. However, the reader can still find solace in seeing the world more clearly. And, if there is hope in either

DeLillo or Ellroy's works it must be founded on the notion that we will no longer skim along the surface of political life. Any optimism for the coming of a better world requires, at the very least, a realistic appraisal of what is actually happening.

Of course, there is an even darker version of conspiracy theory. This one posits a world Byzantine its complexity with conspiracies inside of conspiracies. Life is a depressing fun house of mirrors that distort reality to such an extent that we can't be sure where anything is. Norman Mailer once remarked that the CIA was involved in so many plots around the world, dealing with so many weird people, the leaders of the agency couldn't be sure they were not involved in the Kennedy assassination in some way.[19]

JAMES ELLROY AND THE *UNDERWORLD USA TRILOGY*

To enter into the world of James Ellroy is to cross the threshold into a very dark place. (Indeed, his part memoir and part investigation of his mother's murder is entitled *My Dark Places*.) To friendly readers, his fictional accounts of the world are "uncompromising." To his critics, he is cynical and sordid. Nowhere is this more true than in the *Underworld USA Trilogy*. In these novels, he takes us from November 1958 to May 1972. And, in these works we encounter real figures such as John Kennedy, Robert Kennedy, J. Edgar Hoover, Howard Hughes, Jimmy Hoffa, and various real-life mobsters such as Sam Giancana, Santo Trafficante, and Carlos Marcello, to name the most famous ones.[20] (The Chicago *Outfit* plays the primary role in this account not the *Five Families* of New York.) This inclusion of actual people reinforces the verisimilitude of Ellroy's approach to writing these novels. The feel of the works is often reminiscent of television documentaries—particularly those found on such cable networks as The History Channel or the ID Channel that create documentaries that include reenacted scenes. For instance, in *American Tabloid,* there are sixteen sections in the book that are not chapters but described as "Document Inserts." (There are also "documents" inserted in numbered chapters as well.) These inserts include transcripts of taped telephone conversations of J. Edgar Hoover with other key players, surveillance tapes of mobsters and others, memos written by various characters (usually FBI agents), or headlines and snippets from newspapers. (The technique is somewhat suggestive of the "Newsreels" in John Dos Passos *USA Trilogy*.) Ellroy is trying to give the entire work a feel of authenticity to better reinforce the notion that he is telling the truth about what is happening.[21]

In Ellroy's version of America, it appears true that, as James Madison said, "enlightened statesmen will not always be at the helm."[22] However, unlike

Madison, there is no hope for institutional checks and balances in Ellroy's telling. The moral rot of the men (and it is almost exclusively men) in control is so pervasive, the greed and naked ambition so all-encompassing, that though they and their institutions do clash the result is not a better, or at least safer, world that Madison envisioned. The FBI, the CIA, business leaders, and the Mob are intertwined and work against *and* with each other to essentially debase the mythic ideals of the nation. To Ellroy, an entrenched and nefarious elite works solely to realize its own ends. The idea of the greater good emerging from the clash of interests is a laughable proposition. One cannot draw a pluralist defense of Ellroy's conflicts. In fact, Ellroy seems to be revising Madison's dictum about enlightened men. According to Ellory, it is not, "that enlightened statesmen *will not always* be at the helm." Rather, the depressive conclusion must be that "enlightened statesmen will *never* be at the helm."

My main focus will be on the first novel, *American Tabloid*, since it deals directly with the Kennedy assassination. Though the aftereffects of that event will reverberate in the subsequent novels much as the actual murder of JFK continued, and remarkably continues, to color later political life. (In October 2017, when President Trump announced that he would not stop the legally required release of Archive records of government files related to the assassination, there was a great deal of media coverage. And, as if on cue to continue the feeding of conspiracy-minded people, the president withheld the release of some documents that government agencies wanted redacted "because of national security, law enforcement, and foreign affairs concerns." The saga will never end.)[23]

The driving force that commences the trilogy are three fictional characters: Pete Bondurant, Kemper Boyd, and Ward Littell. Indeed, the first three chapters are the only titled chapters in the book and those titles are simply the names of these three characters. Ellroy signals, in these opening chapters, not only his focus on these three protagonists but that truth will be revealed by looking closer to the ground. We are wasting our time in focusing on Oswald and who he was. Oswald is actually a bit player in the bigger scheme of things. The real action, and the explanation for what is really going on, takes place in the intersection of mid-level operatives and their higher-ups.

Pete Bondurant is an ex-LA police officer who, as the novel opens, works for Howard Hughes as a security man and all-around assistant. Boyd and Littell are FBI agents and friends. In years past Boyd, Littell and Bondurant met one another, and not in a cordial way. Kemper Boyd described Pete thusly:

> Big Pete: shakedown man and Howard Hughes' pet goon. He [Kemper Boyd] and Ward Littell arrested him once—he beat a Sheriff's inmate to death. Littell's comment: "Perhaps the most fearsome and competent rogue cop of our era."[24]

Bondurant is skillful, venal, manipulative, without any sense of morals, and is physically imposing—a huge man. He thinks about money often, but more importantly craves action and is easily bored At one point, Ellroy describes Pete's thinking about some trip: "Miami felt like adventure, Miami felt like money."[25] And, when he is deciding whether to help Nixon or Kennedy in the 1960 election, he thinks, "The smart bet: Don't smear seasoned Red-baiter Nixon. Not so smart, but sexy: Smear him and put Jack in the White House."[26] Given who is he, he chooses the sexy alternative. He is the kind of man who says things like, "It sounds too legal" about training Cuban mercenaries.[27] This last sentence aptly sums up his life in one sentence. Only I should add that Bondurant's adventures are almost always violent by nature. He is quick to violence but he is usually in control of that violence and there is no suggestion that he is sadistic.

Kemper Boyd is charming, manipulative, pragmatic. He comes from a respected, but recently impoverished and tragic, southern family. ("My father went broke and killed himself. He willed me ninety-one dollars and the gun he did it with."[28]) The novel details, in dollars and cents and often in exhaustive descriptions of luxuries (hotel rooms, cloths, elegant meals, frequent martinis), his long-term effort to regain the lifestyle to which he was rightly born. (Chapter 17 opens with a typical comment concerning Boyd, "The Committee booked him into a Howard Johnson's. Kemper upgraded to a two-room suite at the Fontainebleau.")[29] He has been scarred by the lost of status—in discussing his wife, Elroy writes, "He [Boyd] married her for sex and her father's money. She divorced him when the Boyd fortune evaporated . . ."[30] Boyd ends up secretly working directly for Hoover, somewhat indirectly for the CIA, and in pursuing those jobs in eventually works directly for the Kennedys. His employment by the latter is to provide security for the then candidate, some political advice, and secure sexual partners to the sexually voracious JFK. Eventually, he lands a job in the Kennedy Justice Department. All of these activities give him an enormous income for the times ($59,000—over half of a million in today's dollars.) but this still is not enough to maintain the material way of life he wants and to keep company with the cultural and financial elite, as he rightly deserves. He is a man always calm, always in control, and never at a loss—at least through the first half of the novel.

Finally, Littell is an alcoholic, manipulative, somewhat weak, but idealistic believer in making the world just. Littell is also fervently Catholic and an "ex-Jesuit seminarian with a law degree, two years and two months shy of retirement."[31] He is assigned to work on chasing communists but "[I]t was boring, shitty work" because it was concerned with people who "posed no threat to America."[32] His real desire, at the start of the novel, is to be part of the THP (Top Hoodlum Program) rooting out the real corruption generated by organized crime—the Mob. But Hoover only wants the THP to observe organized crime and seeks to make a peace with the Mob. He has no desire to actually stamp out corruption. Indeed, Hoover thrives in a world swimming in corruption—as long as he knows about such corruption and can use that knowledge to maintain his position of power within the system. Littell sees corruption coming from within, within himself and his failings (such as his alcoholism and his ongoing struggles to control his addiction), with the Mob, thus within America, and not some supposed external international threat. He even has sympathy for the leftists he is surveilling as the novel opens "because their philosophy is based on human frailty."[33] Much to his FBI bosses' disgust, Littell even befriends one of the communist leaders he is supposed to be spying on. Littell is in search of heroes who will ultimately disappoint. And when that disappointment takes hold Littell changes and becomes the most sinister of characters.

Boyd and Littell are very close. For Boyd, Littell is, in effect, a younger brother to replace the one he accidentally killed. He looks out for Littell and sees in him the idealism that Boyd doesn't have time for. Boyd lives in a world that is fully compartmentalized (a word that is frequently used by both the narrator and the characters, usually to describe Boyd). Such compartmentalization of life makes a mockery of the demands of any kind of idealism. Yet, Boyd's softness toward Littell is a telling sign that there is something more to Boyd than he is willing to let on—even admit to himself. For Littell, an orphan, Boyd is someone to admire and look up to. Throughout the book, phrases such as "Boyd always said X" are a constant Littell refrain. Boyd is someone who helped him "achieve what I must fatuously describe as my manhood."[34]

As Ellroy documents, in the end, none of these men will come to a good conclusion. No one's fate, or the fate of their beliefs, will be triumphant. The only finality is one of corruption or death. The search for power and money (and money can be converted to power if used correctly) will continue as greed and ambition rule men's lives. There is no redemption in Ellory's accounting of how the world works. Ruthlessness becomes its own reward. Any glimmers of hope flicker briefly and then fade out.

Given this collection of characters, it is not surprising that *cynical* is one of the first words that comes to mind when reading Ellroy. Cynical means believing people are motivated by self-interest, rejecting society's insincere standards of morality and ethics, and being distrustful of other people's stated motives. But to think that Ellroy is cynical invites us to consider the history of cynicism and the philosophical school of thought known as cynicism. The origin of the word "cynic" comes from the Greek word *kunikos* and means "dog-like." There are a number of possible sources to explain the reason for dog-like but one is that the cynics were perceived as crude and even rude. They engaged in dog-like behavior by doing in public things that should be done in private, according to the Greeks. In many ways, this is something that Ellroy is apparently doing—making public what has hitherto been private or secret. And his style of writing spurns societal niceties another key point in cynical thought. Indeed, the cynics question all conventions (*nomos*) of Greek life. For instance, cynics praised the idea of freedom but particularly in terms of *parrhesia* which is the freedom to speak frankly. Ellroy will speak (write) frankly about politics. And it is important to note that while cynicism tends to have a bad connotation in today's society—attempting to tear down the good and offer nothing in return—the ancient Greek notion is connected to the ideal of seeing clearly, beyond society's conventions and to the truth.[35] Ellroy's goal is, if not to offer a solution to our political woes, to diagnose the rot that exists at the core of our political world. Moreover, he wants us to see this rot as going much further back in time than many would like to imagine. In a sense, this must be the only hope Ellroy can offer his readers. The knowledge to see beyond the myths we have been taught and too sadly cherish.

The story that Ellroy tells is an intricate one in which Bondurant, Littell, and Boyd all become involved in the intersection of the Kennedy campaign and later administration, the Mob, and the CIA in efforts to depose of Castro and retake Cuba. The Mob (again, mostly consisting of the Chicago Outfit) wants its casinos back and may even have worked with Castro, if he had not destroyed said casinos. For the Mob, it is just business, as a famous Mob-inspired movie character once said. For the CIA there is the cold calculus of being anti-Communist but this is not really ideologically driven—it is simply their job—their business. Weaving in and out of the narrative are Howard Hughes, as a drug-addled tycoon seeking to further his wealthy position ("half lucid and half nuts—and only cagey where coin was concerned"[36]), a grotesque and uncouth, comically anti-Kennedy Jimmy Hoffa, and J. Edgar Hoover (who is genuinely anti-Communist but this is completely intertwined with his own need to maintain power). As he tells Kemper Boyd when Boyd informs him that Kennedy will retain him as FBI head if elected,

> Of course he is. Every President since Calvin Coolidge has, and you should temper your distancing process with the knowledge that Prince Jack will be in office for a maximum of eight years, while I shall remain in office until the Millennium.[37]

With Hoffa and Hughes, Ellroy is telling us that being vehemently anti-Kennedy is ridiculous and not because the Kennedys are great. Rather, it is just that to passionately believe in anything is a sign that something is amiss in either your thinking or your character. Of the initial Kennedy haters (Hughes, Hoffa, and Hoover) only Hoover with his detachment and ability to see beyond his own hate comes off, if not admirable, at least with a weird kind of respectability. One knows that Hoover will endure. The other two come off as either pathetic or ignorant of what is truly going on. (Hoffa, for instance, is deeply connected to the mob and rants against Kennedy to Trafficante and others after the Outfit has already decided to secretly throw in with Kennedy during the 1960 election. He is contemptibly out of the loop.)

As I stated earlier, the story is very intricate and there are many divergent subplots that all somehow connect. The main outlines though run along the following route. The Mob, the CIA, and Hoover all either support (in the case of the Mob) or acquiesce (in the case of the CIA, which clinically accepts, and the FBI, which grudgingly accepts) the election of John F. Kennedy. They all have their own motives. The Mob wants to remove Castro and get their Cuban casinos back. They also think that President Kennedy can be influenced by a rapprochement. Their real anger is with Bobby Kennedy and his intense, almost manichaean, inspired pursuit of corruption and the Mob. (As Kemper Boyd remarks, "Bobby's a true judger and hater.")[38] The CIA wants to fight in Cuba largely becomes that is what it does—it fights wars against enemies. Finally, Hoover just wants to keep his job—and maintain his power. Eventually, this coalesces around what would become the Bay of Pigs operation. Pete Bondurant and Kemper Boyd represent the main characters on the ground in creating and training of the operational forces. Also, along the way Bondurant and Boyd see numerous ways to make a lot of money (this involves the procuring and selling of drugs). At this point, all seems to be coming together for these two main characters. They are going to get adventure, they are going to do the right thing in getting Cuba back, and they are going to get rich. Yet, this all falls apart when the Bay of Pigs fails and the blame falls largely on the shoulders of President Kennedy for not going all in on the invasion. The failure of the Bay of Pigs also signals the fall of various characters. The always calm and composed Kemper Boyd is described, as the Bay of Pigs is happening, as "mildly flustered" by Ward Littell.[39] "Flustered" is the one word you would never use to describe Boyd. As Boyd continues his descent he will become addicted to drugs and even, horrors, "disheveled in appearance." Yet, in his official capacity in the Kennedy Justice Department, he does honorably devote himself to the cause of civil rights. This ray of goodness continually baffles his associates and even surprises Boyd himself. ("No. I [Boyd] like the Negro people with just as much as you [Bondurant] like our Cubans, and offhand I'd say that their grievances are considerably more justified.")[40]

Elsewhere, Ward Littell in pursuit of the corrupt discovers and takes secret Mob accounting books that show a vast criminal enterprise that runs through the Teamsters. Namely, a fraudulent loan sharking operation exists that implicates hundreds of famous and important people. What is even more astounding is that Joe Kennedy was an initial funder of that scheme. The Kennedy fortune is linked, and not tangentially, with organized crime. Littell will keep this secret and do good if only he gets a job in the new Kennedy administration. But Bobby Kennedy, as attorney general, rebuffs his desires. Littell then descends to complete darkness and out of his fall (he is brutally fired by Hoover, who scotches whatever chances Littell had with Bobby Kennedy) a new hardened and vindictive Ward Littell emerges. The newly sober Littell eventually becomes a lawyer for Carlos Marcello and more generally a go-to legal adviser for other mobsters.

Eventually, this all comes crashing down. In the pieces of the Bay of Pigs fiasco a second attack, in the form of a hit, on Castro is planned. But this plan seems clownish and never appears to get off the ground. Bondurant and Boyd steal a fortune in heroin from the Mob. The Mob finds out about the theft and in return for sparing (maybe) their lives, Bondurant and Boyd must help plan a hit on the president. The mob has completely soured on Kennedy—he not only screwed up their hopes for Cuba he is an ingrate to boot for failing to appreciate their help in getting him elected. Ward Littell, whose hatred of all things Kennedy, helps create this operation and takes the lead ordering Bondurant and Boyd around. But all along there were actually two parallel assassination plans being put forth by the Mob. The one involving our main characters, set in Miami, is canceled and a second one organized by Guy Bannister (another real person, ex-FBI, who figures in many conspiracy theories about the assassination and a prominent character in Oliver Stone's *JFK*) in Dallas goes forward. Boyd is finally killed, while staying at "a discount motel" by Littell himself, as he is no longer useful and must be punished anyway for his drug theft. Peter Bondurant still proves of value but he will be relegated to pushing drugs in Las Vegas and he awaits the assassination in a dive bar in Dallas; however, he is away from the action he craves. Littell stands triumphant as a Mob lawyer. He is sober, corrupted, and now controlled by the mob as well. The weakest of the three main characters now appears "commanding" to his once more powerful accomplices—Boyd and Bondurant. Yet, his idealized goals have now become twisted and his original love of Robert Kennedy (his first encounter with Bobby was in the 1950s when Bobby as McClellan Committee counsel goes after mobsters with an intensity that inspires Littell) has turned to a sickening and brutal hatred. And by helping to kill President Kennedy he can maim the brother. In the end, only an all-powerful Mob and an all-knowing J. Edgar Hoover remain standing.

One of the hard lessons that Ellroy appears to be teaching is that neither pragmatism nor idealism can be our guiding principle. In many ways, Kemper Boyd and Ward Littel offer parallel commentaries on their more famous "twin." Boyd, with his compartmentalized professional life, his never-flustered demeanor, always elegant persona is the Jack Kennedy of the three main characters. JFK was known for his cool bearing and detachment. He was also known to be a more pragmatic politician of the era. Yet, at the same time, he could be inspiring—not just in rhetoric but in action. As E. J. Dionne observed is his column on the hundred anniversary of Kennedy's birth:

> Across our increasingly rigid political divides, we still treasure his cool and ironic perspective on life that coexisted with an infectious sense of public service. He drew thousands to government and tens of thousands to a Peace Corps that was one of his proudest creations.[41]

Kemper Boyd, like John F. Kennedy, has that mixture of coolness and a sense of public service. Boyd becomes more and more committed to the civil rights movement. In fact, the relentless narrative, which Ellroy crafts, that catalogues endless corruption, there are not infrequent scenes—almost detached from the main story—of Boyd becoming increasingly enthusiastic for this work. Yes, Boyd and Kennedy have many less-than-laudatory characteristics. Yet, along side that is the "infectious sense of public service" that Dionne recalls when all else fades from memory. However, sadly both men are killed. And as Ellroy writes, "Kemper died thinking of Jack."[42] Detachment, pragmatism, cool irony with a commitment to some greater ideal is snuffed out just as the goodness begins to emerge.

Littell is the Robert Kennedy of this book. He yearns to work with RFK early on and clearly has a nonsexual love for the man. Robert Kennedy was always the hot to JFK's cool. He was intense, moralistic, driven. He was driven by an idealism, a longing to do what was right no matter the cost. Many may consider him a hater—but he was a hater for the greater good. He wanted to punish but only because he wanted things to be better. This was already apparent to many in 1960 and would become publicly clear in his tragic 1968 run for the Democratic nomination. Littell is all those things—a man who at one time wanted to be a Jesuit priest, to hate sin, to worry about human frailty that exists so evidently in a broken world. However, Ward is also weak, brittle even. He also longs to do good but in so doing he becomes corrupted. He is rejected by his hero and all that drive to do something must go somewhere. Possibly forecasting physically what will happen to Littell internally, he is attacked and badly disfigured, particularly his face.[43] In a kind of middle period, after losing his job but still not a mob lawyer, Littell is already warped. For instance, in a very brief chapter Littell describes a life already set for the final corruption. In talking to Boyd, Littell observes, "Kemper calls his civil rights work "moving." It's that cheap noblesse oblige the Kennedys evince so condescendingly."[44] Ellroy is telling us that without being tethered to something greater and good Littell is easily (and out of desperation) transformed into the very things he fought. His commitment to the good is so thoroughly corrupted he comes to work for the very people he once hated. Unsurprisingly, Ellroy will not offer idealism as a way out. As he says elsewhere, about these books and America, "Anybody who doesn't know that politics is crime has got a few screws loose."[45]

DON DELILLO, OSWALD, AND LIBRA

If the world of Ellroy is the world of barely controlled violence bubbling up from below with mobsters and corrupt politicians in control, the world of Don DeLillo is a place of middle to high-level bureaucrats engaged in precision planning and the sweep of history guiding action. Meetings, committees, and a knowledgable detachment defines the novel. Whereas Ellroy will describe in graphic detail, with blood splatters and such, action scenes concerning the Bay of Pigs or the training beforehand, DeLillo has moments like this:

> He [Win Everett, a main character and CIA agent] and Larry Parmenter had belonged to a group called SE Detailed, six military analysts and intelligence men. The group was one element in a four-stage committee set up to confront the problem of Castro's Cuba. The first stage, the Senior Study Effort, consisted of fourteen high officials, including presidential advisers, ranking military men, special assistants, undersecretaries, heads of intelligence. They met for an hour and a half. Then eleven men left the room, six men entered. The resulting group, called SE Augmented, met for two hours. Then seven men left, four men entered, including Everett and Parmenter. This was SE Detailed, a group that developed specific covert operations then decided which members of SE Augmented ought to know about the plan. Those members in turn wondered whether the Senior Study Effort wanted to know what was going in stage three. Chances are they didn't. When the meeting in stage three was over, five men left the room and three paramilitary officers entered to form Leader 4.[46]

Along with this bureaucratic ballet there is the allure of history. DeLillo's Lee Harvey Oswald is a creature of history. He longs to be a part of *history*, to be an actor in the inevitable, relentless movement:

> Maybe what has to happen is that the individual must allow himself to be swept along, must find himself in the stream of no-choice, the single direction. This is what makes things inevitable. You use the restrictions and penalties they invent to make yourself stronger. History means to merge. The purpose of history is to climb out of your own skin.[47]

Later, while working with a Soviet spy, handler, "he could almost believe he was being remade on the spot, given an opening to some larger and deeper version of himself."[48] When he is, at first, denied in his attempt to stay in the Soviet Union he attempts suicide. When asked about it later by his Soviet handlers, he says, "I wanted to let someone else decide. It was out of my hands."[49] He writes a journal which he entitles, "Historic Diary."[50] Oswald has spent a lifetime in little apartments, hectored by his mother and her suffering at petty slights and larger failings, misunderstood by all around. Yet, he aches for significance and finds it in communism and being part of some larger moment. At times, he mouths the ideas about the injustices of Western capitalism. He also extols certain aspects of communism and the Soviet Union. And they appear to be sincere beliefs, particularly about the injustices of the world he lives in. But those moments are less frequent and less compelling than the idea of being a player in the unfaltering march of history to a new world. It is not that he doesn't care about the possible justice of Marxism so much as he sees this as secondary.[51]

These reflections on history are not confined to Oswald, though. Larry Parmenter, one of the main characters and a CIA agent, in contemplating the interconnection between the CIA and corporations observes:

> There were men related by blood and by marriage; there were company directors who were former high-ranking intelligence officers; there were government advisers who were once company directors.It was a society he recognized as a better-working version of the larger world, where things have an almost dreamy sense of connection to each other. Here the plan was tighter. *These were men who believed history was in their care.*[52]

Of course, it is worth noting the ambiguity of Paramenter's thoughts. These are "dreamy" connections and such powerful men "believed" they were in control. DeLillo's own character both admires and yet half consciously casts doubts on what this sense of history is and who is actually in control. And given the failures of so many operations, the Bay of Pigs and, as the novel documents, an attempted assassination of the president, one is left to wonder whether anyone is actually in control. For Paramenter, though, there is always the beauty of the Guatemala operation. In that case, through the use of a radio broadcasts that included, "[R]umors, false battle reports, meaningless codes, inflammatory speeches, orders to non-existent rebels" an unfriendly government collapses in nine days.[53]

Finally, Marguerite Oswald, a remarkably self-centered woman always explaining and justifying herself, closes the book:

> Lee Harvey Oswald. No matter what happened, how hard they schemed against her, this was the one thing they could not take away—the true and lasting power of his name. It belonged to her now, and to history.[54]

The last word of the book—*history*—defines so much of the way characters think and why they act in this book. The Kennedy assassination is a sadly exceptional moment in history. Much went into making it happen and much of exceptional importance would flow from it. This is true no matter who was behind it. To take a hold of someone, as Marguerite does with her son, is emblematic of why people act. It is to meld oneself into greatness no matter what constitutes that historical moment. DeLillo opens the book with a quote from the actual Lee Harvey Oswald, "Happiness is taking part in the struggle, where there is no borderline between one's own personal world, and the world in general."[55]

The premise of *Libra* is that disaffected CIA agents, upset over the failure to take back Cuba, plan to attempt an assassination of Kennedy. However, the initial plan is not to actually kill the president but to have "a surgical miss."[56] This will galvanize the American public and force the president and the nation to act with vengeance against Castro. That is the original plan formulated by Win Everett. In the process of fashioning the plot, Everett enlists the help of two other CIA operates, Lawrence Parmenter and T. J. Mackey. Parmenter is the sophisticated, Georgetown living, comfortable with the Washington scene one. The kind of man who dressing up as Castro for a costume party a month before the Bay of Pigs.[57] In some ways, he is reminiscent of Ellroy's Kemper Boyd. T. J. Mackey is "a roving paramilitary" man who "they use to pay to teach other men the fundamentals of deadly force."[58] In other ways, Mackey parallels Peter Bondurant. And, although Mackey has fallen from grace he is quickly employed to help in the operation. In the process, we encounter Lee Harvey Oswald, Guy Bannister, and David Ferrie to name a few of the real-world figures DeLillo casts in his story.[59]

In Ellroy's telling Kennedy's fate is controlled by the Mob and three law enforcement types driven by events that predate Cuba, Castro, and the Bay of Pigs. Yet, the Bay of Pigs is still important as a kind of accelerating event that will help bring the narrative to its logical conclusion. Kennedy must die and until his failure to support the Bay of Pigs, he is in danger of becoming approved by too many people. In DeLillo's version, the Bay of Pigs is the foundational moment which demands correcting. That which was wrong must be made right again. The CIA must make it right. As Larry Parmenter tells his wife:

> It's the job of an intelligence service to resolve a nation's obsessions. Cuba is a fixed idea. It is prickly in a way Russia is not. More unresolved. More damage to the psyche. And this is our job, to remove the psychic threat, to learn so much about Castro, decipher his intentions, undermine his institutions to such a degree the loses the power to shape the way we think, to shape the way we sleep at night.[60]

The Mob, in *Libra*, is just a set of side players in the drama; whereas they are the main characters for Ellroy. For Ellroy, the criminals are in charge.

For DeLillo, the bureaucracy, and not even the highest levels, are the ones forcing matters.

The key moment, though, in the novel is when T. J. Mackey changes the plan. Mackey sees that Everett had made a brilliant move in switching from taking out Castro directly and focusing instead on Kennedy. "Everett had seen the logic of staying home. The idea had power and second sight. Of course, Everett did not plan to shoot Kennedy in the strict sense."[61] Mackey sees the flaws in such a plan. The original plan is too complex, "mazes that extended to infinity."[62] So, Mackey makes the second leap and knows the president must die:

> They had to take it all the way. It was a revelation to him that in the moment he saw what had to be done, feeling the crash of the air on the hood of the car,he felt the oddest goddamn sympathy for President Jack.[63]

There is no indication that Mackey particularly hates Kennedy, though he resents him for not backing the Bay of Pigs. He is really just taking things to their logical conclusion. And, importantly, Mackey will bring in Cuban shooters to do the job. Oswald is part of the plan and he is a patsy of a sort. He is a willing participant in that plan eventually. He is both central as a fall guy and shooter. Though, his participation as shooter is secondary to the real assassins.

The conclusion of the book is a typical tour de force of writing by DeLillo. He weaves together people, important and incidental, as they witness the final day in Dallas. Somewhat earlier in the book, while David Ferrie (a man of surprising if odd philosophical views) is talking to Oswald, Ferrie observes:

> "Think of two parallel lines," he said. "One is the life of Lee H. Oswald. One is the conspiracy to kill the President. What bridges the space between them? What makes a connection inevitable? There is a third line. It comes out of dreams, visions, intuitions, prayers, out of the deepest levels of the self. It's not generated by cause and effect like the other lines. It's a line that cuts across causality, cuts across time. It has no history that we can recognize or understand. But it forces a connection. It puts a man on his path of destiny."[64]

Later, Ferrie observes, "That building's been sitting there waiting for Kennedy and Oswald to converge."[65]

Through the book we are also privy to the work of "a retired senior analyst of the Central Intelligence Agency," Nicholas Branch. He is "hired on contract to write the secret history of the assassination of President Kennedy."[66] Early in the book we learn "he is in the fifteenth year of his labor."[67] One of the main themes of Branch's role in the story is to highlight the way we can never fully understand what happened. Yet, there is all this information.

> Everything is here. Baptismal records, report cards, postcards, divorce petitions, canceled checks, daily timesheets, tax returns, property lists, postoperative x-rays, photos of knotted string, thousands of pages of testimony, of voices droning in hearing rooms in old courthouse buildings, an incredible haul of human utterance.[68]

Branch is privy to any information he wants to have and he believes all of it is somehow important. At first, it might seem that with just enough concerted effort all these facts will tell a story—the complete story to explain the event. He will be able to understand and then explain "that moment in Dallas, the seven seconds that broke the back of the American century."[69] Yet he is overwhelmed by it all and has not moved very far in actually writing the report.[70] Part of the problem is the very enormity of all these facts that somehow must be made to cohere.[71] That problem is noted early in the novel. Later, though, Branch observes that even the facts won't stay still. "One of the first documents he examined was the medical report on Pfc. Oswald's self-inflicted gunshot wound. In one sentence the weapon is described as 45-caliber. In the next sentence is is 22-caliber."[72] Later still, near the final pages of the novel, Branch begins to worry that the agency is not giving even him all the information.

> There's something they are not telling him. The Curator [who sends Branch all the material he needs and asks for] delays, lately, in filling certain requests for information, seems to ignore other requests completely. What are they holding back? How much more is there? . . . .Now he wonders if the Agency is protecting something very much likes it identity - protection is own truth, its theology of secrets.[73]

Is Branch on to something—the agency is holding back information? Or, is he losing it a bit in the sea of data? It is possible that Branch represents DeLillo himself or maybe the reader. There is all this information to be reviewed—has anything in American history ever been as documented as widely as the Kennedy assassination? Yet we can't make sense of it. With each new piece of evidence, it seems that one thing is cleared up but two more unanswered questions arise.

CONCLUSION

The stories we tell about our politics are important. All stories need heroes and challenges, triumphs and failures. Americans, in this time as much as any, would like to think of heroes. Our hyper-partisan era, with its intense tribalism, lacks heroes that can transcend our political divides. That alone can explain a great deal about why we look back to Kennedy and dwell upon his death. That is why people are still drawn to him. And, probably why they believe that if we could only unmask and explain who really killed Kennedy the world can be made right again.

To Ellroy, this is a fool's errand. The unmasking will only end in heartache as we only learn that "politics is crime." The Kennedy assassination is only an important event in the first novel of a trilogy that reveals this stark fact. America is corrupt and politics is not going to save us. Heroes don't exist. Everyone is in for themselves. At the center of Ellroy's thinking is, I believe, a rejection of politics. We are foolish to place our hopes in such things and the sooner we learn that the better. It may be painful but it is also the only realistic—adult—thing to do.

For DeLillo the mythic is real. It does have a great deal of pull. However, the stories we tell about ourselves and key events can never be fully explained. The unmasking of the conspiracy cannot happen with any finality. There are too many facts, too many possibilities. DeLillo tells us a story, it is plausible; however, as the character of Nicholas Branch reminds us, we cannot really know. DeLillo places in the novel itself a character who throws doubt on everything else that DeLillo is presenting. Even the motives of the characters are complex. Oswald only hesitantly joins the plot that is designed, by others, around him. And, after it is all over, Oswald seems to genuinely suggest multiple explanations for what he did. Maybe he is rehearsing stories he can tell the police—but it seems just as likely he believes them at some level. He tells himself three plot lines—deny he did, say he did it, but he was part of a greater plot that was the real evil, or accept his fate as the lone gunman. The last almost seems to be the best way to go. "He and Kennedy were partners."[74]

DeLillo tells us that like the Kennedy legend itself, there are so many possibilities. We are, in a way, paralyzed by possibilities and left unsure. Politics is pregnant with too much meaning. For DeLillo, we cannot know and that is bound to be frustrating. For Ellroy, it is almost too easy to know. We just need to realize that politics is simple—simple corruption.

NOTES

1. https://fivethirtyeight.com/features/the-one-thing-in-politics-most-americans-believe-in-jfk-conspiracies/

2. http://www.esquire.com/news-politics/a13099987/jfk-assassination-conspiracy-theories/

3. For a review of various conspiracy theories and Bobby Kennedy, see https://www.irishcentral.com/roots/robert-f-kennedy-believed-jfk-was-killed-because-of

-him?utm_source=zergnet.com&utm_medium=referral&utm_campaign=zergnet_2183247

4. http://www.centerforpolitics.org/crystalball/articles/public-rates-presidents-jfk-reagan-obama-at-top-nixon-lbj-trump-at-bottom/

5. Like any politician of his era Kennedy faced a highly diverse party—the Democratic party was an uneasy alliance between ideological liberal Northerners and more conservative Southern Democrats, at least when it came to issues like civil rights.

6. Thomas Mallon, *Jack be Nimble, The New Yorker*, May, 22, 2017, p. 85.

7. As Alan Brinkley highlights, a Defense Department policy paper argued that "The United States needs a *Grand Objective*. . . . The Key consideration is not that the Grand Objective be exactly right, it is that we *have* one and that we start moving toward it." Quoted in Brinkley's Atlantic Monthly essay, https://www.theatlantic.com/magazine/archive/2013/08/the-legacy-of-john-f-kennedy/309499/

8. Quoted in https://www.theatlantic.com/magazine/archive/2013/08/the-legacy-of-john-f-kennedy/309499/

9. https://www.jfklibrary.org/Asset-Viewer/LH8F_0Mzv0e6Ro1yEm74Ng.aspx

10. This case is made most forcefully by Ira Stoll, *JFK, Conservative* (New York: Houghton Mifflin Harcourt, 2013). While Stoll's case is fairly weak—few people at the time saw Kennedy as a conservative and it requires being somewhat anachronistic to make the case—it is nonetheless telling that conservatives today sometimes make this argument.

11. https://www.theatlantic.com/magazine/archive/2013/08/the-legacy-of-john-f-kennedy/309499/

12. https://www.theatlantic.com/magazine/archive/2013/08/the-legacy-of-john-f-kennedy/309499/

13. Some exception to this assessment must be made for Ronald Reagan. Reagan was certainly bold and one cannot say his administration ended in failure. However, the onset of his personal dementia and the fact that he has not, as of yet, transcended the partisan nature of his support means Reagan has not reached such mythic levels of presidential greatness. He may someday do that—but it remains to be seen. I think the key factor is the partisan angle. Truly great and admired presidents are no longer seen primarily as Democrats or Republicans first. Although Democrats today (Obama for instance) have said nice things about Reagan no Democrat embraces the Reagan legacy.

14. See https://www.theatlantic.com/magazine/archive/2013/08/the-legacy-of-john-f-kennedy/309499/

15. Also, one possibility is when all the documents are released and all the evidence is considered, what we will find is: first, that our government is hiding a lot, to protect its image and cover up a lot of bungling. Second, that we will never know for certain anything. Third, that it is still a distinct possibility that one man acted alone.

16. DeLillo, Libra, p. 181.

17. https://www.vox.com/science-and-health/2017/4/25/15408610/conspiracy-theories-psychologist-explained. For an interesting take on the political movies that trade in JFK and conspiracy, see Art Simon's *Slate* essay on the 1970s movie, *The*

Parallax View, http://www.slate.com/articles/arts/conspiracy_thrillers/2017/07/the_parallax_view_is_a_70s_paranoid_classic_about_evil_corporations_and.html

18. https://www.vox.com/science-and-health/2017/4/25/15408610/conspiracy-theories-psychologist-explained. Of course one of the most frustrating things about dealing with conspiracy theorists is that any evidence contrary to the conspiracy is rejected—often as a sign of the conspiracy itself. Hany Farid, a photo forensic expert, did extensive work on the famous photograph of Oswald holding a gun in his backyard. The photograph does look odd, but his research showed that it was, in fact, an authentic photo and not a forgery. But, Farid simply "became part of the conspiracy" in the eyes of many. See Joshua Rothman, "Afterimage," *The New Yorker*, November 12, 2018, p. 43.

19. Josh Marshall of TPM wrote about this in his posts there and in personal communication to the author.

20. For a discussion of the reality underlying the fictional account provided by Ellroy, see Selwyn Raab (*Five Families*, New York: St. Martin's Press, 2005), pp. 146–154.

21. Another example of this is with the precision that Ellroy often employs. When FBI agent Ward Littell steals some money from a mid-level mobster it is not described as about 80,000 or even 81,000, it is "81,492." This is the kind of precision that underlies the way Ellroy can write.

22. James Madison, *Federalist Papers, # 10,* in *The Debate on the Constitution*, (New York: The Library of America, 1993), p. 407.

23. https://www.nytimes.com/2017/10/26/us/politics/jfk-files.html?_r=0 Not much of importance was actually found in these documents and the essential outlines of what we know stays intact. However, there were tantalizing bits of information that give color to events and people—someone calling the FBI to threaten the killing of Oswald the day before Oswald was murdered, for instance.

24. James Ellroy, *American Tabloid* (New York: Random House, 1995), p. 24.

25. ibid., p. 83.

26. ibid., p. 312.

27. ibid., p. 230.

28. ibid., p. 147.

29. Ibid. p. 124. There is also a description of a party given by Joe Kennedy which takes place at Caryle in Kennedy's "magnificent suite" with a view of "the breadth of Central Park" (p. 110). The party is populated by the famous and infamous.

30. ibid, p. 25.

31. Ibid, p. 31.

32. ibid. p. 31.

33. ibid. p. 34.

34. ibid. p. 337.

35. Much of this discussion of cynicism comes from Julie Piering http://www.iep.utm.edu/cynics/.

36. ibid.p. 311.

37. Ibid., pp. 297–298.

38. ibid., p. 362.
39. ibid., p. 400.
40. ibid., p 400.
41. https://www.washingtonpost.com/opinions/jfk-the-forever-young-president-100-years-on/2017/05/28/f62ac0f2-4188-11e7-9869-bac8b446820a_story.html?utm_term=.7ee3d2d40fcb
42. Ibid., p. 572.
43. ibid, see chapters 46 and 49.
44. Ibid., p. 355.
45. Stephen Capen, Interview with James Ellroy, https://web.archive.org/web/20060323195230/http://www.worldmind.com/Cannon/Culture/Interviews/ellroy.html.
46. DeLillo, Libra, p. 20.
47. DeLillo, Libra, p. 101.
48. DeLillo, Libra, p. 113.
49. DeLillo, Libra, p. 158.
50. DeLillo, Libra, p. 179. Later, DeLillo writes of Oswald, "He believed religiously that his life would turn in such a way that people would one day study the Historic Diary for clues for the heart and the mind of man who wrote it" (p. 212).
51. At one point, Oswald muses on the coincidences that seem to be tying everyone together. He lists five coincides in quick succession. Some of them are banal and silly, a desperate attempt to see connections. "Lee was always two or three books, like Kennedy." Yet they all suggest Oswalds need to see such connections as fraught with meaning. His life is saturated with greater meaning. Libra, p. 336.
52. DeLillo, Libra, p. 127. Italics added.
53. DeLillo, Libra, p. 125. This is, of course, the very real CIA backed coup of the Guatemala government in 1954.
54. DeLillo, Libra, p. 456.
55. DeLillo, Libra, p. 1
56. DeLillo, Libra, p. 219.
57. DeLillo, Libra, p. 129.
58. DeLillo, Libra, p. 220.
59. Ellroy is quite candid and appreciative about the influence DeLillo had on him. He praises Libra specifically and says, "I've learned from Don DeLillo, I discovered Delillo and I credit him every chance I get . . ." See M. G. Smout, http://www.barcelonareview.com/24/e_lunch.htm. See also, Stephen Capen, https://web.archive.org/web/20060323195230/http://www.worldmind.com/Cannon/Culture/Interviews/ellroy.html. In referring to Libra, Ellroy says, " I read that book and got hooked on the Kennedy assassination. I had never been interested in it before."
60. DeLillo, Libra, p. 258. Of course, just before telling his wife about the psychic need to handle Castro, Parmenter laments the loss of some potentially lucrative oil fields he might have had if Cuba had stayed under Batista's control.
61. DeLillo, p. 219.
62. DeLillo, p. 219.
63. DeLillo, pp. 219–220.

64. DeLillo, p. 339. A little later in the book, pp. 351–353, Guy Bannister and Ferrie continue to talk about Oswald and his fate. Oswald has yet to finally make the leap to what he has to do. Ferrie reassures Bannister that Oswald will eventually do what he has to, "Leon's a type he is willing to relinquish control at some point down the line. . . . It just has happened yet."

65. DeLillo, p. 384.

66. DeLillo, p. 15.

67. DeLillo, p. 14.

68. DeLillo, p. 181.

69. DeLillo, p. 181.

70. DeLillo, p. 301.

71. DeLillo, p. 378. "There is nothing in the room he [Branch] can discard as irrelevant or out-of-date. It all matters on one level or another. This is the room of lonely facts. The stuff keeps coming."

72. DeLillo, p. 300.

73. DeLillo, p. 442.

74. DeLillo, p. 435.

BIBLIOGRAPHY

Brinkley, Alan, *Legacy of John F. Kennedy*, Atlantic Monthly, August 2008.

Capen, Stephen, *Interview with James Ellroy, Worldguide*, January 17, 1997.

DeLillo, Don, *Libra*, New York: Penguin, 1988.

Dionne, E. J., *JFK, the forever-young president, 100 years on, Washington Post*, May 28, 2017.

Ellroy, James, *American Tabloid* (New York: Random House, 1995).

Enten, Harry, Most People Believe in JFK Conspiracy Theories, 538, October 23, 2017.

Hallemann, Caroline, *The 5 Biggest Kennedy Conspiracy Theories, Esquire*, October 26, 2017.

Irish Central Staff, *Robert F. Kennedy Thought JFK was Killed Because of Him*, June 1, 2023.

Kennedy, Joh, F., *Televised Address to the Nation on Civil Rights,* June 11, 1963, JFK Library.

Madison, James, *Federalist Papers, # 10,* in *The Debate on the Constitution*, New York: The Library of America, 1993.

Mallon, Thomas, *Jack be Nimble, The New Yorker*, May 22, 2017.

New York Times, *J.F.K. Files Released, Highlighting Hoover, L.B.J. Among Others,* October 26, 2017.

Piering, Julie, cynics, Internet Encyclopedia of Philosophy.

Raab, Selwyn, *Five Families*, New York: St. Martin's Press, 2005.

Resnick, Brian, *The Dark Allure of Conspiracy Theories, Explained by a Psychologist, Vox,* May 25, 2017.

Rothman, Joshua, *Afterimage*, *The New Yorker*, November 12, 2018.
Simon, Art, In *The Parallax View, Conspiracy Goes All the Way to the Top—and Beyond,Slate,* July 27, 2017.
Smout, M. G., *Lunch and Tea with James Ellroy, The Barcelona Review,* April 15, 2001.
Stoll, Ira, *JFK, Conservative*, New York: Houghton Mifflin Harcourt, 2013.
UVA Center for Politics, *Public Rates Presidents: Kennedy, Reagan, Obama at Top, Nixon, Johnson, Trump at Bottom*, February 15, 2018.

Conclusion

"James Ellroy and the Dark Criminal Vision of American Politics"

Darrell A. Hamlin

THE WORLD TURNED UPSIDE DOWN

Former Colombo crime family *caporegime* Michael Franzese has claimed that an interview on the morning news show *Fox & Friends* sparked the genesis of a duty to warn Americans that their government operates as an organized crime enterprise. Claiming to be gripped by moral obligation from the insight, in 2022 the convicted felon published *Mafia Democracy: How Our Republic Became a Mob Racket.*[1] Franzese writes that like most Americans, he watched government officials line their own pockets, reward high-dollar donors with access and anonymity, and unplug corruption reform with loopholes. "But unlike most citizens, I can see our elected officials' behavior for what it really is—a Mafia-style Democracy. Our elected leaders have become racketeers proficient in carrying out Mob-like rackets, and we are all suffering as a result." At least he said it was still a democracy, which is something, unless you are aware that even actual pirates apparently operated with more commitment to democracy than the wealthy aristocratic societies they plundered.[2] Underscoring the irony of an extended lecture on civic virtue from a convicted gangster, the Foreword for Franzese's book is provided by none other than former Mob prosecutor Rudy Giuliani, whose license to practice law was suspended in New York and the District of Columbia in 2021 for ethics violations related to the *kraken* of legal challenges released under his direction after the 2020 election.[3]

There is, of course, a long tradition of corruption critiques in scholarship, journalism, and popular culture. Generally, the criticism is aimed at excesses of capitalism that infect the institutions of public life. Yet Franzese's indictment of government-as-organized-crime is leveled at regulatory practices that intrude upon the excesses of capitalism. Franzese's argument reads more like a former high-earning mobster testifying in the court of public opinion against people doing what he used to do. *Mafia Democracy* is a book functioning as the witness for the state—with a letter of recommendation from the prosecutor who put him behind bars. The Franzese finesse here is that Mafia members like himself broke the law, while the systemic practices he describes as a Mafia-style operation are legal.

Regulatory corruption is, in fact, a kind of political corruption, an opportunistic force in American public life that we often must drag into the light—to punish criminal conduct, but also to shame the sabotage of public policy. Explanations of the nature and depravity of corruption have been a staple of investigative journalism, cataloging the rogue behaviors of both opportunists and regulators. An ironic strain of such critiques has been present in popular narratives of American public life throughout our history. This critique suggests that opportunist roguery in the regulatory process is not about bad apples that can be culled from the barrel if we aim the right reform at the right loophole, it's entwined in the DNA of American capitalism. Working the system, cheating, even breaking the law is not the dirty exhaust of the system, according to this critique – it's the fuel.

We can see this second critical thread in a variety of popular media from the nineteenth, twentieth, and twenty-first centuries—in newspaper features, mass audience political reporting, and feature-length film documentaries, each of them representing popular expressions of the day. Examples include Tammany Hall boss George Washington Plunkitt, filmmaker Michael Moore, and former *Rolling Stone* contributing editor Matt Taibbi. What is identifiable in these three is the attempt to explain fundamental and driving elements of American life by explaining the momentum of corruption in American capitalism. The style is characterized by narratives about corruption that are popular because they use humor, sarcasm, and irony to make their points about American capitalism; offering a kind of moral critique of how America works, for good or for ill; offering a bleak yet uncynical perspective of the relationship of individual citizens to the larger system, arguing essentially that citizens have more authority on the question of political corruption than the prevailing narratives seem to allow.

George Washington Plunkitt is the best example here.[4] Like Franzese, he gave the public an insider's view of corruption. Unlike Franzese, Plunkitt had a sense of humor. Plunkitt was born in New York City in 1842 and died there in 1924. Starting in the 1860s until his death, Plunkitt was a boss in an urban political machine that is synonymous with corruption—Tammany Hall. Plunkitt is known to us now for a famous little book he was part of publishing in 1905, a book that started out as a series of popular newspaper features written in his voice with the help of a local journalist named William Riordon. The articles, and later the book called *Plunkitt of Tammany Hall*, are described by Terrence McDonald as "not simply an exact record of the words of Plunkitt, however; it is rather the product of a collaboration between a life-long politician with a carefully crafted public image and a journalist seeking to write a book that would sell."[5] Everybody involved in the project of capturing the essence of Plunkitt wanted the book to be a commercial success. The book did become successful and has remained a touchstone of this literature because it had the charming effect of simultaneously explaining corruption and winking at it. Even more impressive is that Plunkitt provides the nuts and bolts of political power and personal pocket-lining with a narrative that operates to instill the virtues of loyalty, statesmanship, and civic purpose.

For Plunkitt, the success of political life is measured, ultimately, by whether elected officials take care of the citizens who elected them. Politicians are only principled actors if their guiding principle is constituent service and well-being. Looking too closely at how that service is delivered, however, is like inspecting the process of sausage-making. *Is your objective a clean sausage room, or do you want sausage?* The problem with civil service reform, he argues, is that the most it can deliver—and it is a short-term delivery—is a system that operates toward following the precisely defined rules of a clean system, but not toward delivering results for the underlying needs of citizens.

It takes clever politicians to get you what you want from the system. Resourceful, imaginative, ambitious professional political operators. When you get that kind of skill and craft, you also get operators who deploy that skill set toward personal ends. For Plunkitt, the clever and resourceful politician—in the natural course of taking care of constituents—is also well-positioned to discern ways of enriching himself. The important factor is whether he enriches himself in the service of others, or whether he enriches himself in the service of self. This distinction is the most famous part of Plunkitt's worldview, which he sums up as the difference between *honest graft* and *dishonest graft.*

> *There's an honest graft, and I'm an example of how it works. I might sum up the whole thing by saying, "I seen my opportunities, and I took 'em."*
>
> *Just let me explain by example. My party's in power in the city, and its goin' to undertake a lot of public improvements. Well, I'm tipped off, say, that they're going to lay out a new park at a certain place. I see my opportunity, and I take it. I go to that place, and I buy up all the land I can in that neighborhood. Then the board of this or that makes its plan public, and there is a rush to get my land, which nobody cared particular for before.*
>
> *Ain't it perfectly honest to charge a good price and make a profit on my investment and foresight? Well of course it is, and that's honest graft.*[6]

It is critical to note that what Plunkitt has just described was not illegal at the time. It is now, but not then. Then, it was illegal to literally steal from the treasury, or blackmail gamblers or saloon keepers. Plunkitt operates with a moral code. How you get rich must be legal, one should be sober, and faithful to one's wife, because a man who cheats on his own wife is not to be trusted with anything else. Be grateful. Be humble. Above all, take care of the people who elected you to take care of them. In other words, SERVE. Your public role may position you, from time to time, to privately profit from questionable but legal opportunities. But your public purpose is to serve the public good with the best of your energy, imagination, and ambition.

This moral code underlying the just operations of public life is crucial, as one can learn from Moore and Taibbi.[7] The central, driving feature of their critiques of American capitalism is that it has become un-moored from moral purpose even as the deregulation of American economic life made it legal to achieve phenomenal wealth through immoral business practices because of a corrupt relationship to government regulation. Yet, for Plunkitt, while this is legal graft, it is not honest graft, because those who were elected to take care of their constituents instead began to take care of their contributors. Instead of citizens being served by their representatives, the fix came in against them.

It is in the space between Plunkitt and Franzese that we can consider the effort of James Ellroy, through his *USA Underworld Trilogy*, to explain the real American system. It is a project to expose the criminal purposes and control of government operating to steer public choices toward their own interests. It is a retelling of history with real Mafia dons making decisions and financing the direction of American commitments from an underworld wielding power and influence.

RECKLESS VERISIMILITUDE

We know the *USA Underworld Trilogy* is a retelling of American history because James Ellroy announced it at the beginning of *American Tabloid*.[8]

> *America was never innocent. We popped our cherry on the boat over and looked back with no regrets. You can't ascribe our fall from grace to any single event or set of circumstances. You can't lose what you lacked at conception.*
>
> *Mass-market nostalgia gets you hopped up for a past that never existed. Hagiography sanctifies shuck-and-jive politicians and reinvents their expedient gestures as moments of great moral weight. Our continuing narrative line is blurred past truth and hindsight. Only a reckless verisimilitude can set that line straight.*

The real Trinity of Camelot was Look Good, Kick Ass, Get Laid. Jack Kennedy was a mythological front man for a particularly juicy slice of our history. He talked a slick line and wore a world-class haircut. He was Bill Clinton minus pervasive media scrutiny and a few rolls of flab.

Jack got whacked at the optimum moment to assure his sainthood. Lies continue to swirl around his eternal flame. It's time to dislodge his urn and cast light on a few men who attended his ascent and facilitated his fall.

They were rogue cops and shakedown artists. They were wiretapper and soldiers of fortune and faggot lounge entertainers. Had one second of their lives deviated off course, American History would not exist as we know it.

It's time to demythologize an era and build a new myth from the gutter to the stars. It's time to embrace bad men and the price they paid to secretly define their time.

Here's to them.[9]

The idea that some versions of truth can be better than others calls to mind Karl Popper, Stephen Colbert, and more recently, Kellyanne Conway.[10] But Ellroy's focus on Kennedy and *Camelot* is telling. JFK and *Camelot* offer the most direct point of departure for the epic demythologizing demolition Ellroy plans. It is the perfect leverage point from which to pry the grate off the gutter and bring not just the characters of *American Tabloid* onto the stage but also the hidden character of America into what he considers a worthy perspective. There is another reason. The *Camelot* myth and JFK himself are the product of another project to tell a story unknown to the public. The story Jackie Kennedy fashioned shortly after her husband's show-stopping state funeral, possibly the first television mini-series.

A funeral is basically a "hot take" on the history of a life. The funeral form advances the interpretation of a life to an audience that often relearns the facts of a life in an emotionally purposeful way. The catharsis of grief and loss is a powerful sealant of perspective because the funeral itself is a narrative device. The emotional context of the funeral narrative operates to shape the reality that you take away. That's where the interpretation becomes a place where we make sense of the life history. Yet when that emotional catharsis and narrative power intersects with a moment of great historic significance, the story cauterizes into the culture itself. After the shocking assassination of the president on November 22, 1963, what followed was three days of constructed televised mourning, with iconic images such as JFK, Jr.—little John-John—stepping out to salute his father's passing casket. It is one thing to take part in the memory of the funeral events this way—as an audience grieving with others. But the power of this mythology is much more problematic when it literally changes what future generations take on as historic reality.

The legacy of John F. Kennedy's presidential administration as *Camelot* mythology is *the* great example. The origin is a *Life Magazine* interview shortly after the assassination.[11] November 29 (five days after the funeral events) Jackie invited two photographers and a writer to the family compound in Hyannis port. She revealed that President Kennedy himself would play the songs in the residence, following along with the words,

Don't let it be forgot
That once there was a spot
For one brief shining moment
That was known as Camelot.[12]

Like the moments after a funeral, the haze of emotion in her storytelling lingered as the prevailing reality. JFK's administration became a time of innocence and purpose with a young vital president tacking to a clear moral line on the horizon, grounded in family held together by a wholesome dedicated marriage. The problem is that this narrative is very much at odds with the facts. We have not needed Ellroy's *reckless verisimilitude* to learn that JFK was a man with a variety of almost debilitating health challenges, that he was a pathological adulterer, that his family operated a political machine with a shady, criminal past, and that the true horizon line of his administration was always his re-election. Yet mythology is more powerful, more useful, and more comforting, so *Camelot* is the story that lives on.

The wave of grief over the loss of JFK, and the psychological need to make elegiac sense out of it, unleashed a spasm of expression in popular culture. Tribute music is just one thread. In the weeks and months after the assassination, there were dozens of sentimental songs that flooded the airwaves, many of them so utterly misrepresenting of the reality that the underlying project of revision is a powerful psychological force.

Tragic Songs of the Grassy Knoll, a collection of JFK tribute music, is the most efficient way to go through this wormhole.[13] A collection compiled for release in connection with the 50th anniversary of the assassination, the playlist includes sixteen songs, all originally released as forty-five RPM. Fourteen of them were released within a year of the assassination. One was released in 1968 in tribute to Robert Kennedy after his assassination. Genres include Country Western, Rockabilly, and Gospel. Performers include names like The Justice Brothers, Hayden Privitt and the Patriots, Hasil Adkins and his Happy Guitar, and the Honorable Bob Peters. These were quick, cheap, low-budget recordings that hit the airwaves in the aftermath of the funeral events. This was TikTok in 1964, when AM radio *was* social media.

The songs proceed through recurring themes and imagery. Dallas. Jackie's wedding ring placed on her dead husband's finger. Heaven's gain of a great leader and patriot. The last one, however, is a song released in 1988 and covered several times in the 1990s. It jumps out in a jarring way, like a drunk cousin who tells inappropriate stories at a wedding reception. "Lee Harvey was a Friend," by Homer Henderson and the Dalworthington Garden Boys, disrupts the work of mythology, because it is an ode to revisionism itself.[14] Revising history operates the way building implosion revises the skyline. In this story, Lee Harvey Oswald is a good guy, friendly neighbor, a favorite of the kids. He's a regular fellow who just could not have shot the president. It's all just a frame-up, fake news. The song is about the disbelief that has healed the pain of reality. Its power is the earnest, reflexive resistance to the believability of anything bad you hear about Lee Harvey, much like Jackie preempting whatever you will hear in the future that speaks ill of JFK and those glorious days.

Politically, what is interesting or important resides not simply in the power of the JFK *Camelot* myth but in what that need to revise reveals about the vulnerabilities in our civic capacity. About this weakness for constructed reality in the American psyche. Can democratic life survive this need to implode the structures of reality, to just keep erasing facts from the skyline of our history? These questions, perhaps not surprisingly, lead to the attempt to make sense of the historic reality of the Trump presidency. Less as analysis of public policy and governance, more as the cultural moment of MAKE AMERICA GREAT AGAIN, which I would argue is a dark, updated, set-the-controls-for-the-heart-of-the-sun version of *CAMELOT*.

What *Camelot* and MAGA both do is undermine the history we have about our past that is based on the idea of truth as facts, not as mythology. However, the difference between MAGA and *Camelot* is that *Camelot* is looking back, trying to convince you that something mediocre was glamorous, exciting, noble. MAGA is misrepresentation used to implode, or at least shout down, any argument that greatness itself is about anything other than winning. *Camelot* and MAGA are both "truthy" stories of American greatness. Alternative facts. *Camelot* is sentimental revisionism, and it speaks to how we can be convinced, over the course of a traumatic funeral weekend, that a marginally accomplished administration was a shining moment we should never forget. But MAGA is an alarming worldview precisely because it is not really about the past at all. MAGA is a dark, active political vision of the future, a fully envisioned retro-fascism, not just a gauzy myth about our past.

SYMPOSIUM

Circling back to this book's introduction, we told you that these essays offer neither a full biography of Ellroy nor an exhaustive analysis of his work.

Just as every thousand-piece puzzle comes together from the sorting of color patterns that somehow fit together, the contributors here have huddled to identify puzzle pieces related to one pattern—*darkness*. We show you pieces of a story, not the whole picture. For one thing, James Ellroy has told his own history, and as he relates it, there is loss beyond words and without justice. There is an ugly story, against great odds, of the survival of one man from his demons. And there is redemption from the committed labor of art. Our essays say not much of anything that should shock Ellroy or his readers. Disagreement and eye rolls are the price of our own labor. Even the negative response of readers is redeemed by the very presence of readers.

These essays exist as context for what is tragic, shocking, horrifying, drawn from the memory and imagination of an artist who has survived damage. The ideas and arguments here consider the lure of corruption in the human heart. They come for connections to cops, criminals, and those who die in American streets only because they appear suspect in the gaze of authority. The essays are here to warn. To look at the crime scene of American history with more honesty than what is already in the books many parents are seeking to ban because even that largely sanctified history—both joke and punchline to Ellroy—might make their children uncomfortable. Uncomfortable with events for which they bear no responsibility but responsibility for the future. But is it really because children might feel bad about horrible stories of the past? Or is it anxiety for some, straight-up fear for others, that those children, informed of complex history and damaged human beings, might acknowledge that history and that humanity? That they might even help to dismantle structures maintained to privilege their future as it privileged their ancestors in the past. These essays look at the crime scene of American history that Ellroy has called his readers to examine. A mess of gore and implication. To see the clues, get back into the cold case evidence, maybe even identify the ones who got away. To see that even having drawn the worst childhood hand, one can emerge from the damage with the redemption of sober, productive labor in the world, to find some kind of joy in the experience of being human.

We have worked to help readers consider how crime and politics could fuse in the next part of the American story. If Ellroy's *reckless verisimilitude* is a retelling of American past, what might be the reckless truth of American future? Is it the addiction to MAGA-level rage or the addiction to *Camelot*-level mythology? Is it a return to Jim Crow? Tactical McCarthyism? We know our society is capable of both erecting Jim Crow and dismantling it. We know our native or learned political impulses are capable of both eroding into McCarthyism, yet also, at long last, recovering decency. Will it be some form of emergence from the damage done to us by our past—a past as recent as January 6, 2021—into the political sobriety it takes to overcome political rage? Or is it a government that lies about science and history, wobbles with election instability, deploys violence as the public policy of intimidation—*mobsterism* as both the philosophy and practice of the state?

James Ellroy has told the story of his life and the stories that came out of that life. What really happened to him as a child is horrible beyond words. His stories are violent, so dismembered that there are moments of degradation from just reading them. Yet James Ellroy came through the darkness of violent crime in childhood, then the darkness of addiction. He made his darkness the medium and the message of his art. He made a life emergent from the darkness, such that, believe it or not, he has survived and thrived as encouragement for others to overcome the crimes of the past to tell a new, redemptive story. We could say it is somewhat like the story of a Mafia *caporegime* forced to accept the consequences of his own criminal history, emerging from prison to earn legitimately for his labor producing books. Like Ellroy, we may not enjoy his stories, but we can acknowledge a redemptive truth that he lived to tell them. Such alternative facts may be reckless calls for a reckoning with new realities of civic virtue.

NOTES

1. Michael Franzese, *Mafia Democracy*: How Our Republic Became a Mob Racket (Carson City, Lioncrest Publishing, 2022), 25.
2. Colin Woodard, *The Republic of Pirates*: Being the True and Surprising Story of the Caribbean Pirates and the Man Who Brought Them Down (New York: Mariner Books, 2007).
3. Myah Ward, www.politico.com, July 7, 2021, https://www.politico.com/news/2021/07/07/rudy-giuliani-suspended-washington-dc-498653.
4. William L. Riordon, *Plunkitt of Tammany Hall: A Series of Very Plain Talks on Very Practical Politics*, Bedford Books of St. Martin's Press, 1993 (originally published in 1905).
5. Riordon, p. 5.
6. Riordon, p. 3.
7. Examples, among many, are Matt Taibbi, *Griftopia*: Bubble Machines, Vampire Squids, and the Long Con That Is Breaking America (New York: Spiegel & Grau, 2010). Michael Moore began his career of film documentary critique of capitalism with *Roger & Me*, directed/performed by Michael Moore (Los Angeles: Warner Brothers, 1989), documentary. His succeeding work follows a similar critique.
8. James Ellroy, *American Tabloid* (New York: Alfred Knopf, 1995).
9. Ellroy, *American Tabloid*, p. 5.
10. Karl R. Popper, *Conjectures and Refutations*: The Growth of Scientific Knowledge (New York: Basic Books Publishers, 1963), p. 27; Stephen Colbert, *The Colbert Report*, New York: Comedy Central, October 17, 2005. https://www.cc.com/video/63ite2/the-colbert-report-the-word-truthiness; Kellyanne Conway, *Meet the Press*,

NBC, January 22, 2017. https://www.nbcnews.com/meet-the-press/video/conway-press-secretary-gave-alternative-facts-860142147643

11. Lily Rothman, "Jackie Kennedy's Post-Assassination Interview with LIFE, www.life.com, https://www.life.com/history/jackie-movie-life-magazine/, retrieved July 27, 2023 (interview published December 6, 1963).

12. Rothman.

13. *Tragic Songs from the Grassy Knoll*: John F. Kennedy 50th Anniversary Collection, New York: Norton Records, 2013. Compact disc.

14. *Tragic Songs*, track 16.

BIBLIOGRAPHY

Colbert, Stephen. *The Colbert Report*. New York: Comedy Central, October 17, 2005. https://www.cc.com/video/63ite2/the-colbert-report-the-word-truthiness.

Conway, Kellyanne. *Meet the Press*, NBC, January 22, 2017. https://www.nbcnews.com/meet-the-press/video/conway-press-secretary-gave-alternative-facts-860142147643.

Ellroy, James. *American Tabloid*. New York: Alfred Knopf, 1995.

Franzese, Michael. *Mafia Democracy*: How Our Republic Became a Mob Racket. Carson City: Lioncrest Publishing, 2022.

Moore, Michael. *Roger & Me*, directed/performed by Michael Moore, 1989 (Los Angeles: Warner Brothers) documentary.

Popper, Karl R. *Conjectures and Refutations*: The Growth of Scientific Knowledge (New York: Basic Books Publishers, 1963).

Riordon, William L., *Plunkitt of Tammany Hall: A Series of Very Plain Talks on Very Practical Politics*, Bedford Books of St. Martin's Press, 1993 (originally published in 1905).

Rothman, Lily. "Jackie Kennedy's Post-Assassination Interview with LIFE." www.life.com, https://www.life.com/history/jackie-movie-life-magazine/, retrieved July 27, 2023 (interview published December 6, 1963).

Taibbi, Matt. *Griftopia*: Bubble Machines, Vampire Squids, and the Long Con That Is Breaking America. New York: Spiegel & Grau, 2010.

Tragic Songs from the Grassy Knoll: John F. Kennedy 50th Anniversary Collection, New York: Norton Records, 2013. Compact disc.

Ward, Myah. "Rudy Giuliani suspended from practicing law in D.C., weeks after similar action in New York." www.politico.com, July 7, 2021, https://www.politico.com/news/2021/07/07/rudy-giuliani-suspended-washington-dc-498653.

Woodard, Colin. *The Republic of Pirates*: *Being the True and Surprising Story of the Caribbean Pirates and the Man Who Brought Them Down*. New York: Mariner Books, 2007.

Index

About the Contributors

Erik Anderson is Chair and Professor of Philosophy at Drew University in Madison, NJ. He works in metaphysics, aesthetics, and environmental philosophy. He also loves animals, bicycles, and jazz.

Paul Babbitt, PhD, is Chair and Associate Professor of the History and Political Science Department at Southern Arkansas University, where he teaches courses in American government and political theory. His current research focuses on Cold War liberalism.

Susan McWilliams Barndt is Professor of Politics at Pomona College. McWilliams is the author of *The American Road Trip and American Political Thought* (2018) and *Traveling Back: Toward a Global Political Theory* (2014). She is also the editor of *A Political Companion to James Baldwin* (2017) and a coeditor of several books, including *The Best Kind of College: An Insiders' Guide to America's Small Liberal Arts Colleges* (coedited with John Seery, 2015) and *A New History of American Political Thought* (coedited with Nicholas Buccola and Roosevelt Montás, forthcoming). McWilliams is the coeditor (with Jeremy Bailey) of the American Political Thought book series at the University Press of Kansas and a past editor of the peer-reviewed journal *American Political Thought*. For her work, McWilliams has received recognitions, including the Graves Award in the Humanities and the National Endowment for the Humanities Fellowship.

Lexey A. Bartlett is Associate Professor of English at Fort Hays State University, with primary teaching and research interests in nineteenth to twenty-first-century British literature, literary theory, and literature of crime. She has served as Area Chair of Mystery/Detective Fiction for the Southwest and American Popular Culture Association since 2014.

Jeffrey Becker is Associate Professor of Political Science at the University of the Pacific. He is the author of *Ambition in America: Political Power and the Collapse of Citizenship.*

Deirdre M. Condit is Associate Professor of Political Science in the College of Humanities and Sciences at Virginia Commonwealth University. As a feminist political theorist, her research interests engage work in the areas of women and politics, the politics of reproductive and genetic technologies, maternal political theory, sex and gender identity, and the nexus between complexity theory and trans-corporeality. Her interdisciplinary interests span and integrate studies in political theory, feminist theory, law and public policy.

Born and raised in Oklahoma, **Caitlin B. Coulter** has lived in Virginia and North Carolina, but now lives in Kentucky where she is a PhD candidate at the University of Kentucky and teaches English courses on detective fiction and female narratives in contemporary literature. Her research is specifically interested in how contemporary American detective fiction by women of color juxtaposes itself with the Chandlerian hard-boiled ideal: through the detective's redefined liminality, capacity to maintain relationships, expression of emotional trauma, and critique of cultural systems of harm. Just a few plaid-jacket elbow patches away from the stereotypical aesthetics of Chandler, Tracy, and Macdonald, she enjoys smoking her Nording tobacco pipe, sipping black coffee, and trading an occasional dry witticism over bourbon.

W. John Green is an historian and Editor and Director of the *Latin American News Digest*. His most recent book is *A History of Political Murder in Latin America: Killing the Messengers of Change* (2015).

Darrell A. Hamlin is Associate Professor of Political Science and Senior Fellow at the Center for Civic Leadership at Fort Hays State University. He is the former managing editor of the *eJournal of Public Affairs*. Previously Hamlin was Associate Professor of Criminal Justice at Fort Hays State University and Assistant Professor in the Department of Political Science and Law at Spring Hill College.

Joseph Romance is an independent scholar who taught political science and political theory for more than twenty years at Drew University and Fort Hays State University. He has written or coedited a number of books, including *The Challenge of Politics*, *A Republic of Parties?*, *Democracy's Literature*, and *Democracy and Excellence*. His most recent publication is *Primary Elections and American Politics.*

www.ingramcontent.com/pod-product-compliance
Ingram Content Group UK Ltd.
Pitfield, Milton Keynes, MK11 3LW, UK
UKHW041452071026
15587UKWH00010B/813

9 781666 926002